Remaking the Hexagon

Remaking the Hexagon

The New France in the New Europe

EDITED BY

Gregory Flynn

Westview Press

BOULDER • SAN FRANCISCO • OXFORD

Copyright © 1995 by Westview Press, Inc.

Published in 1995 in the United States of America by Westview Press, Inc., 5500 Central Avenue, Boulder, Colorado 80301-2877, and in the United Kingdom by Westview Press, 12 Hid's Copse Road, Cumnor Hill, Oxford OX2 9JJ

Library of Congress Cataloging-in-Publication Data
Remaking the Hexagon : the new France in the new Europe / Gregory Flynn, ed.
    p.   cm.
  Includes bibliographical references and index.
  ISBN 0-8133-8919-4 — ISBN 0-8133-8927-5 (pbk.)
    1. France—Civilization—Philosophy.   2. France—Politics and government—1981–   3. National characteristics, French.   4. Europe 1992.   5. Social change—France—History—20th century.   6. France—Relations—Europe.   7. Europe—Relations—France.   I. Flynn, Gregory.
DC58.R36   1995
944.083'9—dc20   94-46249
                                                                            CIP

Printed and bound in the United States of America

10   9   8   7   6   5   4   3   2   1

Contents

Part Three
Social Change and Political Institutions

Part Four
France in the New Europe

Tables and Figures

Figures

Acknowledgments

This book has resulted from collaboration between the Center for German and European Studies in the Edmund A. Walsh School of Foreign Service, Georgetown University, and the Fondation Nationale des Sciences Politiques in Paris. Our work together exemplifies the best in academic collaboration. Special thanks are due to Alain Lancelot, the president of the fondation, and to Françoise Sauvage, the director of international programs at the fondation, for all of their support in making this project happen.

The first drafts of the book's chapters were presented at a very productive two-day conference held at Georgetown in October 1993. The authors gathered with many of the top specialists on France from both sides of the Atlantic. Numerous people were involved in making possible this conference and subsequent completion of the book manuscript. Contributions for both the conference and project were received from Air France, the Embassy of France, Mrs. John French III, the W. Averell and Pamela C. Harriman Foundation, the Anna-Maria and Stephen Kellen Foundation, the Philip Morris Companies, Inc., and Time Warner International. We are extremely grateful to them all for their generous support. Special thanks are owed to Paula Dempsey of Air France for her efforts well beyond the call of duty when an untimely strike by Air France personnel in Paris conspired to keep the conference from taking place. I also wish to thank Ambassador Jacques Andréani and his staff at the French Embassy for their logistical help, without which this conference would not have been possible.

In the end, people always make the difference in every project, and I have been especially blessed with outstanding help from my graduate student assistants during the life of this project. I have frequently convinced myself of how much they learned in the process; while this may well be true, they also gave generously of their time and energies. The greatest burden was borne by Daniel Powers, who organized the conference in October 1993 and who served as my right hand in the early phases of editing. His talents and professionalism were praised more than once by the collaborators in this volume; his care and mature judgment greatly facilitated my own work. Henry Farrell joined me during the final editing phase and several texts owe a great deal to his sharp mind and skilled pen. The privilege of working with these two fine young scholars has been all mine. I also wish to thank Joseph Mellott and Richard Wiggers who provided additional help at crucial moments. Lastly, Marlene Niefeld has over-seen the preparation of the photo-ready manuscript with the kind of attention and adeptness that one can only dream of. All have made this a better piece of work and have my lasting gratitude.

Gregory Flynn

1

Remaking the Hexagon

Gregory Flynn

All of the nations of Europe have had difficulty adjusting to the dramatic changes that have transformed the continent in recent years, but none more than France. In the case of France, the changes in the European context have coincided with deep-seated structural changes in French politics and society. Europe has emerged from its division during the Cold War and new questions are being raised about the purpose and form of European integration. Together with the challenges of modern society and the demands of contemporary economic management, these new conditions are forcing a reexamination of many assumptions about how France is governed, the objectives of national policies, and ultimately what it means to be French. The result has been a national preoccupation with French identity.[1]

At first blush, the outside observer may be forgiven for viewing all this with a certain cynical skepticism. There is nothing new about France's preoccupation with its own cohesion and its own role and image. At numerous moments throughout the last century France has been both deeply divided over political and social issues affecting the very heart of the nation's character and distressed by its decline internationally. Since World War II, France has endured not only the humiliation of defeat and the consequent deep, emotional divisions separating those who resisted from those who collaborated, but also the indignities of decolonization and the fratricide it engendered at home. Under the Fifth Republic, however, France has also witnessed a phenomenal economic, social, and political renaissance; this was accompanied by an assertiveness abroad that constantly sought to remind others as well as itself that it remained a major international force. Thus, national identity has been a consistently revisited issue for the French during the last fifty years.²

This book has not set for itself the task of resolving either the philosophical or the methodological issues associated with the study of French national identity.³ Rather the group of scholars gathered here have had another agenda: to understand better why France has seemingly had such difficulty as it seeks to chart its course into the next century. The challenge of remaking the hexagon, that is refashioning the French approach to governance and the management of international relationships in response to structural changes in society and the international system, is substantial, but on the surface at least, no more substantial than that faced by many other countries. It would certainly seem, for example, that the magnitude and difficulty of adjustment for Germany after reunification is greater than that faced by France. And yet the public proclamations of France's difficulties would seem to imply that something particular has been transpiring in this country.

To explore the underlying dimensions of this problematic, the authors of this volume have undertaken an examination of today's France from the perspective of history, economics, comparative politics, and international relations. They share a belief that some of the answers to France's current difficulties lie in its history, some in its competitive position and approach to economic management, some in its political structures, and finally, some in a changing international role.

In the first part of this volume, three historians explore how the different legacies of history are affecting the way France confronts the issues with which it is currently challenged, specifically how past traumatic experiences, socioeconomic and cultural patterns, and the traditions of an assimilationist state shape the approach to contemporary political dilemmas. The second part of the book then looks at how the choices in favor of a more open stance toward trade and a strong franc have changed the French approach to economic policy making and have brought to a head many of the political dilemmas about the role of *l'état providence*, the state as a guarantor of welfare. The third part of the book examines the changing domestic political milieu: changes in elite structures, particularly the disappearing barrier between bureaucratic and political elites; the attempts and failure of the party system to modernize; and the fusion of a perceived loss of economic and social control at home with the uncertainties of the international environment, resulting in widespread pressure for the political class to erect new barriers to the threats from the outside world. Finally, the book examines directly how the fracture of the international framework of the postwar world has affected French security thinking, the country's relationship to the European Union and the future of European integration, and ultimately, basic notions of the state and sovereignty.

One of the most interesting results of this exercise has been that no matter what the original formulation of the questions, most of the authors ultimately came around to the same underlying theme: to understand the problems they were discussing, it was necessary to understand that they were dealing with challenges to French identity. Independent of their various points of departure, several authors actually end up explicitly taking the analysis beyond the problems with which they started to argue that the core problem involves concern about how domestic and international change have called into question what it means to be French. And for those authors that do not, they well could have, as their analyses point in the same direction. This book did not start out to be an analysis of French identity, but a book about the challenges of change to French economic, social, and political structures; and yet it has ended up with challenges to identity as a central theme. This opening chapter provides a structure that helps tie together the different strands of that identity theme.

The current identity crisis of the French may not be the most acute the nation has had, in the sense that failure to deal with today's crisis of identity does not threaten the nation in the same way crises of the past may have; France is not on the verge of even a cold civil war. In an important way, however, France does face a profound crisis of identity in the sense that France is today being forced to confront directly a central element in the glue that has held the nation together in the past -- specifically, the nature and role of the French state. The changes to the world in which France must navigate as a nation have made it necessary to modify the traditional role of the French state. The good news is that the state no longer appears to be an indispensable element in the glue holding the nation together -- France has been in the process of becoming less "exceptional" in this regard for some time. Nonetheless, the transition toward a less centralized, less homogenizing state will be rough and encounter considerable opposition.

Historically, France has not been like other nations, at least in regard to the special relationship between the nation and the state. France has often been referred to as the state that was in search of the nation, in juxtaposition to Germany, the nation in search of a state. While the comparison may be overdrawn, there is no doubt that the French state has played a critical role in molding if not creating the nation. As modern France was created out of the many peoples that inhabited its lands, a powerful, centralized state helped to bring a nation into being where none had previously existed.[4]

Even in recent times, many French have gone so far as to contend that a strong, centralized state was essential to France's existence as a nation. Indeed, as late as the early 1980s when the Socialist Government introduced decentralization into political life once again, it was not at all uncommon to hear the argument that this was the beginning of the end of France, that the French did not possess a sufficient commitment to what they shared in common to override that which divided them. The fact that this statement was an exaggeration did not stop some people from believing it. The myth of the state and the myth of the nation have been intimately interwoven in France.

Part of the explanation for this intimacy is to be found in the fact that the main threats to sovereignty in France, as Stanley Hoffmann reminds us in his chapter in this volume, historically came from within. The role of the state in uniting the nation was reinforced by the depth of the political divisions over how the nation should be governed. After a point, a united French nation clearly existed in the sense that key loyalties of its peoples were given to the central authorities of the French state (as opposed, for example, to the regions). But the contending visions of that France were sufficiently at odds with one another that there was a constant need to reknit the nation together. Something had to substitute for the absence of a shared image, and the state, which helped society to function as a whole, performed this role.

Today, France is no longer divided, at least not in the same way, by the demons of the past, which long plagued it. These legacies are discussed in the chapters that follow by both Jean-Noël Jeanneney and Alain-Gérard Slama. To be sure, traumas such as that of World War II and Vichy are still very much alive in French political life and will seemingly remain so for some time, even though the number of those with personal involvement in the events is rapidly declining. But even though these traumas continue to affect the political agenda and the political fortunes of individuals, the divisions they create almost certainly do not challenge the condition of the French nation in the same way as did past divisions over the Revolution, the institutions of the Republic, or even modernization. The need for the state constantly to knit the nation together is no longer there. The challenges to the French nation today are of a different order than they have been in the past. These challenges are linked, however, to the fact that the Jacobin state has served as a key element in the glue for so long that for many it has become identified with the nation itself.

The basic challenges to the French nation today are new and originate from within and from without. Internally France no longer confronts either direct challenges to its institutions or the challenge to modernize, but rather it faces the challenges that come from the consequences of successful modernization. This is not to say that modernization is either complete or even. As is made clear in several chapters that follow, particularly those by Ezra Suleiman and Yves Mény, there is considerable unevenness to the modernization process, especially when it comes to political structures themselves. In a broader sense, however, France has indeed modernized; the last several decades have witnessed a profound transformation of the country's economic, social, and demographic patterns. And with modernity has come a set of problems, also experienced in other countries, that originates in the breakdown of traditional structures and values, and a fragmentation of economic and social life.

These problems pose a double difficulty for the French. On the one hand, the modernization process erodes qualities that have been associated with the character of the nation and that helped bind it together. Richard Kuisel discusses these at length in his chapter on "The France We Have Lost." Something has been left behind that helped France to identify itself. In a sense, that is what the debate in France over modernization -- a debate that has had more than one phase and has occurred at more than one moment over the past century -- was about. For some, there would be not only winners and losers with modernization, but substantial elements of France's coherence as a nation would be jeopardized. For others, most importantly Charles de Gaulle in the period after World War II, failure to modernize was seen as having been responsible for France's relative decline in Europe, a decline that itself challenged another element central to French identity -- its role among the first rank of nations. Stopping the clock thus also carried a substantial risk, and in many ways World War II had brought this lesson home to a larger number of French. Nonetheless, modernization has diluted or dissolved many features of what it meant to be French and it is not yet obvious what will replace them as elements in the bonding agent of the French nation.

The other problem modernization has posed stems from the mismatch between the problems created by new economic and social fragmentation and the capacities of a highly centralized state. The Jacobin state coped well with the challenges of integration in nineteenth century France and it may well be true that postwar modernization could not have occurred as effectively in the absence of a strong state role. The problems of contemporary economic and social management, however, are much less susceptible to being dealt with effectively through solutions imposed from or even designed by the center. Economic decision making demands a flexibility that is hard to reconcile with ministerial leadership and state ownership. The problems of modern society demand a sensitivity and tolerance that is hard to reconcile with the aspiration for conformity. France thus faces a situation where its state remains strong, but where the state's capacities to deal with the new range of problems are weak.

The challenges to France from beyond its borders are no less intense, although they too differ fundamentally from those encountered in the past. Historically, the most important dangers for France from the international environment were threats to its independent existence, were military in nature, and came from its neighbors. Today, the challenges cannot really even be expressed in terms of independence (which may well be why the word has taken on special meaning in France's search for a response to the new conditions), they are more economic than military in nature, and they are diffuse in origin. Changing international conditions have made it far more useful to think of challenges to France in terms of the country's ability to achieve national goals rather than its ability to preserve its independence. France's existence is not really threatened at all today, but in both military and economic terms, France, along with the rest of Europe and much of the rest of the world, has become dependent on others for its ability to achieve basic national goals. The threats are not to its borders, but come through its borders. Interdependence has made borders porous.

Interdependence poses a range of difficulties that are not unique to France, but they have a special effect on France because of the way France has chosen to represent itself to itself. What is distinct about the French case concerns the special power and prestige that was vested in the national state, and the expectations that the state should be able to respond to the new conditions. The French are particularly uncomfortable with the notion of forces operating within the state that are not subject to the state's control. The control of national territory has been particularly important in France, stemming from the nature of the struggle to unify the French nation. Indeed, national borders have had a particular symbolic value in France that goes beyond that of most countries because they have served not only or even primarily as a means of distinguishing from "the other" or "the foreign" but more importantly as a means of declaring the unity of that which lies inside the borders. Indeed, France may well be the only country to have adopted a geometric figure -- the hexagon -- as an expression of the nation and its identity. No other nation refers to itself in terms of the shape of its borders. A challenge to French borders, even one that does not try to change the borders as such but simply makes them permeable, is thus an important challenge to the way the French nation has chosen to represent itself. The need for well-defined limits between France and the outside world is thus unusually strong and this need is increasingly difficult to fulfill.

The capacity of the French state to play the role it has traditionally played is thus challenged from without as well as from within by the changes that have taken place over the postwar period. As that role has been central to France's self definition as an *etat-nation*, it is the identity of France that is indeed challenged by these new conditions. The range of challenges can best be understood in terms of three basic issues: the state as the agent of assimilation; the state as the guarantor, as well as provider of last resort, of wealth and welfare; and the state as protector. Each of these three goes to the heart of the specific compact that the French have made with their state and thus the sources of loyalty to the state, a core of most definitions of identity. The chapters that follow provide evidence of the various ways in which each applies, but the following discussion highlights how the analyses relate together around the issue of identity.

The first and in many ways deepest challenge to the French sense of nation comes from the difficulties the country faces with its traditional doctrine of assimilation. The most observable dimension of this problem concerns the failure to integrate into French society many of those who have come to France from abroad, most specifically those from the former colonies. France's approach to immigration paralleled its approach to its colonies. Based on a *mission civilisatrice*, French policy foresaw a transformation of local populations through education and an extension of French culture. Individuals from the colonies would gradually become French. As French men or women, their ability to integrate easily in the *metropôle* was assumed. The reality, of course, is that France today faces the same problem as many other countries with large immigrant populations: ghettoization (in this case sub-urban); disputes over rights; and a backlash on the Right.

This is a real problem in contemporary France, and at the same time, it is only a piece of a much larger problem. France's approach to its colonial experience was governed by the same doctrine of assimilation that guided the unification of the nation under the Republic. It is not only immigrants that challenge the French state's ability to be an agent of assimilation, but the evolution of the economic and social system of the country itself. As Alain-Gérard Slama explains in his chapter, the challenges to France are no longer those that required a central, homogenizing state, nor is such a state well adapted to dealing with the issues of the new agenda. The state is being required to move from acting as the agent of assimilation to playing the role of arbitrator between different interests and the guarantor of the rights of different groups. This is far more like the role of the state in other Western countries, but a major change for France. As Slama points out, the transformation carries the risk that attempts to regulate will become a form of authoritarianism, given that the French state has only limited experience as an arbitrator and an underdeveloped instinct to act as such.

Even if this fear is not realized, the process of France moving from one conception of the state to another will force a parallel adjustment of national identity: from a homogeneous to a more heterogeneous concept of the nation, from a society with a dominant culture to a multicultural society. The problems France will confront along the way are likely to be profound and divisive. It will require a further evolution of the relationship between the state and society in France, a modification of the basic compact between the people and the state. The Jacobin state was the centralized expression and expressor of the common will, indeed of what it meant to be French. The tasks of articulating the common will and of continuously reknitting the nation will move from the state to the political system, a system that may not, as will be discussed below, be well prepared for this task (for precisely the same reason that the state was vested with this role to begin with). The glue that binds the new France together will clearly be a blend of old and new elements, the precise chemical formula for which has clearly not yet been discovered.

The second basic challenge concerns the role of the state as a provider or at least guarantor of welfare and economic security. Perhaps the single most important blow to the French psyche during the last decade has not been the reunification of Germany but the unprecedented levels of unemployment that France has been forced to endure. Successive governments have attempted to find solutions to increasing structural unemployment, but have met with little success. Unemployment continued to grow throughout the 1980s and has reached 12 percent, a level not known since World War II.

Not all the economic news has been negative. One of the great successes of French economic policy during the 1980s was bringing inflation under control, indeed bringing it down to a level that even dipped below that of Germany at one point in the early 1990s. The French economy is also more open than at any time in its history, and as William James Adams demonstrates in his chapter, this appears to have produced a more competitive French economy. The question mark that remains is whether France will be sufficiently competitive in the faster growing export sectors in order to bring down structural unemployment through export-driven growth. The analysis of Jacques Le Cacheux shows us how France's monetary strategy was aimed precisely at creating the preconditions for this export-led growth, and that France had been reasonably successful in the 1980s in building up a competitive advantage through fiscal "virtue." However, the devaluation of several key European currencies within the European Monetary System may have robbed France of much of the competitive advantage it had painfully built, leaving it to endure high unemployment with limited prospects of export-led growth solving the problem.

The inability of the state to resolve France's economic difficulties, indeed the weakening of confidence that the state has a capacity to deliver or at least provide an answer as to how France's structural economic problems can be solved, challenges directly a central tenet in France's sense of self. The effect of this situation comes from the comparison with the experience of modernization during the postwar period, which was less a period of traumatic dislocations than it was one of spectacular economic growth by historic standards. The period is regularly referred to as the *Trente Glorieuses*, the thirty years of economic reinvigoration. This has made the subsequent two decades simultaneously easier and more difficult to endure: easier because the economic base and welfare net have become wider; more difficult because expectations are higher and the contrast with the recent past makes the state's current impotence all the more evident.

The situation is of course not as clear cut as a simple incapacity of the French state to solve its economic problems. Indeed, the reality is that two objectives of French policy have been in competition with one another, each of which is linked to a central part of the contemporary challenge to French identity. As David Cameron so carefully explains in his chapter, there is a direct link between the new levels of unemployment and the decisions France made for moving Europe toward a monetary union. The decision to pursue a strong franc and create the conditions for monetary coordination and eventually monetary union was clearly a decision in favor of a specific vision of France's economic future; coordinated monetary policy among member states of the European Community would provide them all with a more stable, predictable environment for economic policymaking. At the same time, however, there is no doubt that this was also first and foremost a political decision about France's future role in shaping Europe. To this extent, some have even been tempted to portray the problems France currently faces with unemployment as having been caused by its perceived need to combat its loss of international status. The decline of France as a major power could only be compensated for through a major role as an architect of Europe, the precondition for which was an ability to play the economic game as well, and on the same terms as Germany. *L'Etat Providence* is placed in direct competition with *Grandeur*, a potentially dangerous form of national schizophrenia.

The final challenge to the French sense of nation is linked to the role of the state as protector. In France, protection has naturally had the same meaning as in most states, that is as defender of the national territory. But in France, the nation's sense of itself has also required the state to be the protector of the nation's status and the propagator of its values. France has always seen itself as having a role larger than other states, based on a universalist conception of its values and culture, and a consequent entitlement to influence beyond its borders. At both the level of defense of borders and the level of international role, French leaders face new questions, to which old answers will be inadequate; the new answers, however, raise uncomfortable questions about how the French have defined themselves.

Under Charles de Gaulle, France found a formula to reconcile the country's need for security, its demoted position internationally, and its need to rehabilitate a self-image of *grandeur*. Nuclear weapons were simultaneously a means to ensure that France could never again be occupied, and an expression of being a nation of the first rank, a position to which France clearly could not have aspired on any other grounds. The national declaration of *independence* helped the country to overcome its debilitating internal divisions and undertake the modernization that de Gaulle also saw as the prerequisite to the nation's future *grandeur*.

In the post-Cold War world, security and status problems once again impinge on the French state, but not in a way that can be easily reconciled, and certainly not with the formulas that worked for de Gaulle. Nuclear weapons still provide France with a defense of last resort, but their relevance to the problems of the new Europe is problematic. Their possession alone thus no longer guarantees the same kinds of influence among either friends or others. At the same time, France does seem to have a possibility, as Frédéric Bozo argues in his chapter, to continue to exert a leadership role in European councils. The greatest difficulty in this domain may well be the fact that no state has the answer to conflicts like that in Bosnia. Such conflicts do not directly threaten French security, but once again the impotence of the French state in the face of new challenges, although not alone in this regard, is graphically demonstrated.

A more important challenge to the state as protector is the heightened sense of vulnerability to the outside world that comes from the difficulties of assimilating immigrants discussed earlier, and most importantly, popular perceptions of an economy out of control and the belief that the enemy is to be found abroad. As Suzanne Berger analyzes so well in her chapter, the problems of unemployment and general feelings of uncertainty have produced a feeling that the state has failed and have created demands for protection at the borders. The debate over the economy and the debate over identity have fused. Adams may well be correct in his assessment that the French economy has become so dependent on the global economy that it cannot only withdraw slightly, and that a radical withdrawal would entail too high a price in foreign policy and security terms to be attractive. Nonetheless, as the capacity of the state to act as a guarantor of economic welfare declines, the demands for it to perform in its role of protector have grown. The internal political pressures for protection will likely continue, once again placing the French state in a virtual no-win situation unless and until improvements in the global economy begin to have a growth effect in France and thus reduce the sense of threat that currently prevails.

The strategy that France has pursued to achieve its need for both security and status, political and economic, has been European integration. Yet as both my own chapter and that of Stanley Hoffmann explain, France has more problems than most of its partners (Britain being an obvious exception) with concepts of shared or pooled sovereignty because of the history of the French state. And even as the French state is demonstrating clearly that it does not have the answers to many key questions confronting the country, political leaders are nonetheless having great difficulty making the case that the answers must be sought collectively. The solutions to many of modern society's problems in today's world, if solutions exist, will not be national; the scale is wrong. Some answers will surely be found at the local or regional level, and some at the European or even global level. But the national state in France has fought so many battles for so long against the concept of dividing sovereignty that it will adapt only slowly, if ever, to the idea that sovereignty can be layered. This is the external parallel to the adjustment that must occur if France is to move from the concept of the assimilator state to that of the arbiter state.

The relationship between the French and their state is seriously called into question by the way in which both the domestic and international context has developed. Given the role that the state has played in fostering and then reknitting the nation, these new conditions also provide a deep challenge to the identity of the nation. It may well be that France no longer needs a strong state to act as a critical element of the bonding agent that holds the nation together because the nation is no longer in danger of fragmenting in the same way it was in the past. Certainly, there are no challenges to sovereignty from within in the way there once were; and there are no longer the same kind of fundamental, ideologically driven differences in vision for the nation such as those that forced the state to compensate for the absence of a basic unity of underlying national vision in the political system.

The French have always been ambivalent about their state, even as it helped bond them together. A strong centralized state almost by definition did overreach from time to time. But even as the French would react against too much control, they also became uncomfortable if their state appeared to be too weak. Currently, France faces a situation where the state is structurally still strong but the structure is weak in its ability to deliver in the face of the new problems its confronts. National identity is challenged because the state is no longer capable of playing the role it once played. Something must take the state's place as the guardian of identity.

The state came to its special role in shaping the French nation in part because deep divisions in the political system prevented political elites from unifying the nation around a shared image. France now finds itself with a political system that is no longer as deeply divided. The question is whether the political system will be capable of providing a shared vision for the new France, one that takes the challenges just enumerated and shapes a response that unifies the French nation. The evidence would suggest that this will be difficult.

The French political system may no longer be so deeply divided, but Yves Mény's analysis indicates that it is precisely the political structures of France that have been least successfully modernized over the past several decades. Both Charles de Gaulle and François Mitterrand attempted to create modern mass parties and both succeeded for a time in circumventing traditional political elite structures. But both the right and the left have drifted back toward quasi-feudal political structures, with real political power being located initially in local power bases and the national political standing of individuals being built through a cumulation of mandates, not through service to a party. A system of *notables* may actually be reasonably well-suited to dealing with problems at the local or regional rather than national levels. It will almost certainly have difficulty, however, in fostering a unified sense of the nation in the face of contemporary challenges.

Historically, the French state has compensated for the weakness of its political parties by fostering an elite bureaucratic structure that ensured the operation of the state in spite of political fragmentation. Ezra Suleiman's analysis indicates that these elite structures have changed little on the one hand, but fundamentally on the other. French elites still are a self-selecting group and tend to co-opt the best and the brightest. But the barrier between the bureaucratic and political elites has now all but disappeared: even the bureaucracy has now been contaminated by partisan links. This leads one ineluctably to the conclusion that the bureaucratic elite will no longer be in the same position as they have been historically to help provide a unifying national perspective for a fragmented political system.

France thus finds itself at an particularly interesting juncture. In many important ways, the French nation is actually more united than at any time over the past several centuries. At the same time, the country has entered a phase where the problems it confronts and the adjustments it must make do challenge profoundly a core piece of French identity: the nature and role of the French state.

In a sense, there have been three phases of the search for France, to borrow the phrase of Stanley Hoffmann and his colleagues in their 1963 volume.[5] The first and perhaps longest involved internal challenges to sovereignty and disputes over how the French nation should be governed. In some ways, these issues were not completely resolved until the institutions of the fifth Republic finally succeeded in achieving the broad-based legitimacy they now enjoy. The second phase, which overlapped with the first, involved the debate over modernization. *In Search of France*, written at the very beginning of the fifth Republic, explored whether the new institutional framework would finally be capable of facilitating modernization and whether the nation would be capable of reconciling modernization with what it meant to be French.

Today, France has entered a third phase in its search. The nation no longer faces the question of modernization, at least in economic and social terms. The work of James Hollifield, George Ross, and their colleagues demonstrates how much has been accomplished in the first thirty years of the fifth Republic.[6] Now France must confront the problems of adapting to the consequences of modernization and a changed international environment, which will require an adaptation of the French state. This is the same state that was so crucial to the resolution of the dilemmas confronted in phases one and two of the search. Having succeeded in both helping create the nation and reknitting the nation at successive points subsequently, it must now find a way to modify itself, and in the process the French must find a new relationship between themselves and their state that is compatible with their identity as a nation. Perhaps the state's new role will be, as Suzanne Berger has argued, one of protecting the weak against the strong. In any case, the chapters that follow help the reader understand better the specific issues the French must confront in their continuing search to remake the hexagon.

Notes

1. One must be clear about terminology. This national preoccupation does not imply that large segments of the French population have suddenly stopped feeling French, or are about to do so. There is no evidence that the French are beginning to identify more with other objects of loyalty, either at the subnational or supernational level, than with their national state. Indeed, it is not even clear that the average French man or woman is really spending a great deal of time pondering the nation's identity at all. At the same time, it is undeniable that over the past few years, concerns about French identity have surfaced regularly among political elites, in intellectual circles, and in the media, engendering impassioned public debate over national political choices in both domestic and foreign policy. In the late 1980s, France even went so far as to establish a Commission on National Identity to look into whether fundamental characteristics of the nation could be identified that would provide a bridge between the past and the future.

2. The basic positions during this period have always been a variation on standard themes. Many are worried that essential elements of the French national state, elements that have bound the nation together, either are being sacrificed or are brought into question by political decisions. Others worry that their compatriots are attached to traditional values and cultural patterns that have become outdated and misplaced, if not outright counterproductive in today's economic and social environment.

3. Indeed, framing the debate about national choices in terms of identity can mask more than it reveals. When used loosely, identity is a catch-all concept that all too easily absolves one from having to understand what is going on at a deeper level in a society. The public discourse about national identity is a sphere of representation and myths. The origin of nations has long been a subject of controversy between those who believe in the

inherent qualities that define each nation versus those who consider a nation's identity to be constructed. This debate may never be resolved, and there certainly remains much work to be done before we grasp the deeper relationship between a nation's identity and the continuous evolution of its economic, social and political environment, both at home and beyond.

4. This is not meant to take sides in the debate over whether the state was the single most important factor in knitting modern France together. There can be no doubt that other elements were important, particularly changing commercial flows and communication patterns. But it is equally undeniable that political centralization and a strong state were fundamental to nation building in France.

5. Stanley Hoffmann, et al., *In Search of France* (Cambridge, MA: Harvard University Press, 1963).

6. James F. Hollifield and George Ross, eds., *Searching for the New France* (New York: Routledge, 1991).

PART ONE

The Weight of History in France Today

2

The Legacy of Traumatic Experiences in French Politics Today

Jean-Noël Jeanneney

The driving force of History is History. Although many interconnected forces act in concert to define the "present" (or, more accurately, one "present" after another), actors' representations of the past are always of fundamental importance, whether those actors be famous or obscure. These images may appear well-informed or anecdotal to the academic, relevant or fanciful, well thought-out or careless. No matter. Representations may have profound consequences, and are social "facts," even when they are mistaken or naive. Subjective certainties can motivate action.

Still, it is certainly difficult to measure the influence of these representations. Even if one limits oneself to France, the task is immense. This chapter discusses only the clearest aspects of the French case: the marks that key national traumas have left on contemporary political thought and behavior. It begins by setting out some general approaches through which one can examine the current effects of these national traumas, followed by some observations on their variable life cycles. The chapter then looks at particular traumas that have had an impact on French political life during the Fifth Republic: the divisions of Vichy France, the repressed shock of the Algerian revolt, the upheavals of 1968, and even the French Revolution itself. It concludes by offering a typology of traumas and their respective influence on French politics today.

Approaches to the Study of Trauma

Over the past decade or two, French historians have begun to pay closer attention to the study of trauma. Several factors have served as motivation: these historians have begun to appreciate the political influence of their own work and the importance of their social role; they recognize how knowledge of the past and present reflect one another, as in a game of mirrors; and perhaps they are also attracted by the glamour of various commemorations, which afford an unprecedented opportunity to study the phenomenon.

Recently, their line of inquiry has become more focused. Although the abstract notion of "collective memory," can be difficult to define, it has proven indispensable in characterizing communities, regions, and individuals. Philippe Joutard's works have revealed the depth of the hurt still felt by the Protestants of the Cévennes: the violent shock of the war of the Camisards left marks that still shape common memory and political tendencies.[1] Other scholars, given impetus by the celebration of the Bicentennial, have studied the Vendée counter-revolution, the memory of which is still exploited by local leaders seeking moderate votes. It has also been possible to study (though not without many nuances and subdivisions), a "Jewish memory," a "Catholic memory," a "Freemason memory," and various "immigrant memories," all of which perpetuate a specific image of the dramas and conflicts that drastically changed the destiny of their forebears.

In theory, we can analyze memories on the individual level, examining citizens one by one. One can, for example, scrutinize French leaders' personal images of the past. The legacy of French political cleavages is -- or was -- quite different, for example, to each of the successive presidents of the Fifth Republic.

In this context, one could examine the speeches delivered at the Hôtel de Ville in Paris on 21 May 1981 -- the day of François Mitterrand's inauguration -- by Jacques Chirac and the new president. Chirac, the mayor of Paris and the head of the Rassemblement pour la République (RPR), described the capital's role in the great confrontations of the past thus: "Paris was indeed the place chosen by destiny when the city, heeding the call of Sainte Geneviève, the shepherdess of Nanterre celebrated in the poems of Péguy, rose up to save the West; this was the case when Joan of Arc mounted her assault on the Porte Sainte-Honoré, prefiguring France's return to unity and independence; this was the case when Henry IV put an end, inside the walls of the city, to the Wars of Religion, restoring the State and illustrating the necessity of tolerance; and this was the case when the Estates General proclaimed the rights of man, before the nation and before the universe."[2] Then Chirac suddenly skipped 150 years, noting General de Gaulle's arrival in the capital in August 1944, and the establishment of the Fifth Republic in 1958.

For his part (apart from a mischievous reference to Etienne Marcel and resistance to central government by the provost of the merchants), François Mitterrand paid tribute to the birth of the Republic in 1792, the Revolutions of 1830 and 1848, the Paris Commune of 1871 and ... Victor Hugo. He thus put the long struggle of the "party of movement" against the party of "the established order" back on the record.[3] The only shared reference in these two chronologies, which seem to have nothing else in common, was the Liberation of Paris.

In comparison, Valéry Giscard d'Estaing wished, as he put it, to "defuse" French politics and was eager to inaugurate a "new era," in which the great conflicts of the past -- regardless of any progressive effects they might have had -- would be transcended amid a harmonious consensus of "two out of three Frenchmen" that would benefit the center-right and a peaceful business climate. Giscard let it be known that his favorite historical period was that of Louis XV, well before the turmoil of the Revolution. His references to the age of the "*juste milieu*" (an expression he tried to revive) call to mind the power of the bourgeoisie in the age of Louis-Philippe, a bourgeoisie mocked by Daumier, Stendhal, Chateaubriand, and all of the Republicans who wished to halt democratization, and who relied on a voting system based on the poll tax and a coalition of satisfied interests. In 1981, events caught up with the man whose main handicap, Raymond Aron cruelly said, was "failing to realize that History was tragic."

Another line of inquiry leads to a well-thought-out delineation of the different vectors transmitting the memory of French conflicts: family tradition, the press, the audiovisual media, education, and so forth. Everything is presented as though the most contemporary events and the most recent historiography could not profoundly weaken, except in a few exceptional cases, the solid foundation of childhood and adolescent experiences -- itself determined by the education of teachers several decades earlier. At a meeting of historians, Jean-Jacques Becker recently pointed out how, in November 1947, right in the middle of the Communist Party's offensive against the Marshall Plan, *L'Humanité*, the party newspaper, published a notice in block letters that read: "Watch out, they want to assassinate the Republic! A draft law *more abject than the ordinances of Charles X* would suppress union rights, individual liberties, freedom of the press and parliamentary immunity."[4] The newspaper showed remarkable confidence in the historical culture of the working-class milieux targeted by this propaganda! Forty-five years later, the effectiveness of such a relevance would be questionable, and it would probably not be used.

All of this illustrates the value of studying history textbooks. The "generation of fire" was influenced by the famous *Petit Lavisse*, which Pierre Nora examined in *Les Lieux de mémoire*.[5] The *Petit Lavisse*, with a circulation of several million, spread an interpretation of the "Franco-French war," or internal conflict in France between Munich and Liberation, that has gained wide acceptance, at least *in fine*. It explains that the Third Republic succeeded in creating an equilibrium that transcended these conflicts and allowed the nation-state to rally around Republican values. However, there were what one might call "combat manuals" both to the right and left of the *Petit Lavisse*, some propagating the counter-revolutionary tradition in religious schools, others taking a more or less socialist tack. In comparison, today's textbooks are far more confused about French "passions," regardless of whether their intent is to provide a unifying ideology or to organize the past according to a particular bias.

Time and the Effects of Trauma

This area of study is too broad to be summarized adequately in a single chapter. Discussion will therefore be limited to a few key themes.

It is a truism that time eases the intensity of past traumas. But it does so according to variable rhythms. Some events that seem pregnant with meaning soon become less vivid and diminish in importance with the passing of time. One could point for example to the war in Indochina, and the defeat at Dien Bien Phu. These resulted in intense turmoil in the French consciousness of the time, but their effects have now practically vanished from public life. Other events return to the limelight because of unexpected developments in the news. The larger national papers have recently published a number of letters from readers referring back to the "rising threat of war" before 1914, the "Balkan powder keg" and the (unfortunate?) dismantling of the Austro-Hungarian Empire by the Treaty of Versailles. The removal of the iron fist of communism that held collective passions in check means that the long-overlooked clash of nationalities in Central Europe, from the French Revolution to 1917, suddenly becomes relevant again.

Other harrowing events seem to recede into the past for good, because the wounds they caused have been healed by subsequent events. The shock of the loss of Alsace and Lorraine in 1871 was mitigated after the victory of 1918, and then nearly completely disappeared. (I should note, here, that memory does not correspond perfectly from one country to the next; thus although the occupation of the Ruhr by French troops from 1922-1924 has been completely forgotten in France, it has left a profound mark on Germany.)

The fading of the myth of the Commune (as shown by the rapid decrease in the size of the crowd that flocks to the *"Mur des Fédérés"* each spring) was hastened by the decline of "proletarian internationalism," and has probably been given its deathblow by the collapse of communism. The general public is now willing to accept historians' analyses, and to view the event in its true light. The Commune was indeed crushed by the social fear of Versailles, but it was motivated by the patriotism of traditional Parisian artisans, rather than by a modern industrial proletariat.

Impressions that were not suddenly dispelled by some reversal of fortune have taken much longer to fade away. To take an example from economic history, Law's bankruptcy under Louis XV was reflected for many years in investors' inveterate attachment to gold and distrust of stocks and bonds; the default of Russian loans revived this distrust in the 1920s and 1930s. However, this phenomenon is disappearing in the wake of the "*Trente glorieuses*" -- the thirty-year economic boom after World War II -- and the Left's rally around the spirit of entrepreneurship in the 1980s.

And what about politics? The Second Empire no longer generates the repugnance it did for a century. In a recent thesis on the effects of the past in political life from 1885 to 1900, Jean El Gammal demonstrated that the failure of the Boulangist movement was partly because the general and his supporters were forced to take the defensive -- a strategically dreadful situation for a movement of that type -- to clear themselves of the accusation of "Caesarism" at a time when Bonapartism had been rejected by the vast majority of the French elites. Moreover, it is significant that François Mitterrand never published the book on the coup d'etat of December 1851 that he promised Gallimard some thirty years ago. On the right, Philippe Séguin, who certainly could not be accused of anti-republicanism, recently published an almost hagiographic work on Napoleon III.[6] Moreover, his inordinate praise for the emperor did not provoke the strong reactions it would have at one time. This political "neutralization" of the Second Empire reached its final stage when de Gaulle reintroduced the referendum, a principle that had previously been discredited by the precedent of imperial plebiscites.

The Legacy of Vichy

As time passes, historical traumas are recast according to their current influence. Their greater or lesser consonance with contemporary political and societal cleavages is an essential factor in their influence; especially now, when the historical duality of Left and Right is (temporarily) losing its meaning in the eyes of many French people.

The "Franco-French war" is even now the most important historical event in terms of its influence on civic consciousness and political behavior. It is probably the single most frequent point of reference in discussions on diplomacy and war. It is striking that the so-called "*munichois*" are even harder to find than posthumous "*vichystes*." This is because the argument between the two is simplified to the point of caricature. Edouard Daladier and Georges Bonnet struggled in vain throughout their later lives to win some acknowledgment of the complexity of the choices they had faced. But the counter-current was too strong, flowing from a collective guilty conscience, and retrospective awareness of the subsequent course of events.

The cry of "Munich!" in France no longer merely refers to the energy and courage that must be mustered against all aggressors. It is used so frequently as justification that bravery becomes replaced by empty posturing. This was clearly the case with Guy Mollet and Anthony Eden -- a precedent that played a considerable role when they embarked on the disastrous Suez campaign in 1956. Over the past few years, Munich has been invoked, appropriately or inappropriately, in every great crisis up to and including Saddam Hussein and the Gulf War, where the comparison indeed had some relevance.

One can continue by examining the violent civil rift of the last war. When Henry Rousso wrote a recent book about the "Vichy syndrome" (i.e., the evolution since 1945 of the national memory of those years), he knew that he would be called upon to publish numerous follow-up studies in an ongoing process.[7]

Indeed, hardly a month goes by without some striking episode reviving the controversy: the Touvier affair, the attack on Jean Moulin's character, or the assassination of René Bousquet -- and these are only the most recent. Of course it is hard to find important figures who trumpet their fidelity to Pétain. But the memory of Vichy is intense. Public debate is replete with allusions to it, from the most subtle to the most insulting.

True, for many years there have been calls to open a new chapter. They are reminiscent of a French hit from the sixties that goes "Let's forget what happened/Let's forget we hurt each other."

Georges Pompidou was one of those who wished to let go of the past. Asked in September 1972 about the pardon he granted Paul Touvier, he cried, "Must we forever perpetuate the bloody wounds of our national discord? Has not the time come to draw a veil over them, to forget those days when the French did not love each other, tore each other to pieces, even killed each other?"[8]

François Mitterrand himself has sometimes observed that the trials following liberation ended a chapter -- for better or for worse is not at issue -- and that, while we must acknowledge acts of heroism, we must also cease disturbing civil order. He repeated this assertion when he himself was criticized in November 1992 for laying a wreath on Pétain's tomb, as he has done every year.

None of these efforts seems to diminish the fierceness of retrospective passions, and yet attempts to alter this state of affairs will continue. Most recently, Annie Kriegel and François Furet have become the principal academic standard-bearers of a new approach to the experience of Vichy. Journalist Thierry Wolton's recent book, in which he absurdly denounces Jean Moulin as a Soviet agent,[9] gave these two renowned historians (who noisily praised the tome) an opportunity to assert their authority. The two more or less explicitly advocate a radically revised reading of France's commitments during the war, in historical and moral terms. This is a slippery slope. Drawing no distinctions between the horrors of Nazi and Stalinist barbarities (let everyone draw their own conclusion), they anachronistically challenge the circumstances of the French Communist Party's struggle after 1941. Furthermore, they dispute the profound gulf between the philosophy, motivations, and acts of the Communist militants, and those of pro-Hitler activists in France during the war. This "demonization by permutation," to borrow François Bédarida's expression, in which "the universe of suspicion replaces that of science,"[10] attempts to equate the agreements between Vichy and Hitler's forces, and those signed between the Communist and other elements of the French Resistance.

These could be the first forays of a campaign aimed at radically calling into question the political and moral heritage of the Resistance as a whole. Yet I think it unlikely that these arguments can have a major effect, even if they are supported by a few big names and disseminated to the general public by politically motivated hack writers. Indeed, it is to be hoped that civic good sense and intellectual rigor will prevent them from having effect. There are some hopeful signs of an intellectual counteroffensive that should win out and ensure that the memory of that dramatic period continues to influence the geography of traditions and behaviors in the near future.

That influence is complex. The Left knows it cannot legitimately claim the legacy of the Resistance as its exclusive property. The name of de Gaulle, who transcends the rift between the two camps, would be enough to forestall any such attempt. So would the now-better-known ideological diversity of his first entourage in London. One could also point to those individuals on the Left who rallied around Pétain -- a minority the importance of which has nevertheless been overestimated by moderate historiographers. To the right, the RPR -- which only recently retired the Lorraine Cross from its "logo" -- also had some illustrious resistance workers among its ranks. Those who worked together for the liberation, and who now have political affiliations, span the spectrum from Left to Right. Whenever a public controversy seems designed to divide the *Résistants*, Jacques Chaban-Delmas makes his ritualistic appearance on television, wrapped in his personal prestige and legendary raincoat, calling for harmony and peace.

Nevertheless it is still on the Right, and only on the Right, that we find not just the last of those who are nostalgic for Vichy (though, given their age, they soon will all be dead), but also those who make excuses on behalf of it. In foreign policy, they tout the implicit cooperation of the sword (de Gaulle, fighting outside France) and shield (Pétain, protecting the nation from inside) during the occupation. They continue to do this even though de Gaulle himself rejected this analogy on countless occasions. (François-Georges Dreyfus's book on the "French State" recently demonstrated that this false notion is still alive, even among some university historiographers.)[11] They also stress the wisdom of various domestic measures taken by Pétain's regime, and exaggerate the continuity between Vichy and the Republic that may have existed in some areas.

Due to the natural dialectic of political battles, it is mainly the Left that denounces these loose alliances and spurious balancings of the account of Vichy. The Left sees them as the resurgence of a Vichy spirit. Indeed, this argument has some basis in truth, even if the analogy is exaggerated for partisan reasons. And perhaps it is here that the trauma of Vichy is most alive. The feminist movement, although enfeebled by its own success, continues to stigmatize the notion of the "housewife." And the manifold debates on racism, anti-Semitism, and immigration revive the horrid memory of Jews and foreigners being hunted down or delivered to the Nazis. Less dramatically, current discussions on whether aid to private schools should be increased recall the Catholic hierarchy's well-proven complacency toward the Pétain regime. Memories of Vichy continue to reach into all corners of French political life.

The Legacies of the Algerian Conflict and the Protests of 1968

If Vichy and the collaboration constitute the dominant trauma affecting French politics, two subsequent traumas -- Algeria and the protest of 1968 -- have largely lost their effect on French political life.

One could call the Algerian war the repressed trauma. With regard to Algeria, the "moderate" Right has lost its taste for nostalgia. It leaves that to the party of Le Pen and some defeated, marginalized leaders. On first impressions, the Left could react differently. It has its references, its proof of noble heritage, its veterans of decolonization. The Socialist Party's "generation of Epinay," was shaped by the memory of student battles for Algerian independence and the vigilance of draftees fighting within the army to preserve its republican traditions. Today's Left is swift to honor the battles fought by publications such as *L'Express*, *France-Observateur*, *Témoignage Chrétien*; by men like Pierre Mendès France; by groups such as the Partie Socialiste Autonome (PSA) that fought regardless of risk for peace in Algeria, against the use of torture, and for the defense of republican values. Nor has it forgotten the influence of colonial interests on the parliamentary right, or this group's flirtation with the temptations of a military putsch. But in spite of all this, the Left has many reasons to be modest, and to refrain from using the memory of the Algerian war as ammunition. The policies of Guy Mollet, the last Socialist prime minister before Pierre Mauroy in 1981, were painted as the latest manifestation of the colonial Left's civilizing ambitions under the Third Republic. But in fact, they did not stop the government from distancing itself from its campaign promises and the values that constituted its very identity.

Furthermore, it was ultimately de Gaulle who pulled France out of the quagmire, and kept it from becoming embroiled in civil war. The Left may still discuss the general's motivations in retrospect and quibble about his motives, but it cannot deny his effectiveness as contrasted to its own impotence at the time. The subsequent history of Algeria under Boumedienne and his successors, which has culminated in today's unrest and the dangers of fundamentalism, gives no reason for retrospective pride. And political realism has led the Left to come to terms with the electoral clout of the repatriates who, over time, have slowly rediscovered the diversity of electoral choices that belonged to the "Europeans of Algeria" before the war of independence.

The Left continued to blame de Gaulle for the "troubled" origins of the Fifth Republic until the 1970s. Even though de Gaulle's accession to power in 1958 was entirely legal, the Left continued to wax indignant, with some justification, about his use of the threat of a military invasion. In so doing, it continues to overlook the fact that Socialists took part in the June government. As long as the Left refused to accept the legitimacy of government institutions, it harped on the theme of their questionable beginnings. But now that the Left has used those institutions and found in them the means of lasting power, these complaints have ceased. It is significant that Maurice Duverger and Georges Vedel, the prestigious jurists chosen by *L'Express* and *Le Monde* to criticize the Constitution, and to point out its defects, have now become its vigilant defenders and do not advocate changing more than a few details.

There is hardly half a generation between the militants who manned the barricades during the Algerian crisis, and those who found politics on the barricades of the Latin Quarter in May 1968. However, the two groups are separated by a gulf the depth of which is explored by Hervé Hamon and Patrick Rotman's book on leftism before, during, and after the "events."[12] 1968 was traumatic for France, but its traces, while they have been significant, have also been of an entirely different quality.

Anniversaries serve as mirrors, and the anniversary of the end of the Algerian war is of necessity a low-key event, when it is marked at all (the unhappy exception to this rule is the bloody police attacks on immigrants in October 1961). Alternately, the anniversary of May 1968 is celebrated at every opportunity -- often with a healthy irony, to be sure, but always with genuine emotion just below the surface. The anniversaries in the years 1978, 1988, and 1993 were celebrated with neither bitterness nor derision. The tensions arising from the divisions of 1968 are disappearing.

Now that the dust has settled, we can, generally speaking, identify two main aspects of the spirit of 1968. The first is a watershed in mores, firstly with regard to the situation of women in society and the workplace, and also with regard to sexual freedom, which affects everyone. Even the threat of AIDS, while it has introduced new caution and constraint, does not take back this freedom. Those young men and women at the University of Nanterre who wanted to have the right to visit one another have finally triumphed. But the breadth of this change (which May 1968 crystallized rather than sparked in France), prevents it from becoming a true wedge between Left and Right. This is particularly true now, when surveys indicate that many Catholics cheerfully deviate from the prescriptions of John Paul II on chastity outside of marriage and on birth control. A few troublemakers have demonstrated against abortion, but the scale of their protest is nothing like the situation in the United States. Only a fringe element of hardliners is still hostile to the heritage of 1968, hoping against hope that the State restores the proper order.

Secondly, the 1968 attacks on the "consumer society" seem quite antiquated to the sons and daughters of the protesters, whose main concern is the threat of unemployment and economic stagnation. Similarly, many key players of the movement of 1968 now hold rather glamorous positions in publishing, academia, journalism, and politics, and view their youthful activities through the spectacles of controlled irony and gently affectionate smugness.

The Present Relevance of the Revolution

If both Algeria and the events of 1968 have thus receded in their impact on contemporary French life, the Revolution still constitutes one of the strongest polarizing elements in French behavior. Contrary to conventional wisdom, the memory of 1789-1794 remains a source of dissent in French society and politics. Recent arguments that its importance is receding may be correct at one level, but this is all clearly relative.

When, after the death of Edgar Faure, I assumed responsibility for the Bicentennial Mission in 1988, I myself had nearly accepted the validity of these reassuring assertions. My predecessor had espoused the doctrine that reconciliation was now possible. He advocated "moving beyond" a period whose brutality repelled him, and enjoyed saying that only two men could have spared France the Revolution: Turgot, who had already died, and he himself, who had not yet been born.

From my point of view, the commemoration demonstrated that the Revolution no longer constitutes a radical break between Right and Left, inasmuch as the Right has more or less rallied around the great principles of 1789-1794 in a series of steps since the Centennial in 1889. Nonetheless, there remain those who continue to contest the Revolution, and not only the hard-liners huddled angrily in the traditionalist church of Saint-Nicolas du Chardonnet in the fifth arrondissement of Paris.

In his recent book *Adieu 89*, Steven L. Kaplan raises some interesting and convincing points.[13] The book highlights the importance of local communities' reactions to requests for subsidies, and their attitude toward proposed festivities, such as the planting of trees in March 1989 in commemoration of freedom. In the absence of more detailed research, it seems to me that the RPR generally played a more active role at the municipal level than the Union pour la Démocratie Française (UDF) in the events and celebrations of the 1789 anniversary. Philippe Séguin was regarded in his town of Epinal as one of the champions of the celebration. I would argue that Parisian Mayor Jacques Chirac's bizarre decision not to attend the big commemorative parade in July was not a hostile gesture toward the revolutionary legacy, but rather the uncontrolled bitterness of a presidential candidate who had been defeated the year before and was infuriated at the prospect of what might be construed as François Mitterrand's triumphal procession. Additionally, many French villages controlled by Chirac's party were also unenthusiastic about the celebration.

In fact, one could say that a demarcation line now passes through each of the two right-wing parties in the parliament according to a complex political topography. This topography helps define, from one region to the next, from one department to the next, even from one town to the next, the distinctive characteristics of the Right's history during the revolutionary period and the wars of the past two centuries, the personal preferences of its elected officials and their personal trajectories, and even the weight and influence of religious Catholicism.

During the anniversary celebrations, there were interesting variations in the ways that the different camps interpreted the national motto "Liberté, égalité, fraternité," formulated during the Revolution and adopted in 1848. Some (who celebrated the demise of the guilds with a warmth that contrasted with their numerous other reservations about the Revolution's effects) emphasized commerce and industry and called for the defense of liberty, which they posited as a rampart against the excesses of "egalitarianism." Others agreed with the Left that an abstract notion of liberty can be a vector of oppression and prevent solidarity if its brutal excesses are not compensated for by something more than the profit motive. Still others harked back to the words of Clemenceau, who, at the time of the Centennial, taunted those "economists whose whole art consists of making legless cripples tied up in sacks race against the winner of the Paris Grand Prix. Freedom for everybody! Forward legless cripples, and good luck! The freedom of the weakest is the right of the strongest. Legless cripples, my friends, try to grow legs!"[14]

It is the "right wing of the right wing" that attacks the legacy of the Revolution and the philosophy of the Enlightenment; there is no uniform consensus on this topic among the right wing as broadly construed. The Enlightenment has been attacked, for example, by the cardinal-archbishop of Paris, Monsignor Lustiger. In 1989, he put himself forward (with more or less caution, depending on his audience) as one of the leaders of the camp that holds that the Declaration of the Rights of Man of 1789, which purports to be based on reason alone (meaningless without God), was the infamous fount of all the barbarity of the 20th century. This antagonism has considerable significance, both in the game of doctrinal debate and in the everyday world of politics.

This analysis suggests that the future might see a coalition government of Left and Center, as was proposed when Mitterrand was reelected president, and Rocard was prime minister. A substantial part of the French Right now accepts the legacy of the Revolution as revealed in the Bicentennial celebrations. While the parties missed their opportunity to realign party splits along the cleavage of attitudes to the Revolution, similar opportunities may well reappear in the future.

Conclusion

It is possible in conclusion to make some general arguments about the effects of the traumas discussed in this chapter. Some have receded into history, such as Dien Bien Phu. While every schoolchild knows about them, they have no real political significance. Other traumas are still commemorated and referred to in political debate, but are largely irrelevant to that debate. Here, the memory of 1968 serves as an example. The social legacies of 1968 are either too universal to be the subject of debate, or irrelevant to a changed world. The events of 1968 had a lasting influence on the development of French society, but the societal changes it generated are now so entrenched that cleavages today are no longer apparent: except for a few diehards, for example, everyone accepts the changed sexual mores of modern society. Thirdly, there are traumas that are still unresolved, but which have no major implications for the cleavages of modern-day politics, such as Algeria, which is too problematic to constitute a partisan rallying point, especially now that the Socialists have been reconciled to the institutions of the Fifth Republic.

There are, however, historical cleavages that resonate deeply with present-day cleavages, such as the memory of Vichy. Attempts to affect a national reconciliation have failed: despite the passage of time, memories are still too raw to allow any real rapprochement between those with a tendency to justify the regime and those who claimed they will never be able to do so. Some recent attempts to equate the Communist members of the Resistance with their collaborationist counterparts are intellectually spurious, and even sinister.

The Revolution is *sui generis* in that attitudes concerning the Revolution have constituted one of the major cleavages of French politics for centuries. They still do, although that fact is obscured by a party system that is no longer aligned with the traditional positions for and against the Enlightenment.

This typology has some interesting implications for the study of traumas and their legacies. Those traumas that are still commemorated are not necessarily the most politically important. Indeed, the very fact that they are celebrated often indicates that they are relatively unproblematic; society has reached a general consensus on them. One can gauge their political import by studying the *reactions* to their celebration. The differing responses of local communities to the bicentenary of the Revolution allows one to make a provisional mapping of the attitudes of different strains of the Right to the Revolution. By the same token, some traumas are not celebrated and can not be, but nonetheless will continue to resonate in politics until either the differential rhythms of time, or a new and more profound trauma, stills their voice.

Notes

1. Philippe Joutard, *La légende des camisards, Histoire d'une sensibilité au passé* (Paris: Gallimard, coll. "Bibliotèque des Histoires," 1977).

2. Documentation de la mairie de Paris.

3. Documentation de la présidence de la République.

4. Jean Jacques Becker, "La mémoire, objet d'histoire," in Institut d'histoire du temps

présent, Ecrire l'Histoire du temps présent, hommage à François Bédarida (Paris: CNRS éditions, 1993) pp. 116-117.

5. Pierre Nora, "Ernest Lavisse, instituteur national," *Les Lieux de mémoire,* vol.1: *La République* (Paris: Gallimard, 1984) pp. 247-290.

6. Philippe Séguin, *Louis Napoléon le Grand* (Paris: Grasset, 1990).

7. Henry Rousso, *The Vichy Syndrome* (Cambridge: Harvard University Press, 1991).

8. Georges Pompidou, *Entretiens et discours, 1968-1974* vol. 1 (Paris: Plon, 1975) p. 158.

9. Thierry Wolton, *Le Grand Recrutement* (Paris: Grasset, 1993).

10. François Bédarida, "L'Histoire de la Résistance et 'l'affaire Jean Moulin'" *Jean Moulin et la Résistance en 1943*, Cahiers de l'Institut d'Histoire du temps présent, no. 27 (Paris: IHTP, 1994) p. 162.

11. François-Georges Dreyfus, *Histoire de Vichy* (Paris: Perrin, 1990).

12. Herve Hamon and Patrick Rotman, *Génération* (Paris: Editions du Seuil, 2 vol., 1987 and 1988).

13. Steven L. Kaplan, *Adieu 89* (Paris: Fayard, 1993).

14. Georges Clemenceau, *La Mêlée sociale* (Paris: Charpentier-Pasquelle, 1895) p. 140.

3

The France We Have Lost: Social, Economic, and Cultural Discontinuities

Richard F. Kuisel

The French are supposedly in a "funk." They are, according to journalists, authors, and even government planners, worried about the present and pessimistic about the future.[1] The "immigrant problem" exposes intolerance and defensiveness. Urban disorder and the State's ineffectiveness prompted a distressed Socialist deputy to exclaim, "postwar society is falling apart."[2] The disappearance, or what some call the *désertification*, of the traditional countryside provoked a warning from one senator: "We are spoiling France, we are undermining its identity."[3] And progress toward European integration aroused almost half the electorate to vote against the Maastricht Treaty. Opponents of Maastricht hold the treaty responsible for almost everything that has gone wrong including giving in to U.S. demands over GATT and the invasion of U.S. television programs.

French national pride is a given. But the irritability and pessimism of the "New France" requires an explanation. For the historian, the social, economic, and cultural transformations of the last few decades provide one answer to the current French malaise. Anxiety about "the France we have lost" accounts for much of the testiness of the 1990s. Rupture with the past has caused a keen sense of loss and vulnerability. Perhaps this malaise has been exaggerated by the press and it will quickly pass. Even so the discontinuities analyzed here are profound.[4]

Today the French ask themselves a question that was unimaginable in 1950 -- is France still France? Does France exist if there are no peasants and only a few practicing Catholics? If the French language is bastardized by American phrases, McDonald's sells hamburgers on the Champs-Elysées, Hollywood films dominate French cinema screens, and EuroDisney attracts over 3 million French visitors in its first year? If the price of a baguette rises and Renault becomes a private company? If the State cannot control the exchange rate of the franc and Brussels dictates agricultural policy? The actual answer to these questions is less significant than the existence of the inquiry or reflection. An awareness that their society is passing through a period of profound change makes the "New French" acutely self-conscious and defensive.

The past, in its socioeconomic and cultural dimensions, is important for the French. It survives as a warm memory, as an affinity for a certain society. The vanishing peasantry, immigration, Americanization, and an unprotected economy, among other developments of the postwar era, intersect, or clash, with a collective memory of what France was and, many think, should be again. The legacy of the past comes not from long-term socioeconomic continuity, but from short-term rapid change and a sentimental reluctance to accept this change. Recent trends have so transformed the France of the 1950s, the inward-looking, complacent, and distinctive "stalemate society," that the French have become uneasy about their inherited sense of collective identity, purpose, and direction. There is a tension between what has happened and how the French think and feel about the changes. The malaise of the "New France" is mental and sentimental -- it derives from a sense of *déracinement* or uprootedness that is both real and imagined and that is expressed in several ways ranging from nostalgia to paranoia. Expressed differently, in socioeconomic terms France chose a course of modernization during the 1950s and 1960s, but not everyone has accepted the consequences of this transformation and today few know where France is headed. As one observer has written: "French fears do not prefigure the future, they reflect the difficulty of purging the past."[5]

Social, economic, and cultural change prompt some to seek, define, assert, and protect what they consider to be "Frenchness," while others reflect on this transformation to argue France can, and should, adapt. Those who try to resist contemporary trends include the supporters of the National Front, with its racist and xenophobic agenda that articulates the discontent caused by social insecurity. But the ranks of opponents extend far beyond National Front voters to include at least a quarter of the population who, according to Stanley Hoffmann, retain "the notion of a simple, homogeneous, culturally unified 'hexagon' " and, may even reach out to include many of those who "revolted" against Maastricht.[6] There are also those who may express nostalgia for "the France we have lost" but are resolved to push forward. These people argue for the need to *redefine* national identity in order to *maintain* it as France adjusts to a new international order. The pro-Maastricht electorate belongs in this camp. France, caught today between these two poles of opinion, evokes the central dilemma of twentieth-century France, the dilemma posed by modernization.

This chapter will not offer a *tour d'horizon* of the French society and economy. It will omit much including trends in demography and urbanization or changes in the family and education. There is only space to select a few cases to make my argument for the France we have lost.

The Vanished Peasantry

For a historian, the most striking feature of the "New France" is the disappearance of peasant society. The family farm and the rural life associated with farming have receded or been so transformed that a way of life that historically defined Frenchness has virtually vanished.[7] The social class that still accounted for a third of the workforce at mid-century will soon drop to 5 percent, and this social fragment bears no resemblance to the historic class called "peasants." Since the last war over half the farms, many of which were smaller family units, have disappeared and large farms now provide the bulk of total output. The family farm and diversified agriculture (that made France a country of the proverbial 365 cheeses) have all but vanished because of the need for concentration and specialization. The *terroir* has been replaced by the *bassin*, e.g., *bassin céréalier*. Those who remain in the rural setting are an aging population and the sons of seven out of ten farmers do not intend to continue in agriculture.[8] Many who do reside in the countryside are not farmers (e.g., they are retirees), and farm wives supplement farm income by working outside agriculture.

Even the link between land and agriculture has been broken with crops grown *hors-sol*. Surviving farmers, as Bertrand Hervieu has pointed out, have lost their historic mission of providing food for their fellow citizens. When markets are global, when the French spend less and less on food, when farm products lose their local character and are sold by brand name, when farm commodities become raw material for prepared food, then the link between food and farm is less tangible and more remote. Hervieu concludes, "In the decade [1980s] when France became the second agricultural exporting power [in the world] it ceased to be an agrarian society."[9]

In this context Laurence Wylie's celebrated book entitled *Village in the Vaucluse* is relevant. Wylie tells of how one Provençal village, the town of Roussillon, has been transformed since his initial stay in 1950. Writing in 1987, Wylie explains how the old village, once marked by polyculture farms, isolation, and fear of outsiders, a lack of amenities, and anxiety about the future, has become a wealthy resort community with cosmopolitan residents, boutiques, and a sense of connection with the region, the nation, and the world.[10] In other communes like Roussillon that have become tourist attractions, professional organizers have tried to recreate traditional festivals where farmers play at using old farm tools. When farming becomes entertainment, then a way of life has been abandoned.

Why is this transformation important? Because long-term socioeconomic change in the countryside has so diminished a traditional point of reference that contemporary French men and women have difficulty defining Frenchness. For a society that defined itself by its peasantry for over a millennium, and in modern times kept a larger portion of its population on the land longer than other industrialized nations, this change represents a massive discontinuity. The transformation of the countryside has removed a social stratum that had anchored the French to their past. Rural France is a lived experience for fewer and fewer people and has increasingly become a page of history. How can the French of today continue to locate their identity in a way of life that has vanished? What was possible in 1900, or even in 1950, is not in 1993. In this case "the world we have lost" means a growing sense of *déracinement*.

The logical corollary is that as the differences between present and past have multiplied, nostalgia has intensified. Pierre Nora has observed: "It is very curious, but France is a country for which *la terre* would mean something even if there were no more farmers left."[11] In 1992 and 1993 we witnessed an expression of this sentiment when many urbanites rallied to the cause of farmers in their protest against the GATT negotiations. It might seem curious that farmers, who are such a small fragment of the electorate, possess the power to intimidate their government. There are several reasons for this political potency, including the farmers' skill at organizing demonstrations, agriculture's large share of the country's exports, and the strategic electoral role of farmers in many regions (in almost half of the departments 10 percent of the active population are farmers).[12] Yet none of these touch the heart of the matter. Psychologically, the farmers' plight evokes nostalgia among an urban populace that is sentimental about the countryside. To what extent this nostalgia is based on the experience of a parent, grandparent, or some other relative is an open question. Whatever the case, such experience is disappearing quickly. In 1991 when farmers presented their case to Paris by erecting stands serving wine, cheese, pâté, and other produce, according to the press, "a million Parisians turned out to welcome them as if they represented a threatened species."[13] This whole affair has the aura of a desperate effort to reconnect the mass of urban society with a rural past -- even though the contemporary farmer has only limited connections to this past.

In itself this vanished world does not mean a loss of identity because the French, like every other community, have multiple references for defining themselves. Yet the waning of "la France profonde" takes on added significance when one considers that some of the most fundamental references, for example language and culture, also face serious challenges in the New France.

A Multi-Ethnic, Secular, and Urban Society

A second discontinuity of recent decades has been the realization that French society has lost its capacity to assimilate outsiders. Despite a past marked by

immigration, the French, until well after World War II, dismissed ethnic differences because they believed in the transformative power of French education, the
idea of citizenship, and the other institutions of the Republic. For example, Alfred
Grosser has reflected: "For me, a young German Jew in exile, two years in a
[French] elementary school made Joan of Arc and Napoleon my ancestors and
Goethe a foreign author."[14] The French did not conceive of France as ethnically
divided. But now, because of the recent waves of immigration that have swept
across the country, the ethnic composition of the hexagon has begun to change
and the perception of ethnicity has surfaced. During the early postwar period, up
to the early 1960s, the proportion of *étrangers* among the resident populace was
just over 4 percent, but by 1982 it had jumped to 6.78 percent. There were less
than 2 million foreigners in 1954, but by 1990 their numbers had almost doubled
reaching 3.6 million.[15] Even more striking than the increase in numbers was the
change in the cultural origins of these newcomers. Recent arrivals differ from the
Italians, Portuguese, Belgians, Spanish, Poles, and others who came prior to the
1960s. For the past two decades, immigrants have originated less often from
Christian Europe, and ever increasingly from the Muslim world. In 1954 79
percent of the *étrangers* living in France were of European origin and only 13
percent were Arab/African, but by 1982 the proportion of Europeans had dropped to 47 percent and those of Arab/African background had climbed to 42.8
percent.[16] And these late arrivals, who clustered in certain cities or areas where
they became highly visible, did not "blend" or assimilate into French society as
easily as earlier generations of immigrants had.

What has begun to break down in the last twenty years is the process of
inclusion that historically permitted the French to believe in sociocultural unifor-
mity and to dismiss ethnicity. Almost three out of four French men and women
now complain that there are "too many Arabs."[17] Some politicians have either
exploited or pandered to this anti-foreigner sentiment. The National Front, with
its slogan "France for the French," is only the most shrill exponent of this xenophobic attitude. Former president Giscard d'Estaing has warned of an immigrant "invasion" and Jacques Chirac commiserated with those French men and
women living beside the "noise and smell" of immigrants.[18] Both the Socialists
and the Conservatives have moved toward ever tighter immigration controls.

This awareness of ethnic heterogeneity becomes doubly disturbing when complicated by the waning influence of the Catholic Church, that institution, which,
at least until the French Revolution, served to unify the nation. An increasingly
secularized society -- in which the number of *pratiquants*, that is those Catholics
who regularly attend services, includes only 14 percent of the population (although another 17 percent are occasional in their attendance); in which the church's
ability to set norms for private behavior, even among the faithful, has faded (one
poll indicated over half of practicing Catholics refuse to recognize the Pope's
authority over affairs like abortion); and in which vocations have declined at an
alarming rate (from 1,000 per year in 1950 to 100 in the 1980s) -- is hard pressed

to use the church as a defining institution.[19] Moreover, forty years ago the church controlled aggressive lay affiliates like the *Jeunesse Agricole Chrétienne* or the *Confédération Française des Travailleurs Chrétiens*. This is no longer the case. As Henri Mendras has observed, "the Catholic Church has become an institution like any other" so that the church can no longer claim, as it did as recently as the 1960s, that it was in charge of the spiritual life of the French.[20] Or as Alain Touraine has proclaimed, over the course of "a few decades France ceased to be Catholic." According to Touraine, contemporary Catholics conduct their private lives as others do, and the French in general have replaced religion with morality.[21]

The 1984 struggle over the Socialist-sponsored reform that edged toward incorporating private schools into the state system rallied three-quarters of the public to the church's side. But this groundswell of support had little to do with Catholicism; it was a protest for freedom of choice in education against an aggressive Jacobin State.[22] To pretend France is any longer "the eldest daughter of the Church" seems nearly as hollow as to pretend France is defined by peasant values.

The vanishing village landscape and the increasing secularization of French society relate to a third transformation that has marked contemporary France. This transformation, which can only receive brief mention here, is the urbanization of French society. A demographic map of France in 1900 shows a population widely distributed throughout the hexagon, but today four out of five inhabitants live in cities, with an enormous concentration in the Ile-de-France. Urban life presents challenges that were largely unknown in the traditional village. Insecurity, crime, AIDS, and other urban blights mark life in the city. More importantly, the institutions that traditionally sheltered the individual, and provided social solidarity and security against the vicissitudes of life, have been progressively weakened. As discussed above, the church has faded in importance. No longer is it a central institution in French society. Perhaps more fundamentally, the family, still the most basic social unit, has faced serious challenges in contemporary France. Referring to falling marriage rates and the growth of single-parent households, experts now speak of "the uncertain family."[23] Church and family were important institutions in the life of the village; their weakness or absence today can only complicate the adjustment to city life and to the process of urbanization in general.

In summary, social change has brought additional challenges to traditional conceptions of what it was to be French. One can no longer make easy reference to "our ancestors the Gauls" or "our Christian religion" -- not when large visible concentrations of residents lie outside this paradigm. A criterion that has traditionally defined Frenchness, that of a culturally uniform, Christian population, has lost its force to distinguish in the urbanized, multi-ethnic, secular society of the 1990s.

Americanization

"Americanization" is yet another dimension of the dramatic sociocultural transformation that has created the "New France." One of the transcendent trends of the post-1945 era has been the arrival of consumer society and mass culture, in part inspired and imported from the United States. This change, which began in the late 1950s and enveloped France by the 1960s, has further eroded a traditional sense of French identity. Recently, for example, a number of Socialist deputies attributed France's malaise to its "progressive Americanization," which they described as "growing individualism," the impoverishment of the state, the omnipotence of television, intemperate consumer spending and the emerging power of lobbies.[24] Or, as it is said, "on s'anglo-saxonise de plus en plus."

There are several dimensions relating the concept of Americanization to the contemporary crisis of French identity. First, Americanization has undermined the old France by adulterating linguistic purity. The French language, perhaps the single most important defining characteristic of Frenchness, has had to compromise with Americanization. French has incorporated a multitude of American words and phrases. Increasingly the need to know American/English -- at least for scholars, scientists, businessmen, politicians and others -- has made it, rather than French, the tongue of international communication. American/English is now the second language among the French. This "invasion" has precipitated a continuous series of controversies, such as the one over "Franglais" that erupted in the 1960s, and prompted repeated (and for the most part futile) efforts by the government to defend the language against American/English. In 1992, the government added a clause on the official status of French to the constitution of the Fifth Republic. And under the Balladur government legislation has been offered that would attempt to stem the Anglo-Saxon tide by, among other actions, banning the use of English on billboards and requiring film distributors to translate titles into French. The adoption of the American tongue strikes at the heart of identity. How could it be otherwise in a country, as one U.S. journalist quipped, "where the national spelling bee is conducted on prime time television" and where, according to a French newspaper, "defending or reforming spelling is a national psychodrama."[25]

Americanization has also disturbed confidence in a traditional conception of French high culture. This culture, closely associated with the French language itself, pivots on the humanities, the classics, philosophy, and the fine arts; insiders and outsiders commonly view this culture as synonymous with France. But this old, elite culture has also faced a challenge from Americanization in the form of mass culture. American mass culture means everything from the arrival of *Reader's Digest*, rock and roll and Coca-Cola in the early postwar years to McDonald's, television programs like *Dallas*, and the EuroDisney amusement park in more recent times. This culture, manufactured for everyone on a global scale, has appeared to many French men and women in the postwar era as an affront to "real" culture. The opening of the EuroDisney amusement park in 1992, for example, provoked some intellectuals to complain of an American effort to industrialize leisure. In fact this Americanized mass culture, rather than displacing traditional culture, has merely become a second culture in France, as it has almost everywhere on the globe.[26] But French defensiveness suggests that another pillar of Frenchness, the humanist, elite culture has weakened.

There is yet a third way Americanization has intruded. Some believe that U.S. consumerism is contrary to the French way. Several generations of French intellectuals, both secular and religious, from both Left and Right, have, for example, identified Americanization with consumerism and condemned it because it prizes material acquisitiveness. From this perspective those who elevate the act of purchase and the article purchased to the apex of their values degrade, rather than enrich, human society. For these critics (whose ranks are not limited to the intelligentsia), status in an old society like that of France has been, and should be, defined by family, lineage, education, manners, or style of life -- but not by possessions. Some of these opponents see Americanization as an attack on "bourgeois society" since the French bourgeoisie (*pace* Balzac) has reputedly always been defined by higher attributes rather than by material goods. *Le Monde* dramatized the danger of Americanization as early as 1949, when the Coca-Cola Company began marketing its soft drink in France. The paper stirred rumors about Coca-Cola posters defacing the facade of Notre Dame, arguing that what was at stake was "the moral landscape of France."[27] Whatever the case, consumer society from the traditionalist's perspective corrupts yet one more aspect of French identity.

Finally, Americanization has hastened the decline (though not brought the end) of anti-Americanism, which for decades had been a common way to define Frenchness. For decades, beginning in the interwar years and peaking in the 1950s and 1960s, the French could define their national characteristics by contrasting them with an American "other." The French were individualistic, mature, pessimistic, and civilized, while Americans were *les grands enfants*, naive optimists and uncivilized conformists. The fading of anti-Americanism since the 1970s has a complex set of causes but one of these has been the *banalisation* of America. *Le Monde*, once celebrated for its anti-Americanism, could thus print in 1984 that the French had become so Americanized that it was impossible to be anti-American any longer.[28] By the 1980s anti-Americanism seemed more like a chapter from the past rather than the national posture it appeared to be in the early 1950s or under de Gaulle's presidency.

The question then becomes, if Americanization has so intruded upon the French way of life, including assaults upon the French language, elite culture, traditional social values, and even a collective defense mechanism, that of anti-Americanism, are the French still French?[29] Americanization by challenging an inherited conception of culture and society adds another discontinuity. It has created an uneasiness about *banalisation* that endangers French exceptionalism. And this is a most insidious danger because it is no longer, as once was perceived, an outside threat, but now comes from within -- for today the French themselves revel in the comforts and attractions of consumer society and mass culture.

Economic Discontinuities

In economic affairs there are also discontinuities that disconcert. Surely the most important of these is the end of the national economy. As recently as the 1950s the French Republic could conceive and execute a truly national economic policy, one that largely ignored the international situation. Thus the early economic plans assumed control of the economy within the hexagon (and its colonies). But this closed economy, one that dates back to the nineteenth century, began to open in the 1960s so that de Gaulle had to struggle with the European Community over issues like foreign investment and agricultural policy. By the 1970s expanding trade with the European Community, multinationals, and massive foreign investment had all penetrated the national economy. France was becoming an open trading nation far more dependent on imports and exports than ever before. For example, at the birth of the Fifth Republic, the share of imports and exports in the GDP were 9.7 and 8.9 percent, respectively. By 1980 these shares had climbed to 26.5 and 24.2 percent.[30] The traditional French economy, the inward looking *métropole* that traded mainly with its colonies, has disappeared. Economic globalization during the last few decades has only expedited the process of removing France's economic borders. One lesson of the period 1981-1983 was that the Republic could not steer a course at odds with that of its Western trading partners. Thus one of the major features of the French economy, one that historically characterized economic life, was coming to an end by the 1980s. National economic frontiers were as porous as cultural boundaries. And as the State surrendered its powers the government's ability to protect and act in behalf of this economy also withered. By the 1980s France was more thoroughly immersed in global trade than at any time in its past.

But such interdependence did not come without problems. The French balance of trade, unlike that of Germany or Japan, has been chronically fragile. Between 1946 and 1987, for example, exports equalled or surpassed imports in only sixteen years.[31] Most troubling has been the lag in the export of manufactured goods. France has run a trade deficit in consumer and household products and in intermediate goods and business equipment with most developed countries. Its share of the global export market for such goods fell from 8.6 percent to 6.2 percent between 1950 and 1985.[32] According to Jean-Claude Casanova, French exports of industrial goods have not been price competitive and the few sectors in which France has a comparative advantage, such as agro-food or land transportation equipment, have not grown much in the last twenty years.[33] French manufactured exports are too often state-subsidized, standardized products, utilizing mid-range technology, e.g., armaments, nuclear power equipment, turnkey plants, which are directed at the developing world.[34]   In fact whatever surplus France earns in exporting manufactured goods comes from sales to developing countries. Equally important, the French market share of high-tech exports, such as electronic and aeronautical equipment, is far smaller than that of the United States, Japan, or Germany.[35] The import situation amplifies the problem. Whereas the contribution of industrial goods to the nation's exports has remained unchanged over the years, imports of manufactured products have jumped from half to over three-quarters of total imports since 1950.[36] Thus France continues to suffer from a trade imbalance with the most industrialized countries and debilitating import penetration.

Exposure to the vagaries of the international market has caused doubts, backsliding and protest. Since World War II, U.S. economic domination has been the principal target of Gallic wrath. Even when France was most dependent upon the United States for economic aid, during the early postwar years, majority opinion held that the Marshall Plan was a means of promoting Yankee economic hegemony in Europe. In the 1960s de Gaulle launched campaigns against U.S. investment and the reserved status of the dollar, and the best-seller of the decade was Jean-Jacques Servan-Schreiber's *The American Challenge*. Recent attacks on Washington should be no surprise. The GATT negotiations provoked one French farmer to lament, "The Americans have us by the throat," while other farmers overturned Coca-Cola vending machines, torched Old Glory and poked its ashes with a pitchfork near the U.S. Embassy.[37] Moreover, in one poll four out of five expressed solidarity with the farmers' opposition to the deal struck with Washington.[38]

This new involvement with foreign trade, which has often provoked recriminations against the world's biggest trader, the United States, and caused anxiety about the other global economic giants, Germany and Japan, (not to speak of Brussels and the European Community) adds an economic dimension to the previously discussed sociocultural trends that have undermined a French sense of control of their own destiny. The nation's economic fortunes seem to be determined by outsiders and global forces.

A second rupture associated with the economy occurred because of the abrupt downturn in the business cycle in the 1970s. After nearly thirty years of steady, even accelerating, growth, the economy went into a tailspin in 1974 that has lasted for two decades. Industrial production, for example, which had been growing at almost 6 percent since the 1950s fell to an annual average of 1 percent between 1974 and 1990.[39] Optimism turned to cynicism when governments and experts predicted an end to the crisis, yet hard times continued. Of all the negative effects unemployment proved to be most intractable and debilitating. During the postwar boom unemployment seemed to have been conquered, but once it revived in the late 1960s it spun out of control. First one million *chômeurs*, then two, and by 1993 over three million. Booming businesses like automobile sales went bust; armament sales flattened when Middle Eastern clients cut back their purchases, and the core of the industrial economy, sectors like steel, coal, shipbuilding and textiles, faced the scourge of deindustrialization. Moreover, old structural deficiencies like those in occupational training, research and development, and marketing now haunted the French. So did troubles in the volume and type of exports. Tried and true policies also failed. For example, as Christian Stoffaës has argued, the inherited statist style of financing investment discouraged the free disposition of capital by private lenders and Michael Loriaux writes of the faulty "overdraft economy" that came to an end in the 1970s after it ensnared the State and strangled investment.[40] Twenty years of stagnation have followed the *trente glorieuses* marking yet another way that recent economic developments have brought discontinuity and insecurity.

The Transformation of State Intervention

The transformation of the State heightens contemporary insecurity. All students of the French economy note the heavy hand of the state in its history. And all observers of the present note how France has apparently reversed this pattern since 1983. In fact the decade between 1983 and 1993 represents the acceleration of a shift in the relationship between the state and the economy that began thirty years earlier bringing with it yet another source for the current malaise.

Over the *longue durée* France has had possibly the most interventionist record among all West European countries distinguishing it sharply from the Anglo-Americans. The State, as the guardian of the national interest, has been an energetic economic agent whose activism has been both acclaimed and scorned in a debate that is over three hundred years old. Some have praised the State for its Saint-Simonian or modernizing achievements. The peak of Saint-Simonian agency came during the mid-twentieth century -- from the 1930s to the 1970s, during the decades that spanned the depression, the war, reconstruction, Gaullist statism, and stagflation.

From this perspective interventionism was responsible for the successful catch-up and modernization effort that marked the *trente glorieuses* when the State provided needed investment, promoted productivity, prodded reluctant sectors, upended *situations acquises*, and opened the economy to foreign trade. In these years a nationalized firm like Electricité de France was a source of pride. French economic planning seemed to provide a "third way" between capitalism and socialism, a model for other nations to follow. But others have laid much of France's economic miseries at the feet of the State, blaming it for a suffocating *dirigisme* that stifled competition and entrepreneurship, nurtured dependence, burdened producers with heavy taxes, subsidized lame-duck industries, and protected activities that market forces would have closed down.

Whatever assessment is correct, this *dirigiste* style began to moderate as early as the 1950s, and this trend continued into the 1980s as France moved steadily toward a truly mixed economy. Without stumbling over the difficulty of trying to measure quantitatively the shifting dimensions of the State's reach, the goals and means of interventionism were changing during the Fourth Republic. For example, the public share of investment fell, some prices were deregulated, nationalized firms were "debudgetized," the boundary between public and private sectors blurred, and productivity became the responsibility of private enterprise. In the 1960s and 1970s interventionism did not so much shrink as it changed in form and spirit. It moved from direct to indirect supervision, from constraint to promotion. More important, state intervention was made increasingly to conform to the logic of the market, as for example with respect to taxes, credits, and subsidies. Nationalized companies incorporated criteria of profitability and economic planning waned. By the end of the 1970s deregulation had become government strategy.

Looking back national planning appears not as some innovative "third way" between the market and *dirigisme*, but as a means of readying the French economy for liberalization by making both policy-makers and private managers more expert and confident about forecasting and planning within a market environment. Similarly nationalization may be seen now as a step toward readying certain vulnerable enterprises and sectors for privatization and global competition -- even if this has been, from a certain viewpoint, an unintended result.

The reversal of Socialist policy after the 1981-1983 experiment and the subsequent revolt against the State merely intensified this long-term trend. The ten years between 1983 and 1993 witnessed: the deregulation of many sectors, including telecommunications and the financial market (scrapping practices like the *encadrement du crédit*); the end of a privileged position for certain public agencies like the Crédit Agricole; the privatization of nationalized firms; and a reformed industrial policy that narrowed its scope and refrained from assisting lame ducks. Some of this deregulation seems overdue. Thus the controls that have been lifted on foreign exchange date back to 1939, and some price controls, like those on gasoline, go all the way back to 1928! And the once sharp boundaries between public and private spheres blurred further when nationalized firms began borrowing from private investors or buying shares in private firms as Renault did with Volvo.[41]

Even more important the State has surrendered some of its historic responsibilities and sacrificed some of its traditional powers. The principle of full employment, which has a constitutional basis, has been abandoned. Double-digit unemployment is now accepted as a fact of economic life. Most may blame the government for permitting such social devastation, but few really expect the State to cure it. Meanwhile the advance of European integration increasingly deprives the State of some of its control over the economy and converts it into a negotiator representing French interests in Brussels. The French State has today virtually forfeited its historic right of using interest rates, budget deficits, and exchange controls as means of managing the national economy. The *dirigiste* State of 1950 is no more.

In the grandest terms intervention has shifted from protection and control to promotion. The State's new responsibility is to ready French firms or sectors for global competition, ensure research and development, train or retrain the labor force, and negotiate among economic actors. As Pierre Rosanvallon has argued, the French State has finally stopped what it started during the French Revolution, that is, trying to remake society and the economy.[42] It has dropped its postwar role as a "modernizing State" or "Keynesian State" that educated the French about the value of industrialism and sponsored grand projects. A mature civil society, in this view, no longer needs a pedagogical or paternalistic State. The new task is for the State to modernize itself not for it to modernize the economy.

For the "New France" then, *dirigisme* is dead. But the mixed economy is very much alive. The interventionist tendency may have been transformed over the last thirty years, but it survives today, giving France a mixed economic structure. The notion of the State as an economic guide, as an instrument to lead the economy and to compensate for weakness, as a coordinator of economic activity, and as a source of reward and punishment for economic actors has been and continues to be part of the Gallic credo, even if it is currently spoken *sotto voce* and the *Ecole Nationale d'Administration* has been exiled to Strasbourg. A substantial public sector and system of control mechanisms remain, as does nominal planning and some ministries remain attached to interventionist ways. Moreover, various social groups, like farmers, the medical profession, and business, are still quick to look to the State for help.

In practice the French have moved to the middle, which is to say they have not joined the Anglo-American camp. An "industrial policy," for example, does not frighten the French as it does Americans. For the French have never embraced competition as Anglo-Americans have, or as one commentator writes about the market: "The Socialists are still reticent, the Communists remain stoutly opposed, the Jacobins are allergic, the ecologists are ignorant, and the vested interests have an insatiable appetite for exemptions."[43] One might add that French conservatives, compared to their U.S. counterparts, seem like unrepentant interventionists. Indeed the French, in general, seem to embrace a mixed economy as an alternative to what they term "wild" or "anarchistic" U.S. capitalism with its wasteful competition, its brutal industrial relations, and its apparent indifference to the harsh social impact of economic change. There are advantages to the middle Gallic way and the French wisely seem to recognize its strengths. The late Jean Bouvier used to make the distinction between *faire*, *faire-faire*, and *laissez-faire* in discussing public policy. The French will probably continue to prefer *faire-faire* to *laissez-faire*.

No one should be surprised if a protectionist *cum* interventionist mood reappears in the wake of the retreat from Maastricht and deepening hard times. But the transformation of the State over the last thirty years has ended mid-century *dirigisme*. It seems safe to predict that there will be no further bouts of national-ization, or the imposition of massive controls, or a revival of national economic planning in the style of the 1960s.

The French State of the 1990s, stripped of some of its powers over the economy and committed to a new agenda, bears little resemblance to its paternalistic pre-decessor. But this represents one more "loss" for the French, one more source of anxiety because their traditional protector has now retired. The market has re-placed the plan, the postwar ambition of *aménagement du territoire* has been abandoned and, in general, the French, instead of feeling liberated from the na-tional State, perceive themselves increasingly subordinated to an international market. A passive State, whose principal task is to help its citizenry submit to the rule of international competitiveness, has lost much of its legitimacy and iden-tity.[44]

In addition, the State cannot be relied upon to perform its traditional task of mobilizing national energies. French economic history is marked by a seemingly endless quest for *rattrapage* -- in order to compete with industrial leaders France, usually inspired by the State, has had to launch extraordinary efforts to close a perceived gap. One could go back as far as the 1830s to find episodes of this catch-up fever. This tendency to use the State to overcome perceived backward-ness surfaced most recently during the early years of Mitterrand's presidency. There has been a persistent anxiety about second-rank stature, a sense of relative inferiority in spite of a noteworthy record of economic and technological tri-umphs. But today, even though major structural weaknesses persist and new ones have emerged, the question is whether the means utilized in the past, that of the State leading a national economic effort, can be employed. The issue is whether the changes within France, within Europe and beyond have rendered this tradi-tional means of catch-up obsolete. Here too there are doubts that the State can or should, as it has in the past, act as the agent of renovation.

Fin de Siècle France

Traditional France has passed into history. This passage may end, or at least blur, French exceptionalism, but it does not mean the end of French nationalism. Far from it. In fact the intensity of national assertiveness today reflects the inse-curity caused by socioeconomic rupture and cultural *banalisation*. The ratifica-tion of the Maastricht Treaty is a case in point. Some senators who opposed the accord, for example, announced, as if to convince themselves: "Of the twelve States of the community, France is the one most attached to its identity and na-tional unity."[45] Is this French hubris or self-doubt?

Almost half of the electorate voted against the treaty. Although the reasons for this opposition are numerous, many voters blamed the European Community for expediting the erosion of national identity, for example, by supposedly foster-ing immigration, Americanization, and subservience to outside pressures. Analysis of the Maastricht vote suggests opposition came largely from farmers, workers, and the unemployed, from the countryside and depressed industrial cities, from those who felt most threatened by recent changes, whereas the electorate that approved the treaty were more highly educated, held better jobs, had experience with international travel, and lived in major cities.[46] Almost two out of three Parisians, for example, voted in favor of the accord. *Le Monde* observed the vote divided France in two: "a France of fear, of preserving vested interests, of reject-ing the 'other,' of indifference to the world; and a France, open to the exterior, convinced that responses of the past will not do for the 21st century."[47] Maastricht may not be an altogether accurate measure of resistance to change, but it did reveal the anxieties generated by the massive transformation of French economy, society, and culture since the war. The testy mood of the "New French" expresses the apprehension and defensiveness that comes with recognition of the loss of an "Old France."

In recent years many observers have commented on the French search for the old, ranging from revivals of folklore and village festivals to a passion for pre-serving the national *patrimoine*. One historian in 1987, noting the public's thirst for reading history and nostalgia about the national *patrimoine* wrote: "What we are currently witnessing is a crisis of national identity."[48] The recent publication of Pierre Nora's multi-volume study entitled *Les Lieux de mémoire*, has been called the latest, and best, attempt to recast a national history. It has been likened to Ernest Lavisse's celebrated history in that, like Lavisse's volumes, which ap-peared in the wake of the French defeat in the Franco-Prussian war, the publica-tion and reception of *Les Lieux de mémoire* suggests a nation in crisis, one that finds itself beset by forces like the intrusions of the global economy and distressed by ebbing confidence in such givens as the excellence of the French educational system.[49]

In this time of uncertainty the French again seek refuge in the memories of the nation. Evocations of national history and nostalgia for the past express, in this case, anxiety about "the France we have lost." They suggest a search for anchors in the new fluid and diverse society that lacks the old hierarchies, the old defining institutions and habits, the traditional social classes and elite culture that once gave it its character. At the end of his presidency General de Gaulle, in private, mourned the passing of his France even though he had done much to promote its transformation. Since the war the French have lived in a moment of discontinuity and now, what once was confined to the private musings of a con-servative general, is at the heart of the nation's malaise.

Some of the principal social, economic, and cultural features of the France of the 1990s are indeed new. And they all point in the same direction -- toward the end, and thus the need for redefinition, of what has historically defined the na-tion. This *fin de siècle* France is different from the France of 1900 or even 1950 because its boundaries (economic, social, and cultural) are porous. Because its society now appears to be ethnically divided. Because key institutions and ways of life that identified Frenchness, such as the Catholic Church, the peasantry, linguistic purity and prestige, a bourgeois society, and a paternalistic State have faded. Because society and culture have become, to a degree, Americanized. Because the economy is more embedded in Europe and the world than ever before. The France that was once labeled the "stalemate society," the France characterized by exceptionalism, isolation, resistance to modernity, a peasant base, and bourgeois domination -- that mid-century France is gone. Now the question is how will this multi-ethnic, open, urbanized, Americanized, and secularized society strive to maintain its distinctiveness.

The tension between old and new is captured in Mitterrand's celebrated aphorism "La France est notre patrie, l'Europe est notre avenir."[50] But this is precisely the problem facing the "New France" -- to discover a new design that will sustain French difference. Or as Alain Duhamel has written: "At the end of this 20th century France doubts itself. It knows what it was; it knows what it is no longer; it doesn't know what it is becoming."[51] Perhaps Duhamel is right when he argues that the French need a new collective project that will make them exemplary if they can no longer be exceptional.

Notes

1. See, for example, Alain Duhamel, *Les Peurs françaises* (Paris: Flammarion, 1993); Alan Riding, "The French Funk," *New York Times Magazine*, 21 March 1993; Jean-Louis Bourlanges, *Le Diable est-il européen?* (Paris: Editions Stock, 1992); and Secrétariat d'Etat au Plan, *Entrer dans le XXIe siècle: essai sur l'avenir de l'identité française* (Paris: Editions La Découverte/La Documentation française, 1990). Also note the controversy over anti-racism and national identity entitled "Autour du Malaise français" that appeared in *Le Débat*, 75 (May-August 1993), pp. 116-144.

2. Quoted by Alan Riding in "France Questions Its Identity as It Sinks into 'Le Malaise,'" *New York Times*, 23 December 1990, pp. 1, 8.

3. Hubert Haenel, "La France abîmée," *Figaro*, 26 September 1991, p. 2.

4. I trust my title will not offend. How dare an American write of "the France *we* have lost?" I confess, despite a career of writing about "modernization," that I share in French nostalgia for the past -- thus my identification with "we" in the title. I too am guilty of romanticizing the society I first visited thirty years ago and, in many respects, regret its passing.

5. Duhamel, *Les Peurs françaises*, pp. 15-16.

6. Stanley Hoffmann, "The Big Muddle in France," *New York Review of Books*, 18 August 1988, p. 56.

7. For the transformation of the peasantry since 1950 see Annie Moulin, *Peasantry and Society in France Since 1789* (New York: Cambridge University Press, 1991), pp. 165-199; Henri Mendras, *La Fin des paysans suivi d'une réflexion sur la Fin des paysans*

vingt ans après (Arles: Acte Sud, 1984); and for the current situation: Bertrand Hervieu, "Un impossible Deuil: A propos de l'agriculture et du monde rural en France," *French Politics and Society*, 10 (Fall 1992), pp. 41-59.

8. Hervieu, "Un impossible Deuil," pp. 44, 51.

9. Hervieu, "Un impossible Deuil," p. 58.

10. Laurence Wylie, "Roussillon, '87: Returning to the Village in the Vaucluse," *French Politics and Society*, 7 (Spring 1989), pp. 1-26.

11. Quoted by Riding in "The French Funk."

12. Hervieu, "Un impossible Deuil," p. 45.

13. *New York Times*, 10 November 1992.

14. Quoted in *Entrer dans le XXIe siècle*, p. 152.

15. Patrick Weil, *La France et ses étrangers* (Paris: Calmann-Levy, 1991), annexes. For the history of immigration and the notion of France as a cultural melting pot see: Gérard Noiriel, *Le Creuset français, histoire de l'immigration, XIXe-XXe siècles* (Paris: Seuil, 1988) and *Population, immigration et identité nationale en France 19e-20e siècle* (Paris: Hachette, 1993).

16. Weil, *La France et ses étrangers*, annexes.

17. *The Economist*, 12 June 1993, p. 57.

18. Both Giscard and Chirac are quoted by Riding "The French Funk." One former minister has called for the expulsion of all unemployed immigrants. Michel Poniatowski said "I knew France under German occupation" and "now I feel the same humiliation because we risk a change in our identity under outside pressure" (*New York Times*, 22 June 1991).

19. Data from Henri Mendras and Alistair Cole, *Social Change in Modern France: Towards a Cultural Anthropology of the Fifth Republic* (New York: Cambridge University Press, 1991), pp. 60-65.

20. Mendras in *Recent Social Trends in France, 1960-1990*, Michel Forse et al., eds. (Montreal: McGill-Queen's University Press, 1993), p. 193.

21. Alain Touraine, "Existe-t-il encore une société française?", *The Tocqueville Review*, 11 (1990), pp. 154-56.

22. John Ambler, "Educational Pluralism in the French Fifth Republic" in *Searching for the New France*, James F. Hollifield and George Ross, eds. (New York: Routledge, 1991), pp. 200-02, 212.

23. *Entrer dans le XXIe siècle*, p. 121.

24. Quoted by Riding, "France Questions Its Identity." Individualism and conformity are both associated with American society. This is one contradiction in the French stereotype of Americans.

25. Jim Hoagland in the *Washington Post*, 22 July 1990, pp. C1, C4; Hoagland quotes *Libération*.

26. Todd Gitlin in *New York Times*, 3 May 1992, pp. 1, 30.

27. *Le Monde*, 30 December 1949.

28. Nicolas Beau, "Les Français de l'Oncle Sam," *Le Monde*, 4-5 November 1984.

29. My recent book, *Seducing the French: The Dilemma of Americanization* (Berkeley: University of California Press, 1993), concludes that in spite of Americanization the French remain French.

30. Pierre Rosanvallon, *L'Etat en France de 1789 à nos jours* (Paris: Seuil, 1990), p. 262.

31. Jean-Claude Casanova, "Les Echanges extérieurs; un équilibre précaire," in *Entre l'Etat et le marché: l'économie française des années 1880 à nos jours*, Maurice Lévy-Leboyer and Jean-Claude Casanova, eds. (Paris: Gallimard, 1991), p. 550.

32. Casanova, "Les Echanges extérieurs," p. 558.

33. Casanova, "Les Echanges extérieurs," pp. 566-68.

34. Patrick McCarthy, "France Faces Reality: *Rigueur* and the Germans," in *Recasting Europe's Economies: National Strategies in the 1980s*, eds. David P. Calleo and Claudia Morgenstern, eds. (Lanham, MD: University Press of America, 1990), p. 50; Rand Smith " 'We Can Make the Ariane, but We Can't Make Washing Machines': the State and Industrial Performance in Post-war France," *Contemporary France*, vol. 3, *A Review of Interdisciplinary Studies*, Jolyon Howorth and George Ross, eds. (London: Pintner, 1989), pp. 175-202.

35. According to Casanova ("Les Echanges extérieurs," p. 568) the French share in 1986 was only 6.4 percent compared to 25.7 percent for the United States, 22.4 percent for Japan, and 13.4 percent for West Germany.

36. Data from Casanova, "Les Echanges extérieurs," pp. 556-57.

37. *New York Times*, 10 November 1992.

38. *News From France*, 4 December 1992, p. 5.

39. Christian Stoffaës, "La Restructuration industrielle, 1945-1990" in *Entre l'Etat et le marché*, p. 459.

40. Stoffaës, "La Restructuration industrielle, 1945-1990," p. 471; Michael Loriaux, *France after Hegemony: International Change and Financial Reform* (Ithaca: Cornell University Press, 1991).

41. For the State's economic role in the decades of the 1970s and 1980s see André Gueslin, *L'Etat, l'économie et la société française, XIXe-XXe siècle* (Paris: Hachette, 1992), pp. 199-213.

42. Rosanvallon, *L'Etat en France*, pp. 266-67.

43. Duhamel, *Les Peurs françaises*, p. 43.

44. For an acute analysis of the State's loss of mission and legitimacy, or what is called the "disoriented State," see the report of advisers to the Plan: *Entrer dans le XXIe siècle*, pp. 157-182.

45. Quoted by Alec Stone in "Ratifying Maastricht: France Debates European Union," *French Politics and Society*, 11 (Winter 1993) 82. Charles Pasqua displayed the same anxiety when, in arguing against the move toward monetary and political union, he proclaimed: "In countries like France, where state and nation are inseparable, the very existence of the nation is threatened." Quoted by Ronald Tiersky in "French Foreign Policy Stumbles," *French Politics and Society*, vol. 11 (Winter 1993), p. 97.

46. Stone, "Ratifying Maastricht," pp. 83-84; *New York Times*, 22 September 1992, pp. 1, 16; *News From France*, 25 September 1992.

47. Jacques Lesourne in *Le Monde*, 19 September 1992, p. 1.

48. Jean-Pierre Rioux, "Twentieth-Century Historiography: Clio in a Phyrgian Bonnet," in *Contemporary France*, vol. 1 *A Review of Interdisciplinary Studies*, Jolyon Howorth and George Ross, eds. (London: F. Pinter, 1987), p. 204.

49. Yves Lequin's review of *Les Lieux de mémoire* in *Magazine littéraire*, February 1993, pp. 27-28.

50. Mitterand, "Lettre à tous les Français," *Le Monde*, 8 April 1988.

51. Duhamel, *Les Peurs françaises*, p. 243.

4

Democratic Dysfunctions and Republican Obsolescence: The Demise of French Exceptionalism

Alain-Gérard Slama

The rise of international political, economic, and demographic interdependence, along with the collapse of the Soviet empire and of the Soviet Union, has dramatically changed the problematic of European order. For its part, Germany must deal with difficulties that can be resolved even if they are unprecedented: citizens of the former German Democratic Republic must be given political, economic, and cultural perspectives that are based upon common interests and an evident cultural heritage. France, however, is the country in Europe in which this new situation has produced the greatest shock.

France today is profoundly challenged by a mutation that is perceived as changing radically its traditional conception of independence and sovereignty. The whole pattern of national identity has been turned upside down. A quasi-Copernican revolution is taking place at a very basic level in people's minds as they begin to realize that their scope of individual choices has been dramatically widened by the evolution of technology and by new economic and demographic dependencies. The result is a fundamental shift in the relation between the French and their *état nation*, a relationship that is tightly linked with the assumption and practice of citizenship.

This complete loss of any political compass has led to both the danger of a national-populist reaction, and a paradoxical strengthening of state attempts to control society, in the proper sense of Tocqueville's prediction. A new cleavage is opening between the state and society that is likely to dominate France in the years ahead, one that will challenge the core sense of what it has meant to be French. This chapter discusses the intellectual and ideological dimensions of these trends.

One can point to two closely connected elements in this evolution. The first is the obsolescence of the Republican conception of politics, which has come at the precise time that the main goals of the founders of the French Republic looked to be uncontested. This has resulted on the one hand in a crisis in the Rousseauian conception of law, and on the other hand in a crisis of trust in traditional checks and balances. The second element is the explosion of corporatist, community and differentialist claims, which raises the specter of selective memory, and even of racism, on the one hand, and on the other hand, the replacement of political representatives by a new generation of technocrats, "experts" and "specialists" who undermine the sense of personal involvement essential to citizenship.

The Demise of the Republican Model

Since the French Revolution, the classic cleavage in the country's political and social life has been the battle over the Republican model. A small fringe of elites never accepted the demise of the Ancien Regime and other groups argued that the institutions of the Republic simply replaced one ruling class with another. When one examines France today, however, it appears as if there is now a broad political consensus based on the Republican conception of politics. Moreover, the essential objectives of the French Republicans seem to have been attained. The main conflicts that have defined the political and social landscape of France as a Republic have certainly receded.

The institutions of this, the Fifth Republic are, by and large, universally accepted, thanks to the tardy but real acceptance by the Socialist Party of the "refondation" of the Republic completed by de Gaulle,[1] and to the decline of the Communist Party. The second *cohabitation* of President Mitterrand and a Premier of the Right, while not necessarily comfortable for either man, has functioned properly. On the extreme Right, the National Front does not contest the political system itself. On the Left, only a very small fringe among the ecologists (the "deep ecology" current) maintains a revolutionary agenda.

The old struggle between the Republic and the Catholic Church, especially concerning the status of private schools, was ended in the 1984 agreement between the Catholics (who now acknowledge the principle of secularism) and the Socialist government after the Savary legislative proposal for a "unified education service" was aborted. The demonstrations in January 1994, provoked by the legislative bill on decentralization and national aid for private schools, attested more to the poor health of public schools than to any real hostility to private ones. The news of the government's withdrawal of the bill was met with relief by the Catholic Church.

The Socialist Party has abandoned its call for economic "structural reforms" (so called by Leon Blum) -- i.e., nationalizations -- at least since François Mitterrand put forward the "neither-nor" formula (neither privatizations nor new nationalizations) in the "Letter" announcing his platform for the presidential elections of 1988. The entente between Mitterrand and Prime Minister Edouard Balladur, in the face of the GATT negotiations and hesitation among the political parties (except the Communists and the extreme right), illustrated an increasing convergence among the major decision-makers in the field of foreign affairs, at least insofar as the vital interests of the French economy are concerned. The dispute over the European Community divides all the parties, but has much more to do with the choice of means than with the aim itself. Last but not least, the nuclear deterrent, long criticized by the Socialist Party, is no longer a source of conflict between the Right and the Left.

If one of the founders of the Third Republic were to return to today's France, he would undoubtedly be impressed by this level of consensus. Considering that the only problems that directly oppose the Left and the Right are now immigration and internal security, and that these problems are of mere secondary importance when compared with the great struggles of the time over institutions, religious affairs, and foreign policy, he could easily conclude that the end of the twentieth Century has seen the arrival of the Republican utopia. Observing the enlarged middle class, he would think, along with M. Giscard d'Estaing, that the Republic's project for integration through education, social development, and law had been completed.

There are reasons to believe, however, that the present situation does not represent an authentic consensus. It is neither the result of a real political debate nor of a true political synthesis. In reality, the current political situation is best explained not by consensus -- a word presently used, as seen below, in another democratic meaning than in the former Republican minds -- but by confusion resulting from the destabilization of the Republic's foundations. Before proceeding with this analysis, therefore, a brief review of this foundation is in order.

Mme de Staël, in *De l'Allemagne*, remarked that Germany was a nation in search of a state and France was a state in search of a nation.[2] The overriding purpose of the founders of the Republic was to consummate this bond between the people and the state through the achievement of the main aspirations of democracy: equality and popular participation in the making of law. The Republic itself was to be built upon two bases: the unification of memory and of territory; and the idea of economic progress and social mobility. People, law, memory, territory, and economic and social progress were all linked together and perceived as a continuum.

The means of this national unification process are well known: the school system, the creation of a historical synthesis, conscription, Republican rituals and feasts, and the development of a communication framework, among others. The great lay idea that inspired this policy was put forward by Ernest Renan in his famous 1882 lecture "What is a nation ?"[3] A nation, explained Renan, cannot be defined by a race, a language, a religion, or a frontier. A nation is "a common will," "a spiritual principle," "a daily plebiscite," anchored in the awareness of a common past, a common glory. This communal experience of an identical heritage, added Renan, is conditioned not only by a common memory, but by the "forgetting" (oubli) of the conflicts that divided the nation in the past. This point will be returned to below.

Renan, who spoke for his country and for his time, after the defeat of Sedan in 1870, described the national "common will" as a result of an ancestral legacy transmitted from generation to generation. Among many influences, his analysis highlights the Republican doctrine of assimilation, and its first corollary, the use of the principle of "jus soli" to define citizenship. According to the French system, children of foreign origin born in France become ipso facto French, but they lose this right if they return to their country (unlike a French person born in the United States, who does not lose his U.S. nationality if he decides to live in France). This example illustrates the prevalence in French culture of a conception of nationality founded on individuals sharing the same customs, the same idea of modernization (equating progress and equality), and the same practice of citizenship.

During the last two Republics and, under the Fifth Republic until the seventies, this model had to face two main kinds of challenge, both of which rejected the Republican formulation of modernization. First, the traditionalist and the Bonapartist Right contested modernization, which they characterized as menacing the territorial and historical *continuum* of the nation (*il s'agit du continuum spatio-temporal*). They saw a modern French state as eradicating qualities that were central to their understanding of what was French, including structures of privilege and authority. Herein lies the main source of fascism in France, although it never existed as completely as elsewhere in Europe, thanks to the strength of the intellectual rupture of 1789. The "counter-revolutionary" right was obliged to adopt some of the concepts of the Enlightenment, such as citizenship, the vote, and freedom.[4] Charles Maurras' *Action française*, which attempted a specific and radical counter-revolutionary synthesis, is an exception in the history of the Right, which explains why, at the end of the thirties, many of Maurras', followers confused their *engagement* with fascism.

The second basic challenge came from the extreme Left and was exactly the reverse. It consisted of a denial of the Republican idea of nation from the point of view of social modernization. Pacifists, Anarchists, and communist or Guesdist (but not Jauresian) Marxists, all criticized the formal rights conveyed by citizenship and opposed these rights to "real" rights, from which a part of the society was excluded. They rejected the idea of the continuity of the nation, claiming it was simply a myth propagated by the exploiters, and they appealed to the international solidarity of the poor and of the workers.

In reality, thanks to the double influence of primary school teachers and of the German menace, there was a pronounced Republican imprint on the minds of the French. The most violent attacks against the regime, coming from the extreme Right or from the extreme Left, both had to refer to a common memory, and for France, this memory had been built by the Republicans. The internalization of the Republican culture was so deep, that even after 1940, Pétain was obliged to deal with his image as a "Republican marshall." And it is remarkable that, when these two challenges came to a peak in 1958 under the pressure of the Algerian war, de Gaulle used the traditional Republican pattern to reestablish a base for the regime: the memory of the Resistance stressed both the theme of the national *continuum* and that of modernity (from the Gaullist theory of tanks to the doctrine of nuclear deterrence).

This quick review of the Republican model is necessary to comprehend the depth and to appreciate the consequences of the present rupture. France's political culture was not prepared to face shocks that would strike *simultaneously* at the *national continuum* and the definition of modernity. The whole intellectual frame of reference in which both the supporters of Republican principles and their opponents operated has now been turned upside down. The great event characterized by François Furet as "the end of French exceptionalism,"[5] is a total breakdown of all the categories that were used by the French to think about politics. As a result of this intellectual upheaval, neither the traditional nor the progressive challenges to the Republican model have the same meaning as formerly -- even if the psychological attitudes remain, on the surface, unchanged.

The first shock comes from the weakening of traditional sovereignty in the face of technological and economic change. New European and global realities have resulted in a loss of national control, which has been a serious challenge to the French sense of the nation. When confronted with the obvious restrictions on the scope of national decision-making, the protests of the traditionalists against the programs of Republicans or progressives begin to ring hollow. Equally, the former revolutionary Left, which was perceived as the natural defender of the exploited classes, has difficulty protesting against nationalism when the traditional social classes have exploded and the national State now looks to be the only savior of the poor.

Indeed, the cards of the political debate have been completely reshuffled. The heirs of the earlier traditionalists, obliged to admit that their "France only" propaganda is obsolete, have renounced the greatest part of the Bonapartist program, and declared themselves Republicans. Since the possibility of resisting the constraints of the international economy continues to decrease, they have adapted themes from the traditional Republican spectrum and now focus on the issues of internal security, memory, and the defense of culture. The result is ambiguity, found most readily in their attitudes toward immigration. On the one hand, these modified traditionalists exaggerate their xenophobia, as it is the only proper theme they have; they refuse the principle of "jus soli"; and there is a noticeable return to prewar racism, even prejudice against French Jews, albeit a racism concealed behind very cautious rhetoric. On the other hand, they attempt to hide their xenophobia behind a false use of the Republican assimilationist doctrine: Arabs are rejected because of their supposed allegiance to Islam, and the Jews on account of their supposed allegiance to Israel (the latter was condemned somewhat disingenuously by the National Front). While Jean-Marie Le Pen had hoped that the National Front would gain strength from this confusion, it has been the established conservative Republican right that has in fact benefited.

The heirs of the revolutionary Left, which was internationalist (even if the Communist Party was nationalist during World War II), have also been forced to adjust their approach to the nation and are now divided into two currents of unequal importance: a petit Republican and Jacobin current (Jean Poperen, Jean-Pierre Chevènement), which is no longer internationalist; and a "democratic" current (the "second Left"), which favors substantial decentralization and which is no longer either extremist or revolutionary. On both Left and Right, therefore, the former anti-Republican extremes now either proclaim themselves Republican or fall within the Republican pattern of debate about the nation.

However, although the shock of interdependence and technological progress has helped remove the traditional challenges to the Republic, it has thereby removed a cleavage that has also been a defining characteristic of the French nation. The challenge to the *national continuum* thus results from both the erosion of sovereignty and from the removal of a key element in the common memory of the French Republic, which ironically is the history of the division of that Republic.

The second shock is related to the collapse of collectivist systems in the world and to the emergence of global ecological problems. This has destroyed the basis of the Republican conception of modernity: the utopia of a society of equals (even if it was projected into an indeterminate future); and the dream of a general trend of technical progress, controlled by human will. The decline of this credo has, at the same time, considerably increased fear of the future, and weakened the capability to assume the risks that come with any political choice. Herein lies the origin, not only of a conservative reflex, but also of the difficult crisis, which, in France, affects the Republican doctrine of representation and of law, a subject that will be returned to below.

The Republican model is thus no longer seriously challenged as it once was from within, from a Right and Left who respectively believed that Republican ideas of modernization challenged the continuity of the nation, or saw that continuity as a facade concealing class domination. Today, the model is challenged by forces external to itself that call into question the very basis upon which the Republic has built the nation: the memory of the nation and its commitment to social progress. The consequence is the opening of the question of French identity in the most profound of ways.

As France struggles to respond to a changing economic and social context, a new division of political ideas -- Real democracy versus Republicanism -- has opened and is now more important than the classical struggle between Right and

Left. This division plays itself out in the realms of law and of representation, and is also manifested in the decomposition of the nation into a multitude of conflicting identities. The new demands of democracy require the state to move from its traditional, but now obsolete role as assimilator toward a new role as arbiter. Although this model is well known in Northern Europe and in the United States, neither state nor citizen yet has the instincts necessary for it to function effectively in France. Success in meeting these new challenges will necessitate a complete refashioning of a core element of French identity.

The Dysfunctions of Democracy

The traditionally Jacobin and centralized French polity has been profoundly destabilized by the emergence of European interdependence. The 1993 debate over the Maastricht Treaty, and the transfers of sovereignty implicit in it, was not only rooted in ideological concerns about French grandeur and national identity. It was also because (unlike in Germany or even England) these transfers had implications for the concept of French citizenship and the foundations of French law. The Maastricht debate was in large part a debate about what it means to be French. The arguments that surrounded Maastricht illustrated the new and the old concepts of law and citizenship. It pointed to the changes that both the concept of law and the concept of citizenship are going through at the present time. This section discusses the fading of traditional conceptions of the role of the citizen and the role of law. Deprived of these two crucial underpinnings, the state is no longer able to act as assimilator and unifier of the people. The result has been an upsurge in differentialism, with French identity being decomposed into a multitude of group identities, and a public sphere being paralyzed by its inability to deal with these new actors efficiently.

The Crisis of Representation

Citizenship in France, like the state itself, is indivisible. The French model of citizenship, based on Rousseau, is far more deeply affected by sovereignty transfers than the other prominent model in Europe, inspired by Locke. The opposition between these two conceptions of citizenship is not only theoretical: it has real implications for people's political lives.

In Rousseau's conception of the general will, public opinion is not a sum of private choices, but a relatively autonomous product derived from the will of far-sighted actor-citizens. The general election is the quasi-mystical ceremony through which this general will is expressed, and indeed the only legitimate forum for its expression. In contrast, Locke's theory sees general opinion in arithmetic terms, as a sum of points of view expressed in the short term by self-seeking individuals.

Thus, the vote is a simple measure of the political balance, and public opinion polls between regular elections are reliable and normal indicators of democracy.

In Locke's formulation, political and economic motives are largely identical, and the task of a political system is to set limits to the power of the majority, in order to protect the rights of the minorities. In the United States, the "cohabitation" of a congress and a president elected by two different majorities, is quite normal and proper; the system is based on checks and balances. The expression of differentialist claims, from ethnic, sexual, or consumers' pressure groups, is a standard part of democracy.

In contrast, Rousseau's theory of the general will involves the total submission of the minority to the whole. It strongly implies the specificity of political activity. This has five major consequences for the conduct of politics in France. First, a government's perceived mandate was not a function of the size of its majority (and this was the case until 1981). "Cohabitation," which first occurred in 1986, created a focus on the precise balance of political forces, which was widely perceived as a scandal. Second, public opinion polls until recently were never given the same weight as or were confused with general election results. Third, respect for minorities is, in Marxist terminology, formal and not real. The prospect of giving foreigners the vote, even in local elections as mandated by the Maastricht Treaty, is widely rejected by public opinion. Fourth, the media, which considers itself as part of the general will, is more politicized and consequently less credible than its U.S. counterpart. Fifth, abstention in France has far greater import as political protest than it would on the other side of the Atlantic.

Given the above, one can appreciate the revolution that technological changes and global economic interdependence have brought about in the French political system. The Left's idea of structural economic reform has not so much been abandoned for ideological reasons as it has been recognized, under pressure, as being impossible. The power of television and the multiplication of public opinion polls dictate domestic and even foreign policies in an unprecedented fashion. Minorities -- lobbies, ethnic and religious communities, spontaneous social movements -- have become full political actors and direct interlocutors with the bureaucracy and the government. The political newspapers (*presse d'opinion*) have nearly disappeared and the national newspapers, adapted from the Anglo-Saxon model, have lost a large share of their readership. Last but not least, society is becoming less politicized due to the increased importance of the technical side of politics and of international interdependence. The voters, who no longer feel that their vote is a form of participating in national destiny, take refuge in attitudes that, while frequently contradictory to one another, reveal a common mistrust of the State. Citizens either abstain from voting, or they vote for a protest party, or, most commonly, they identify with local and professional interests rather than the general public interest, which they begin to consider a fiction.

The Crisis of Law

The challenge to the traditional French conception of law has been equally profound. Parallel to the two political cultures just described, one can distinguish, as Laurent Cohen-Tanugi[6] does, between two juridical cultures. The first, deriving from Montesquieu, sees law as emanating from the common will as expressed by the legislature, and gives the judge the role of simply applying that law. This is linked to the Jacobin conception of the superiority of the majority to the minority, and the public interest to the private. "The one-man-one-vote suffrage is the only source of power,"[7] and economic and social liberties are both recognized and constrained by the rules set down by the state, to protect them against themselves.

The other conception of law derives from Madison in the eighteenth century United States, and obtains generally in the West. Executive power applies the law according to the general principles of natural rights. Economic and social activity are less controlled by central authority, than regulated and readjusted by the intervention of a certain number of counter-authorities -- "lobbies," committees, councils, and so on. The judiciary forms one part of the system of checks and balances, and the judge owes his legitimacy to his competence and to his social prestige; rather than being an agent of the general will as expressed in law, he is an arbiter between the rights of the individual and the general will.

In France, the first conception of law is more and more influenced by the second legal culture, with the trend of law following the trend of the economy. As can be seen from the development of the law over the last quarter-century, a series of developments has combined to undermine the autonomy and authority of the law. In 1964 the European Court of Justice asserted the pre-eminence of European law, which in effect argued that the Treaty of Rome was a constitution rather than an agreement between sovereign nation states. In 1971, the French Constitutional Council declared that French law was subordinate to "fundamental principles." In 1974, the conditions under which the high court would hear a case were extended; the French government recognized the European Convention on Human Rights. More recently, the Single European Act of 1985, the cohabitation, which began one year later, and the Maastricht Treaty in 1993 have all played parts in the silent revolution that is inverting the French juridical tradition.

French law is thus becoming less and less sovereign, and the State is less and less the primary source of law. Moreover, the complexity of modern social problems has had substantial repercussions, reinforcing the move from traditional French legal culture toward the law as an expression of the state's arbitration between contending interests. As will be argued later at greater length, the effects of these social problems have themselves also been complicated by the failure of the traditional concept of law.

The Growth of Differentialism

France has seen a resurgence of corporatist, communal, religious, ethnic, and even racist movements in recent years. The reasons for this become clear in light of the above analysis. The growth of differentialism, spurred by the economic crisis, is the counterpart of the crisis in those political and juridical structures that formerly ensured the cohesion of the *Etat-nation* upon the basis of a modernization project. When the political system, law, and economic growth fail to unify a people, primitive badges of identity -- language, religion, race -- become dominant. The common memory of the nation, which previously gave common purpose to its citizens, explodes into a plethora of separate memories, which reignite old quarrels, and oppose groups to each other. The forgetting, considered by Renan as a condition of national cohesion, becomes impossible.

Such a *retour du refoulé*, which took the form of a regression to corporatism and communalism, characterized the fascist and nationalist movements of the period between the end of the nineteenth and the middle of the twentieth centuries. Then, it came from a hostility toward the state, which characterized various elements of society that had been marginalized by modernization: the "uprooted" of the city, ruined petty proprietors and shopkeepers, unemployed white-collar workers, evicted aristocrats, and so on. Today, it is a product of the tensions resulting from the underdevelopment of regions (the Corsican problem), from the social consequences of the economic crisis (National Front), from the more or less artificial reawakening of divisive memories (the Vendée massacre during the revolution, and the Touvier and Bousquet cases), and even from insurrectional movements, which are heirs to the medieval jacqueries (Breton fishermen in February 1994).

Finally, it lies at the root of why Jacobin and absolutist France has the most political difficulties of any country in Europe in dealing with immigrants of Moslem background. Their culture contradicts (and will continue to contradict for the next few generations at least) the assimilationist and secular Republican conception of citizenship.

One should not underestimate the racist tendencies implicit in the present fracturing of French identity. The dialectic between secular and Jacobin France, on one hand, and religious and communal claims, on the other, has produced a primacy of ethnic criteria in political debate. The controversy in late 1993 about Paul Yonnet's book, *Voyage au centre du malaise français. L'antiracisme et le roman national*,[8] and the polemics about the rise of a so-called "national-communism" earlier that same fall, prove that this phenomenon is becoming as widespread as the "political correctness" debate in the United States.

On one hand, the Republican assimilationists are prone to promote an inverted differentialism as an answer to the advent of ethnic, religious, sexual, and consumer minorities: they want to create new linkages that will subordinate these movements and harness them to the national project. In so doing, they forget those particular aspects (customs, social codes, etc.) that are inseparable from their own universalist principles, just as they refuse to admit the universal aspects (for instance Moslems' reference to an absolute moral law) of the particularist claims of the minorities. The minorities, for their part, are prone to raise their differences to universal values, and try to make them compulsory.

This explains the *tchadors* scandals and the rise of the *matrimonial exclusive* (Dominique Schnapper discusses its new popularity among French Jews at the beginning of the seventies).[9] Thus also, the popularization of references in political discourse (and even in law) to religious and ethnic communities. This latter is illustrated by the definition of the "Corsican people" as a "historical and cultural community" (in a law which was struck down by the Constitutional Council in June 1991) and by President Mitterrand's statement: "je remercie les communautés musulmanes et juives de France qui ont donné l'exemple de la sagesse et du sang froid" (I would like to thank the Muslim and Jewish communities who have provided an example in their wisdom and levelheadedness).[10]

The movements of the extreme right, such as the National Front or GRECE, are prudent for many reasons, including the influence of television and the Gayssot law forbidding racist references. But words such as "identity" have become codewords for race, and are used with increasing frequency and ambiguity. Witness this declaration of Jean-Marie Le Pen:

> Je suis de ceux qui pensent que l'attachement à la nation est lié à un instinct de l'homme. Comme nous l'apprennent les éthologues, la notion de territoire est perçue par l'être vivant -- tous les êtres vivants -- comme un besoin fondamental lié à sa sécurité, donc à sa liberté, à sa postérité et aussi, à des niveaux plus élevés, à sa prospérité. Par nature donc, les peuples ne peuvent pas vivre sans idéal et (...) ces peuples et ces êtres, ces hommes et ces femmes continuent à avoir une âme et un esprit avide de pensées et d'identité. Il est donc normal qu'ils se réfèrent au passé, à ce qui les a fondés comme peuples et comme nations. (I am one of those who believes that national identity is rooted in natural instinct. As the ethicists tell us, the notion of territory is perceived by a living creature (indeed by all living creatures) as a fundamental requirement for its security, and thus for its liberty, its posterity, and at a higher level, its prosperity. Thus, people are by nature incapable of living without an ideal and ... these people and these beings, these men and these women, continue to have a soul and a spirit hungry for thought and identity. It is therefore unsurprising that they make reference to their past, to that which has made them as people and nations).[11]

The growth of racist tendencies has spawned an almost obsessive Republican attempt to combat fears for identity through "ideological" assertion -- by co-opting rhetoric and through the use of police action -- rather than tackling its root causes. Not only does such a strategy lead to confusion between the true Republicans and the modified traditionalists, but it gives the supporters of the National Front a new legitimacy, as demonstrated in public opinion polls.

The breakdown of traditional concepts of law and citizenship in France have necessitated a transition to a new set of assumptions about what it means to be French. The turmoil associated with this transition has been reflected in the growth of new differentialist social movements, and a new emphasis on ethnic questions and ethnicity in political debate. These new social realities have confused the guardians of traditional Republicanism, whose answers to these new pressures have almost certainly given legitimacy to the very forces that are most alien to the Republican concept of the nation. The final section of this chapter will examine how the Republic itself has responded to the challenges that are outlined above.

The Challenged State and Its Response

The French State is now in a serious quandary. On the one hand its traditional bases of legitimacy have been questioned by the development of alternate conceptions of law and citizenship. On the other hand, this same general set of developments has resulted in serious social problems and problems of cohesion, which the state is not able to address effectively precisely because its assimilatory function is under threat.

Although other democracies face broadly similar difficulties stemming from the fragmentation of post-industrial societies, the problem is particularly pronounced in France given the sharpness of the break with traditional concepts of the state. Others have tried to counterbalance the change in public attitudes and the breakdown of social linkages by multiplying the processes of economic and social integration. The drive for decentralization and "consensual" decision making in France has a similar purpose. French politics are now based to an unprecedented extent on the principle of negotiation. This practice is normal in federalist or social-democratic political systems but it is not in France, where it has given rise in the last few years to a new cleavage. This cleavage cuts across Right and Left, dividing "Republicans" (the heirs of the Jacobin conception of the State) from "Democrats" (who believe in a wholly decentralized political practice).

This change in the terms of political debate has some perverse effects. They include a proliferation of social movements with counterbidding claims, the precariousness of short-term political bargains, the instability of channels of social representation (the trade unions, for example, being passed over by the new networks), and the substitution of media *coups de main* for the great strikes of former days.

The shift has two consequences. First, any categorical or marginal claim is transformed by the media into a national problem. Political parties cannot afford to ignore any pressure group, and thus put forward catch-all manifestos, which are increasingly interchangeable between parties and actually obscure the fundamental choices of political life. At the same time, economic actors try to tighten their links with the state, so as to maximize rents and protect themselves against the risks of competition; this phenomenon is one of the main causes of present-day corruption. Citizens, given their lack of political motivation, are less and less likely to accept the sacrifices necessary for the public good in any democracy.

The second consequence is the new-found prominence of judges and experts in the decision-making process. They are almost the last actors who have enough prestige to arbitrate conflicts and change, if necessary, the rules of the game. These new arbiters include members of the Constitutional Council, examining magistrates, and members of "ad hoc" commissions, of ethical and valuation councils, and of independent administrative authorities with jurisdictional powers (COB, CNIL, CSA).[12] They have neither formal political legitimacy, strictly speaking, nor political responsibility, but are more and more closely associated with the decision-making process. Even if the government frequently co-opts them, it does so not to "bury" the plans of reform as was the system under the former Republics, but in order to gain public legitimacy for political decisions by having judges and experts play a greater role in decision making. This was, for example, the procedure adopted concerning the revision of the nationality code, between 1987 and 1993. The judges and experts therefore are no longer simply key figures in social regulation, but in a sense have also come to play a major political role.

The rise of judges and experts is not the result of some synarchic conspiracy aimed at increasing the power of elites.[13] It results from a combination of four factors. The first is democratic states' need to find a new basis of legitimacy that can replace the dying concept of the national interest. The function of the democratic election is thus being replaced by the personal credibility of the administrators of law and the bearers of knowledge. This transfer of the basis of legitimacy has its problems for the political leadership -- as is testified to by the relentlessness of some "small judges" in France, or the furor of the "clean hands" campaign that targeted Italy's political class. However, if it is cleverly implemented, it allows the government to defuse particularly dangerous crises and wrongfoot its opposition. Thus, the French government addressed the critical problem of the Nationality Code by handing it over to a commission of experts, which sat between 1987 and 1993. This approach runs the risk, however, of adding the dangers of judges' government to the dangers of *polysynodie*.

The second factor is the way in which technical progress leads to ethical problems. The obvious examples are genetics and medically assisted procreation. This tempts the State to intervene in fields that until recently were entirely subject to individual choice or spiritual authority. The danger here is that by expanding its regulatory competence beyond the prevention of economic abuse, so that it assumes the authority of researchers, doctors, and patients in fixing ethical limits, the law brings atypical borderline cases, which should only concern the individuals involved, into the arena of social debate.

The third factor is the desire to rationalize individuals' behavior so as to reduce collective problems and negative externalities. This argument, which can be traced back to Bentham, provides a useful basis for the justification of state and international regulation to encourage citizens to care about their environment. It encourages the State to intervene in citizens' private lives for their own good, and to legislate for the proper use of substances and objects (tobacco, alcohol, motor vehicles) and social behavior (relations between sexes, language, etc.), so as to prevent social costs and conflicts. Developed societies have evolved from the welfare state to the preventive state, which treats individual responsibility solely in organizational terms.[14]

The final factor, which in a sense encompasses all the others, is the reappearance of very old fears -- the fear of unemployment or bankruptcy, the fear of barbaric invasions, the fear of epidemics, the fear of the end of the world, the fear of drugs and organized crime -- and the priority that the citizens of rich countries now (once again) give to the need of security over aspirations of liberty. Security and continued life have become aims in themselves within which all other values are subsumed. This leads to an obsessive fear of conflict in all its forms, which in turn results in the search for compromise at any price. Such a *Weltanschauung* demands "reasonable" citizens who at the same time are both "virtuous" and politically motivated by rational (and predictable) economic considerations. Political chimeras of this sort, which combine two radically different types of reasonableness, are typical of the periods of moral order. The desire to eliminate tensions leads, nearly ineluctably, to a multiplication of social regulation, with laws becoming intolerant and ever more intrusive. By the same token, the state cannot have a coercive relationship with civil society in a democracy, and the pressures of conciliation thus leads to a diminution of the state into a body subject to the same common law as private citizens, and furthermore obliged to set a virtuous example.

The move of the state toward exercising greater social control has led to renewed interest in the theme of "transparency": a modern buzzword that used to be one of the keywords of totalitarianism. It owes its present popularity to a spurious resolution (which the state itself accepts as valid) of the antinomies of political action, ignoring the Weberian distinction that opposes the ethic of responsibility to the ethic of conviction. Public figures are expected not only to fulfill their duties, but to live exemplary lives, and to be responsible to the public in every detail of their political behavior. In reality, the state's new relationship with society blurs the distinction between public and private to the detriment of both. Laws necessitate the publication of politicians' private financial interests, the verification of electoral campaign expenses to the last penny, and also mandate harsh penalties for the slightest bookkeeping error. Eventually the private lives of politicians will be subjected to judicial monitoring, as in the United States.

These developments reflect more the discredit of political power than the ability to restore faith in it. Public cynicism is reinforced rather than alleviated by these procedures.

The adoption by the state of its new role has also resulted in the ruse of power (in the Hegelian sense), a sleight of hand that consists of preparing and presenting decisions so that they appear to be imposed both on the state and on its citizens. In a society driven by the need to eliminate conflicts, the only way to obtain consensus is to make it appear that decisions have been taken, not by everybody (as in the general will system), but by nobody. The multiplication of commissions of experts, ethical committees, evaluative councils, and independent administrative authorities, are all part of this "nobody" strategy, which is more and more frequently resorted to by heads of government who either fear or are unwilling to lead. Power is both everywhere and nowhere, Panurge and Mr. Nobody. The government hides behind these quasi-autonomous nongovernmental organizations, which it relies on to take decisions that it is incapable of taking itself.

Thus the contemporary French political landscape combines the disadvantages of centralism and decentralization. The minorities, which require legal recourse for their social disadvantages, are encouraged to resort to the tyranny of legislation. The experts, who have the praiseworthy purpose of maximizing social efficiency, undermine human freedom in their worship of administrative rationality. The judges, given their head by the administration, become prosecutors and justice devolves from a balance in the hands of the state to a sword over the heads of statesmen. All of these processes, which presume to advance toleration and/or rationality run the risk of destabilizing the very freedom that they propose to protect.

Conclusion

In summary, the French state is confronted with a new set of problems deriving from the social and ideological changes of the recent past. It still has the same overall task: of ensuring social cohesion. However, it is no longer able to perform this task according to the Republican model: through *assimilation*, which should be construed in its broadest sense as the uniting of potentially disparate social currents into a single, all-encompassing national unity. It thus multiplies linkages between the new differentialist groups and itself in order to ensure that every group is heard, or at least has the opportunity to be heard. The state, which had formerly reconciled the nation through assimilation, now attempts to do so through arbitration.

The major political currents in France today lack any *projet de société* (which form of equality? what kind of liberty? whose justice? etc.). As a consequence, the state is reduced to evaluating its citizens' needs purely in terms of economic rationality. In a system increasingly based in principle on the avoidance of conflict, such as that which France now seems to possess, the confrontation of material interests inevitably leads to never-ending deals and counterbids between the groups, and to a multiplication of rules intended both to prevent and to appease the frustrations and disappointment of the citizenry. This leads to a paralysis of the Republic, and the state therefore resorts to the use of experts and the use of judges as the ultimate arbiters. But this process is not legitimated by the vote. Both the rationality of experts and the impartiality of judges have some universal legitimacy. However, by resorting to these means, which restricts the territory of the political debate, the state acknowledges its own impotence, and runs the risk of further corroding its democratic basis and creating a sort of "soft" authoritarianism.

To return to the theme of the first section of this chapter, the old notion of the Republic is under threat. It has not been replaced by a new political ethos, and the apparent consensus of French politics masks a deep confusion among political actors. The Republican consensus was the minimal agreement concerning institutions, foreign policy, and civic culture, which constituted the background of the political debate. Presently, "consensus" appears as the fragile result, constantly revised, of the permanent deals between more or less representative lobbies, committees, and groups. The divisions about the Republic (which, in a certain sense *constituted* the Republic) no longer dominate French politics, but there is no new assimilatory project around which and upon which new political cleavages can be founded. If there is no national project, there is no basis for opposition to that project either. Therefore the apparent *atonie* of French political life is in reality a manifestation of directionlessness: noone in the mainstream of French politics has a long-term vision or direction with which others can take issue. This is not to say that there is no fundamental cleavage in French politics. However, the new cleavage is not founded *on* a national project and attitudes for or against it, but rather on whether it is desirable to have an assimilatory national project at all. It is a clash between two fundamentally different social logics, which leads to paralysis and is incapable of amicable resolution.

The lack of an all-defining overarching project allows other, potentially destabilizing, nexuses of identification to manifest themselves in the form of rival ethnic, religious, and local identities. The state, shorn of its Republican aspirations, tries to mediate between these various groupings and the result is a vitiating chaos. In the absence of any social linkages, the danger is not only a lack of solidarity, but also the comeback of a cold civil war -- each group refusing to pay for the others. These problems are not unique to France, but the conjunction of these several shocks and the lack of preparedness of French political culture and institutions mean that France faces a particularly difficult adjustment process. France must give a new definition of citizenship without falling back upon discredited notions of ethnic purity, allowing the public sphere to degenerate into a welter of claims and counter-claims, or replacing the fundamentals of democratic identity with a stifling bureaucratization of politics. Success will depend on

France's capacity to create a social and juridical system able to instill a sense of responsibility in the people's minds.

Notes

1. Serge Berstein and Odile Rudelle, eds., *Le modèle républicain* (Paris: P.U.F., 1992) pp. 407 ff.

2. Germaine de Staël, *De L'Allemagne* (Paris: Garnier-Flammarion, 1968) vol. 2, chapter 1.

3. Ernest Renan, *Qu'est-ce qu'une nation?* in Alain de Benoist, ed., *La réforme intellectuelle est morale et autres écrits* (Paris: Albatros, 1982) pp. 88-102.

4. Alain-Gérard Slama, *Les chasseurs d'absolu, genèse de la gauche et de la droite*, (Paris: Grasset, 1980) pp. 54-81.

5. François Furet, Jacques Julliard, Pierre Rosanvallon, *La république du centre* (Paris: Calmann-Lévy, 1988) pp. 29-31.

6. Laurent Cohen-Tanugi, *La Metamorphose de la Democracie* (Paris: Odile Jacob, 1989) pp. 19-26 passim.

7. See *Déclaration des droits de l'homme*, article III: *"Le principe de toute souveraineté réside essentiellement dans la nation"* et *article VI*: *"la loi est l'expression de la volonté générale."* See also *le préambule de la constitution de 1791*: *"Tout ce qui a été décidé par le corps législatif est loi, et mérite le nom de loi (...), quelle que soit la nature de son contenu."*

8. Paul Yonnet, *Voyage au centre du malaise français. L'antiracisme et le roman national* (Paris: Gallimard, 1993).

9. Dominique Schnapper, *Juifs et israëlites* (Paris: Gallimard, 1980).

10. Televised address by M. François Mitterrand, 3 March 1991.

11. Interview of Jean-Marie Le Pen by Jean-Claude Valli and Pierre Cohen, *Le choc du mois,* February 1992.

12. Jean-Noël Jeanneney, *L'Argent Caché* (Paris: Seuil, 1981).

13. *Commission des opérations de Bourse, Commission nationale informatique et libertés, Conseil supérieur de l'audiovisuel.*

14. For further details, see Alain-Gérard Slama, *L'angélisme exterminateur, essai sur l'ordre moral contemporain* (Paris: Grasset, 1993) pp. 229 ff.

PART TWO

Challenges to French Economic Order

5

The *Franc Fort* Strategy and the EMU

Jacques E. Le Cacheux

France's pursuit of a "franc fort" has been one of the single most important characteristics of French economic policy during the eighties and early nineties. The decision to maintain a strong franc, taken after two years of difficult experience with economic policy and exchange markets at the beginning of the Mitterrand presidency, involved fundamental domestic economic and political choices, and fundamental choices about the future relationship between France and its European partners. The new path was to establish a better competitive base for France and to accomplish the preconditions for reinvigorating European integration. France's national interest was to be served by both.

Beginning in 1983, France invested substantially in the stability of its currency, paying significant costs at home as the domestic economy adjusted to the new constraints. In parallel, François Mitterrand also became very active in pursuing a renewal of the European integration process. By the late eighties, there had been a serious payoff on both levels: the franc had become strong, and the Single European Act had set members of the European Community on the path to completing their integrated market by 1992. Then, in response to the challenges brought by the collapse of the East bloc and the reunification of Germany, and based on the propitious economic conditions prevailing in Europe at the end of the last decade, France helped craft the most ambitious step yet attempted in the process of building Europe: the Treaty on European Union signed in Maastricht on 7 February 1992. Although it was by no means the only significant advance in the direction of an emerging European sovereignty, the commitment to create an

Economic and Monetary Union (EMU) before the end of the century was the centerpiece of the treaty.

France thus has made a great investment in this vision of national interest. Its success or failure is intimately linked with the prospects for realizing EMU. By 1994, the optimism that had dominated Europe at the time the Maastricht Treaty was signed had given way to serious skepticism about the future of European Union. This chapter reviews the types of commitments undertaken in Maastricht and the assumptions underpinning the treaty's commitment to achieve Economic and Monetary Union; the movement toward convergence among the economies of member states of the EU; the centrifugal pressures that have challenged French policy specifically and the movement toward EMU generally; and finally, what the current conditions mean for the policy choices France has made over the past decade and a half.

The Challenge of Economic
and Monetary Union

Unlike the agreement to create the European Monetary System (EMS) in 1979 or the Single European Act in 1986 (which decreed the dismantling of intra-EC borders and the completion of the European common market on 1 January 1993), the Maastricht Treaty was deemed to contain such radical amendments of the community's founding treaties that it was to be submitted for ratification to the various national constituencies. There was persistent criticism of Maastricht from some quarters about the specific way chosen to deepen European integration, and more open hostility by the British government to some of the treaty's major goals -- the UK had obtained special dispensations on monetary union and social policies. Nonetheless, pro-European feelings seemed so dominant in all but one or two member states that ratification appeared as a mere formality.

The treaty enshrined precise steps to be taken to achieve Economic and Monetary Union, with dates for each phase including the creation of a single currency, and a final deadline of 1999. The decisions were presented as "irreversible." True enough, the way to EMU implied that member states would have to relinquish their national sovereignty over money. But after more than twelve years of EMS, such an encroachment on national independence appeared to many -- with the exception of the German central bank -- more formal than real. Monetary policy in Europe had been dictated by the German Bundesbank for so long that the creation of a common central bank could be regarded by most states as a way of regaining some control over decisions that had, for many years, been inspired mostly by German domestic considerations. The EMS, with its quasi-fixed exchange rates, was presented as the first step toward full monetary union. In the context of the single market for goods and services -- in particular financial services -- it was planned that the EMS would progressively evolve into a purely fixed rate system, thus "naturally" leading to the creation of a single currency.

The treaty also imposed strict economic criteria for member states to join EMU: some on nominal variables -- domestic inflation and interest rates -- others on national fiscal policies -- budget deficit and public debt. Although many analysts judged them potentially dangerous and barely achievable by the chosen deadline, those countries that were far out of line -- most notably Italy, but also Portugal, Spain, and others -- immediately started to take steps to correct fiscal imbalances.

Two years later, things looked quite different. National ratification processes were anything but easy, with the Danes needing two referenda before succeeding. The deep economic recession in Europe -- together with specific national political turmoil in Italy -- has made the prospects for fiscal consolidation even bleaker than it appeared at the outset. And after more than five years of exchange-rate stability, the EMS was badly shaken by repeated speculative attacks between September 1992 and September 1993. In the fall of 1992, two major European currencies (the sterling and the Italian lira) were forced to leave the exchange-rate mechanism (ERM) and float freely, while three others (the Spanish peseta, the Portuguese escudo, and the Irish pound) had to devalue substantially. In addition, the Danish crown, the Belgian franc, and the French franc were subjected to recurring speculative attacks which tested the resolve of national authorities. As a result, European monetary authorities were forced on 2 August 1993 to widen fluctuation margins in the ERM to ±15 percent.

Although the exchange markets have calmed in the period since September 1993, the repeated exchange crises that rocked the EMS did in fact change things considerably. First, the magnitude of exchange-rate adjustments for some European currencies has been of a level unseen since the beginning of the EMS in March 1979. Second, something more subtle, more difficult to measure, but nonetheless essential to the process of monetary unification, has been shaken and probably eroded: credibility. The whole scenario for achieving EMU described in the Maastricht Treaty appeared feasible at the beginning of 1992. Within two years, it was no longer so.

At the same time, official progress toward EMU has proceeded apace. The implementation of the various institutional steps toward EMU has been scrupulously kept to the schedule agreed upon in the Maastricht Treaty. The second stage of the process began as planned on 1 January 1994. As stipulated in the treaty, the Banque de France has been turned into an independent central bank, and the European Monetary Institute (EMI) -- conceived as the embryo of the future European central bank and a forum for national central banks' cooperation -- has been created and taken up residence in Frankfurt. Moreover, from the perspective of French policy, the exchange rate of the French franc vis-à-vis the deutsche mark was approximately the same in January 1994 as one year before;

indeed, the rate had been almost constant for six years. The strong franc had survived and formally, EMU remained on track.

The Maastricht Treaty offers a fairly detailed account of the way EMU should be progressively realized by the EU. The treaty takes for granted the progress in the fields of market integration since the enactment of the Rome Treaty and, more recently, of the Single European Act of 1986, and of "nominal convergence" amongst member states. It builds upon the achievements of the EMS and proposes a gradual transformation of the monetary system prevailing in the EC at the end of 1991, when the treaty was finalized, into a full-fledged monetary zone endowed with a single currency. The process envisioned is that of "forced convergence" of national macroeconomic policies, a process that looked all the easier in the late 1980s as real economic growth seemed to be back for good, which would make fiscal consolidation much more feasible and less painful.

In many respects, the vision of economic and monetary integration that underlies in the treaty is close to that of the "Werner Plan," adopted in 1970, which envisioned the gradual realization of monetary union in the EC by 1980 (!). In the terms of the debates that have divided economists and European political leaders since that time, both plans chose a rather "monetarist" approach rather than an "economist" approach to European economic integration. The "economists," led by the Germans, have advocated that the processes of market integration and "real" economic convergence be completed before any attempt at monetary unification is made. The "monetarists," who have included most French leaders from the 1970s onward, have regarded monetary union as prerequisite to foster convergence. The negotiations leading to both plans tended to favor the latter by giving prominence to measures in the monetary field. But the recent treaty goes much farther than its forerunner in the specification of the concrete steps to be taken, as well as in the various measures in the "economic" field -- especially fiscal policies -- that would have to accompany the progress toward monetary union.[1]

Just like its forerunner, the Maastricht Treaty may be regarded as another step in the so-called "functionalist" approach to integration: building upon previous advances, it has tried to consolidate progress in the field where it has seemed most urgent and most easily achievable -- money -- which would tend to "spill over" into other fields -- fiscal policy, in particular -- where the advances would generate "unexpected" imbalances that would then have to be corrected by taking further steps in the direction of closer integration.

Economic Convergence in the EU

In addition to the design of a monetary constitution for the EU that closely resembles that of Germany, with a strictly independent, federal system of central banking, the Maastricht Treaty also makes major concessions to the "economists" (the Bundesbank once again) and acknowledges the necessity of achieving some degree of economic convergence for monetary integration to proceed smoothly. The resultant provisions are to be found in the prerequisites for member countries to join the Union in its final stage. Two are in the monetary field: domestic inflation must not be more than 1.5 points, and domestic long-term interest rates not more than 2 points, over the best domestic performance amongst EU members. The other two conditions are meant to discipline national fiscal policies: the public sector budget deficit must be less than 3 percent of GDP and the stock of outstanding, gross public debt less than 60 percent of GDP.[2]

A major postulate of this approach is the hypothesis that tighter monetary integration will, if accompanied by appropriate restraints on other national economic policies, foster economic convergence amongst member states. Although the concept of convergence is, by nature, multifaceted and thus difficult to measure, it may, for analytical purposes, conveniently be split into two distinct processes: nominal convergence, referring to the sphere of money and domestic inflation, and "real" convergence, which includes both aggregate, "real" economic performances (growth, employment, etc.) and economic structures, behaviors, and institutions.

Created in 1979 -- initially with Belgium, Denmark, France, Germany, Ireland, Italy, Luxembourg, and the Netherlands, later joined by Spain and the UK (1990) and Portugal (1992) -- the fixed, but adjustable exchange-rate mechanism of the EMS has been partly successful in achieving what was its major goal, namely fostering nominal convergence.[3] Over the 1980s and early 1990s, in spite of fairly numerous parity realignments in the initial phase of the EMS (twelve between 1979 and 1987), nominal exchange rates have undoubtedly been more stable within the EMS than outside (witness the ample movements of the dollar and the pound sterling exchange rates in the 1980s) and more stable within the EC than during the previous decade, at the time when the European "snake" had been in operation. Success on this front was even so complete in the late eighties and early nineties (no parity change took place between January 1987 and September 1992, except for a minor realignment of the Italian lira in January 1990) that most EC non-members of the EMS (Spain, the UK, Portugal) progressively joined, and several European non-members of the EC such as Finland, Norway, and Sweden, unilaterally aligned themselves. Those realignments that did take place occurred with the agreement of all ERM members, and the magnitude of parity changes was usually fairly moderate, calculated primarily to cancel cumulated inflation differentials, thus carefully avoiding "competitive devaluations" (Figures 5.1a and 5.1b).

This exceptionally long period of exchange-rate stability in Europe has progressively built the credibility of the EMS and induced many -- including those who designed the Maastricht Treaty, as well as most governments in Europe and financial investors -- to believe that the system could be definitively stabilized, and with a number of institutional changes, converted into a full-fledged mon-

FIGURE 5.1a Nominal French Franc/DM, Pound Sterling/DM Exchange Rates, 1979-1994 (monthly averages)

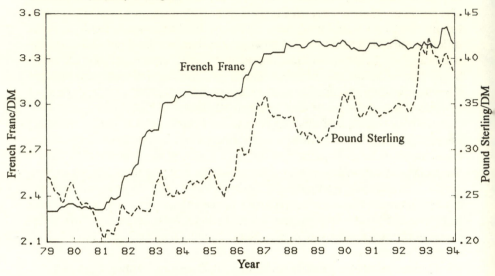

French franc (left scale) and pound sterling (right scale)
Source: OFCE, Département des diagnostics.

FIGURE 5.1b Nominal Italian Lira/DM Exchange Rates, 1979-1994 (monthly averages)

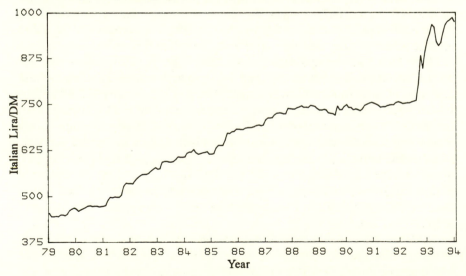

Source: OFCE, Département des diagnostics.

FIGURE 5.2 Domestic CPI Inflation, 1979-1994, France, Germany, Italy, UK

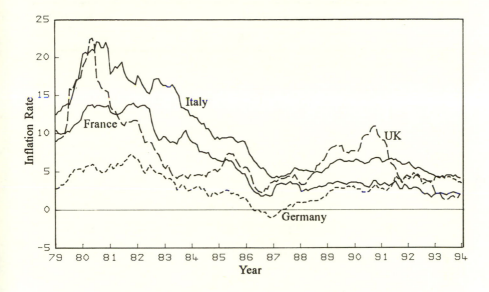

Note: monthly: annual increase over the past twelve months (m/m-12)
Source: OECD, *Main Economic Indicators.*

etary union. The process envisioned less and less frequent parity changes, and a progressive tightening of fluctuation margins, initially set at ± 2.25 percent, but already reduced, unilaterally, to ± 1 percent for the Dutch and the Belgian currencies vis-à-vis the German mark.[4]

However, the EMS was much less successful during this same period at fostering convergence of national monetary policies and domestic inflation rates (Figure 5.2). Indeed, nominal exchange-rate stability was used by the most inflation-prone members of the EMS (France in the early 1980s; Italy, Spain, and the UK more recently) as a tool for domestic disinflation. It was, however, a double-edged strategy, and viable only to the extent that domestic policies were set accordingly and that domestic disinflation was in fact forthcoming. The country embarking on such a strategy of "importing disinflation" from Germany and "buying credibility" by "anchoring" its currency to the German mark, suffered a number of hardships that rocked the domestic economy and threatened the whole experience.

In order to defend the nominal parity, domestic monetary authorities had to maintain high interest rates -- more specifically they had to offer a premium over the German interest rates that served as a reference for the whole structure of interest rates within the EMS. This tended to slow domestic growth performances, thus worsening unemployment, as well as to produce some inflationary effects,[5]

TABLE 5.1 Indicators of Competitiveness (1979-1993)

	France		Germany		Italy		United Kingdom	
	RLC	REP	RLC	REP	RLC	REP	RLC	REP
1979	105	104	85	100	91	85	99	101
1980	110	104	86	98	89	88	121	112
1981	109	100	79	90	89	91	125	111
1982	105	97	83	91	90	91	117	104
1983	105	96	84	92	96	89	106	101
1984	105	97	83	89	93	90	101	98
1985	107	99	81	89	91	90	101	100
1986	109	103	89	98	92	92	94	95
1987	109	104	100	102	92	92	91	97
1988	104	103	99	99	91	89	96	102
1989	100	100	97	97	96	95	94	99
1990	102	103	101	101	100	99	97	100
1991	100	100	100	100	100	100	100	100
1992	102	100	104	103	98	99	96	97
1993	105	99	113	104	82	91	80	95

[a]RLC = Relative labor costs in manufacturing.
[b]REP = Relative manufacturing export prices.
Source: OECD, *Economic Perspectives*, no. 54, December 1993.

and a seriously detrimental effect on fiscal policy via the increase in the interest burden on public debt. Moreover, as long as domestic inflation, although subsiding, was still higher than that in Germany, the domestic currency appreciated in real terms, that is, domestic producers' competitiveness was progressively reduced, resulting in the tendency for the external trade account and the current account to deteriorate. This process of real appreciation, quite apparent in both phases of the French disinflation (Table 5.1) but with only minor consequences on the current account (Figure 5.3a), is extremely pronounced for countries where disinflation has been slow, like Italy (Table 5.1 and Figure 5.3b).

If the disinflation policy is pursued stubbornly to its end, such painful evolutions eventually have beneficial effects. The combination of a rise in domestic unemployment and of fiercer international competition acts to curb producers' cost increases and to stabilize the domestic price level. The policy of low inflation and fixed exchange rates then becomes more credible and domestic monetary authorities can afford to reduce the interest-rate differential vis-à-vis Germany. This is precisely what happened in the case of France. The differential had practically vanished in the fall of 1991, when the Maastricht Treaty was being negotiated (Figure 5.4).

Following such a "virtuous" chain of evolutions (the French disinflation experience is broadly characteristic of the period from 1983 until 1987), the French franc has had a perfectly fixed parity vis-à-vis the German mark. But French policy went even further: in pursuing its orthodox monetary policy, France actually reached a phase of "competitive disinflation."[6] A constant downward pressure on domestic costs permitted France to achieve an inflation rate even lower than that of the "core country" of the EMS, namely Germany.[7] As a result, domestic producers could afford higher profit margins and still achieve better external competitiveness (Table 5.1). The external trade account eventually improved and it was hoped that the combination of stronger external demand and better financial conditions for domestic firms would boost investment, thus reinforcing competitiveness and eventually allowing for a reduction in domestic unemployment and sounder growth.

Italy, Spain, and the UK all embarked on similar disinflation experiments somewhat later than the French, but with much less success. As expected, the policy of fixed nominal parity vis-à-vis the German mark induced a strong real appreciation of these currencies, thus deteriorating their domestic producers' competitiveness. But other domestic policies -- especially fiscal policy in Italy -- were not consistent with the fixed exchange-rate disinflationary option, and the strategy was not pursued long enough for credibility to emerge and produce its beneficial effects on domestic interest rates.

These currencies were therefore extremely vulnerable to any factor that could raise doubts about the future of the EMS or of their domestic disinflationary policies. And numerous such shocks were forthcoming in 1992. The acceleration of inflation and growth in Germany after reunification helped to dampen the hardships of reduced competitiveness in Italy, Spain, and the UK, but it also triggered an orthodox reaction by the Bundesbank. Short-term interest rates were progressively increased in Germany, nearing 10 percent by mid-1992 (Figure 5.4), which pushed rates even higher in the other EMS countries, especially those having domestic inflation rates higher than that in Germany (Figure 5.2). Ample real appreciation of the Italian lira, internal political turmoil and a disastrous fiscal situation in Italy -- implying that the conditions fixed in the Maastricht Treaty for joining the EMU had no chance of being met by the stated deadline -- added domestic reasons to doubt the sustainability of Italy's commitment to the fixed

FIGURE 5.3a External Current Account, 1979-1993, France and the UK
(quarterly figures, U.S. $ billion)

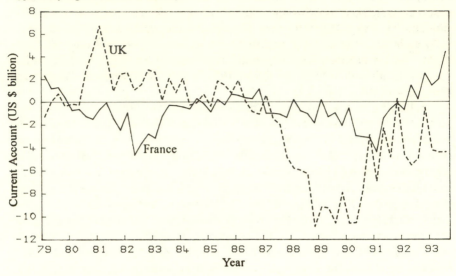

Source: OECD, *Economic Perspectives.*

FIGURE 5.3b External Current Account, 1979-1993, Italy
(quarterly figures, U.S. $ billion)

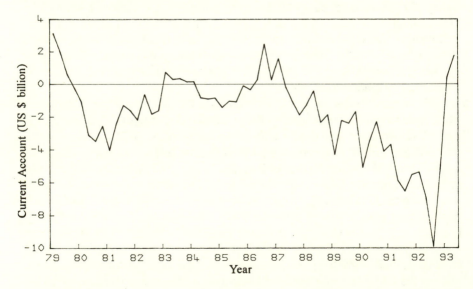

Source: OECD, *Economic Perspectives.*

FIGURE 5.4 Nominal, Short-Term (day-to-day) Interest Rates, France and Germany (monthly averages)

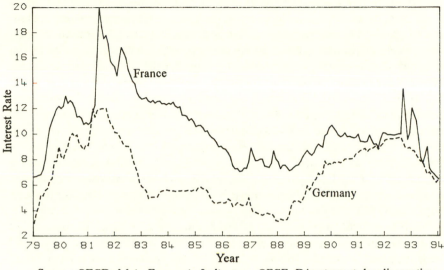

Source: OECD, *Main Economic Indicators*; OFCE, Département des diagnostics.

FIGURE 5.5 Registered Unemployment Rates (Standardized), France, (West) Germany, Italy, UK, 1979-1993 (monthly, end-of-month figures)

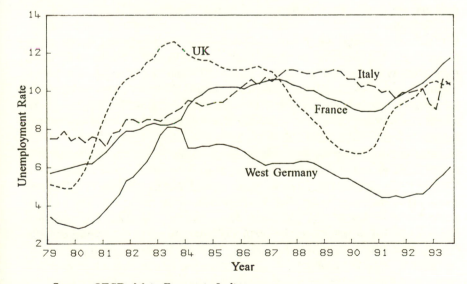

Source: OECD, *Main Economic Indicators*.

exchange-rate option. At the same time, the depth and length of the recession in the UK were shaking the British government's resolve.

The rather unexpected difficulties with the ratification of the Maastricht Treaty -- the open opposition of the majority in the UK, the failed referendum in Denmark in June 1992 and the small margin of favorable votes in France in September -- reignited the fear in the currency markets, which had been beguiled by the long period of nominal exchange-rate stability, that the EMS parities would not last until the completion of monetary union, meaning at least another four years. In addition, the slowdown in European economic activity clearly demonstrated that the fiscal criteria would not be met in most member countries. Finally, external events added to the fragility of intra-EMS parities: the slide of the dollar during the summer of 1992 tended, as usual, to pull the German mark up vis-à-vis the other EMS currencies, making it even harder for their domestic monetary authorities to keep fixed parities. The result was the most intense challenge experienced by the EMS, beginning in September 1992 and running through September 1993.

While one can argue that the EMS, despite recent difficulties, has in fact made considerable progress in promoting nominal convergence among its members, there is considerably more doubt about any such progress toward "real" economic convergence, for example, convergence in "real" macroeconomic performances and economic structures. The assumption behind the chosen approach to EMU has always been that nominal convergence and market integration would foster "real convergence." In the latter part of 1993, some real convergence has indeed materialized. Unfortunately, however, it is mostly in a rather negative way, and not exactly what proponents of "forced convergence" had in mind.

For some time, all EMS countries have been suffering a severe recession, with slow or even negative growth, and all domestic unemployment rates are now increasing and converging to double-digit values (Figure 5.5). In early 1994, registered unemployment was in the vicinity of -- and mostly above -- 3 million people in each of the four large countries of the EU (France, Germany, Italy, and the UK). Tighter market integration and the functioning of the EMS have reinforced synchronization in business cycle fluctuations, although national specificities still make some difference in the timing and magnitude of cycles.[8] There has also been convergence in domestic fiscal policy indicators, but again of a rather negative and cyclical variety: budget deficits have been worsening and have, in 1993, exceeded the 3 percent limit of the Maastricht Treaty in all but one country (Luxembourg); and public debts are everywhere rising, still under the 60 percent limit at the end of 1993 in only five countries -- France (58.2 percent), Germany (51.4 percent), Luxembourg (8.8 percent), Spain (53.4 percent) and the UK (51.9 percent) -- and, in some of them, probably not for very long.

In sum, although far from completed, the nominal convergence process has in fact been considerably advanced over the first fourteen years of operation of the EMS. But it is not clear that disinflation has been any faster or less painful within the EMS than outside, and convergence is clearly not yet sufficient for members to merge into a unified monetary zone and integrated economic area. Substantial "real" convergence has yet to be demonstrated in a positive way.

Centrifugal Forces: Divergent Interests in Varied National Circumstances

The picture emerging from the foregoing is, as could be expected, ambivalent. Seen from a distance, the EC looks more and more like an economically integrated entity, with strong specificities distinguishing it from the other major economic powers, the United States and Japan. But a closer look reveals the persistence of large differences in structures and performances. Will these differences be sufficient to prevent the realization of EMU? From the U.S. experience, it seems that diversity can be compatible with economic integration. But in the EU, diversity is clearly organized along national boundaries, not only with regard to economic structures and demography, but also in terms of culture and values. Perhaps the biggest difference between existing states and the emergent Europe, however, is the absence of any common political authority that can mediate and legitimate trade-offs amongst the various interests. Concepts such as "national preferences" and "national interests" are still the dominant factors in shaping economic policies in Europe. During the period of fast growth in the late 1980s, trade-offs between incompatible national interests were unnecessary because all could be easily satisfied. In the context of marked economic slowdown and rising unemployment, however, various specific shocks and national circumstances have brought the process of European integration to a halt and seem to threaten its future. All of this challenges both the specific policies pursued by the French as they continue to search for economic "credibility," and the general policy of moving Europe toward union.

The major shock of the late 1980s obviously came from German reunification and the movement of Eastern Europe and the Republics of the former USSR toward market capitalism.[9] Initially, both Germany and the rest of Europe were optimistic, as only positive economic consequences of unification and the opening-up of the East were felt, essentially in the form of a growth bonanza in all neighboring countries. It soon became clear, however, that such a large shock had country-specific consequences and induced policy responses that were dictated by national interests.

Additional growth was, obviously, more pronounced in Germany than in the rest of Europe, although countries like France did benefit considerably by expanding their exports to unified Germany. But more importantly, demand pressures in Germany did not lead to any exchange-rate realignment, although a real appreciation of the mark would probably have been required to restore equilibrium.[10] Instead, higher domestic inflation materialized in Germany, which was another way of obtaining the required real appreciation. This induced the Bundesbank to adopt a stricter monetary policy stance, which, in turn, had to be followed in the other countries of the EMS. Similarly, the large increase in public expenditures necessary to keep Eastern Germany afloat were financed, not by additional taxes in Germany, but by additional public debt, which contributed to keeping long-term real interest rates high in Europe.

This occurred in a context where most other European countries were saddled with high unemployment and large stocks of outstanding public debt. Some of them were particularly vulnerable because of their ongoing disinflation attempt (as described above) and efforts at fiscal consolidation in order to meet the Maastricht criteria for public finance. The German unification shock and its domestic policy responses could thus not but have centrifugal consequences for Germany's European partners. The virtual collapse of the EMS in the fall of 1992 and the final blow of 2 August 1993, have been the most visible outcomes of this tension, but it was also clearly felt in the realm of international trade negotiations where the economic slowdown exacerbated national rivalries in such fields as agriculture and steel.

In such circumstances, the temptation is large for many individual countries to "go it alone," as they are inspired by national interest considerations and confronted with diverse national circumstances. Already, the UK, where the recession has been longer and deeper than elsewhere and where European feelings have never been dominant, seems to have opted for an independent strategy. The pound sterling was set free to float, monetary policy was considerably relaxed, and fiscal policy turned expansionary, with the public sector net borrowing exceeding 6 percent of GDP in 1992 and well over 7 percent in 1993. In the other EU countries that have had to devalue their currency (Ireland, Portugal, and Spain) or to leave the ERM (Italy), fiscal consolidation efforts have been maintained, but the severity of the recession has partly cancelled the gains in terms public deficits and debt.

Although the EMS seems to have evolved into a loose target zone agreement, its major discipline devices are still obeyed in practice. European currency devaluations have, up until now, all corresponded to a correction of previously accumulated handicaps -- losses of competitiveness in the course of a slow disinflation process. But persistence of the economic slump and sharply rising unemployment in all countries could yet induce EU member-states to react along short-term national interests by adopting economic policies of a "beggar-thy-neighbor" variety. The major danger would probably come from competitive devaluations, in self-defeating rounds of attempts to restore intra-EC competitiveness followed by retaliations.

Recent depreciations of EC currencies have already cancelled, at least in part, the competitive advantage painfully gained by France in the process of competitive disinflation during the last few years of nominal exchange-rate stability within the EMS. This also demonstrates that the relative success of such a policy was partly at the expense of European partner-countries and was thus, to some extent, non-cooperative. It was all the more successful as other European countries were willing to bear a deterioration of their own competitive position by keeping their nominal exchange rate fixed while allowing domestic inflation to remain higher than in France.

In the 1970s, such non-cooperative policy options quickly degenerated, most notably for Italy and France, into spiralling depreciation, that is national "vicious circles" of accelerating inflation and currency depreciation with very little benefit in terms of domestic activity and employment. The danger in the current European context is not so much a new round of inflation as a general recourse to competitive disinflation, with each country trying to gain a competitive edge over its partners by achieving the lowest possible domestic inflation rate. Restrictive domestic demand policies would be simultaneously pursued in all countries, both for fiscal consolidation purposes and to tame domestic producers' costs, with everyone aiming at export-led growth. But, as is well-known, not all countries can increase their exports and contract their imports simultaneously; at best under this scenario, no country would gain. They might even all lose if this combination of non-cooperative domestic policies, while respecting the words of the EMS agreement and the Maastricht Treaty, would lead to deflation within the EU and an appreciation of EU currencies vis-à-vis the dollar, with an ensuing generalized European loss of external competitiveness. The Maastricht Treaty would then suffer the fate of the "Werner Plan" and EMU would again be postponed for at least another decade. Unless a sudden renaissance of European goodwill and spirit -- as well as a better understanding of the probable long-term best interest of all EC members -- inspires European governments to strengthen their policy coordination, this will likely be the case.

Ever since the early 1980s, France has regularly been tempted by an escape from monetary discipline. During troubled economic times, in a context of rising unemployment, the constraint on domestic economic policies that came with continued participation in the ERM mechanism was major. Successive French governments have all resisted this temptation on the premise that the alternative policy course would undermine policy credibility and reignite inflation, with little or no benefit in terms of additional real growth and employment.

With the complete liberalization of international capital flows in 1990, credibility has become an essential ingredient in economic policy making, insofar as financial markets are perceived as reacting to "rational" expectations of the consequences of policy measures, thus immediately sanctioning mistakes. But the actual ingredients of credibility are not easily identified. Whereas a strict and consistent monetary policy stance has long been considered as a sufficient condition for building credibility, recurring turmoil in the exchange markets from September 1992 to September 1993, a period during which French monetary policy was being kept on course with resolve and inflationary performance was better than ever, has tended to demonstrate that things are not so simple.

Political sustainability seems to have become a major ingredient of this new brand of "credibility" that operators in financial markets have in mind. When monetary and exchange-rate policy -- or perhaps even some other domestic policy -- appears unsustainable for economic or for domestic political reasons, the markets, sensing a change in policy orientation in the near future, begin immediately to discount the consequences of the awaited change. Such betting may actually hasten its occurrence, or at least be profitable, as illustrated by the July-August 1993 exchange crisis. In the last analysis, despite the successes of French policy of the strong franc and competitive disinflation during the eighties and early nineties, the crisis in the EMS demonstrated clearly that the desired credibility was still elusive. And painfully and patiently achieved gains in France's competitive position were substantially devalued by the crisis and subsequent exchange-rate adjustments.

So What?

As emphasized above, the exchange rate of the French franc vis-à-vis the DM had returned to its pre-crisis level by December 1993 and the major decisions inscribed in the Maastricht Treaty concerning the second phase of EMU were implemented on time in January 1994. Nominal short-term interest rates have decreased in Europe, not because France has chosen a strategy of opting out, as the UK did in September 1992, but because the German Bundesbank has progressively lowered its own interest rates and the Banque de France has scrupulously followed suit. And the cohesion of the EU in many ways seemed reborn with the timely conclusion of the GATT Uruguay round of negotiations.

While this may look like a return to the status-quo-ante, however, progress toward monetary unification will not simply resume as originally foreseen. The recession has seriously hampered fiscal consolidation in most European countries, including France. Large public deficits and debts are now the rule rather than the exception, and their reduction might well take much longer than the few years left in the official Maastricht schedule. Given that most member states are not willing to increase taxes very much, consolidation might involve serious cuts in social transfers and a general rolling-back of the European welfare states.

In addition to fiscal criteria not being achievable by the agreed deadline, it has also become evident that EMS parities cannot be expected to remain unchanged until the completion of the EMU. Thus, the condition that no parity change be made in the two years preceding the date of joining the EMU is not likely to be met either.

At the same time, both Germany and France seem presently determined to stick to the letter of the treaty. If they really mean it, there will be no monetary union before 1999 and at that time, it will probably be a very restricted one. Many countries will simply not be in position to meet all criteria by the end of the century. Moreover, the relentless pursuit of monetary and fiscal "virtue" in all major European countries might well make it even more difficult for anyone to succeed, while growth might remain sluggish and unemployment would keep rising. Such a prospect would not only jeopardize the EMU, but might indeed threaten even the basis of European integration.

Thus, prospects for French policy are more somber than they were when the Maastricht Treaty was signed, although not because of any specific failure of French policy. Indeed, France has been successful beyond anyone's expectations in conducting its strong franc policy. Yet, the depreciation of some of the major European currencies has offset, at least in part, the competitive advantage that France had hoped would produce an export-led French recovery, which is therefore much less likely. As a result, the growth and declining unemployment at home and the economic stature within the European framework, which the strong franc was to produce, remain elusive.

The pursuit of French national interest through the creation of the European Union as foreseen in Maastricht is challenged by prevailing economic conditions in Europe. Yet a return to past ways offers little prospect of greater success; indeed, in today's Europe, "going it alone" is not an option, as was demonstrated so clearly to the French between 1981 and 1983. Moreover, the basic issue at the heart of French policy is not only how best to safeguard the economic welfare of the country, but what political role France wishes to play in helping shape the new Europe. A great deal of skill will be required by France and its partners in order to keep Europe moving forward while beginning to resolve the acute economic dilemmas they currently face.

Notes

1. Catherine Bruno, Jacques Le Cacheux, and Catherine Mathieu, "L'Union monétaire européenne: état des lieux, projets et enjeux," *Revue de l'OFCE*, No. 38, October 1991.

2. Jacques Le Cacheux, Catherine Mathieu, and Henri Sterdyniak, "Maastricht: les enjeux de la monnaie unique," *Lettre de l'OFCE*, No. 96, January 1992; and Commissariat général du Plan, *A French Perspective on EMU* (Paris: La Documentation française, February 1993).

3. Bruno et al., "L'Union monétaire européenne;" Rahim Loufir and Lucrezia Reichlin, "Convergence nominale et réelle parmi les pays de la CE et de l'AELE," *Revue de l'OFCE*, No. 43, January 1993: [Special Issue entitled "Europe 93," forthcoming as J.P. Fitoussi, ed., *Entre convergences et intérêts nationaux: l'Europe* (Paris: Presses de la Fondation nationale des sciences politiques)].

4. From 1979 on, the Italian lira had enjoyed wider fluctuation margins (± 6 percent), that were reduced to ± 2.25 % at the time of the last lira's devaluation in the ERM, in January 1990. When they finally joined the ERM in 1990, Spain and the UK were also allowed to use the wide-band option. As of September 1992, when the first exchange crisis rocked the EMS, only the Greek drachma was still out of the ERM.

5. Jean-Paul Fitoussi and Edmund S. Phelps, *The Slump in Europe -- Reconstructing Open-Economy Theory* (Oxford: Basil Blackwell, 1988); and Jean-Paul Fitoussi and Jacques Le Cacheux, "Une théorie des années quatre-vingt," *Revue de l'OFCE*, No. 29, October 1989.

6. Jean-Paul Fitoussi, Anthony B. Atkinson, Olivier E. Blanchard, John S. Flemming, Edmond Malinvaud, Edmund S. Phelps, and Robert M. Solow, *Competitive Disinflation, the Mark and Budgetary Politics in Europe*, First Report of the International Policy Group of OFCE (Oxford: Oxford University Press, 1993).

7. In the meantime, of course, Germany had to suffer the negative consequences of reunification, so that its own inflation had accelerated, making it all the easier for France to outperform it.

8. The UK is quite clearly in the Anglo-Saxon camp, cyclically closer to the United States than to Continental Europe; and the German unification has also had differentiated effects on the various European economies. In general, country-specific shocks and external shocks do not have uniform consequences on the EC members.

9. Jean-Paul Fitoussi, et al., *Competitive Disinflation, the Mark and Budgetary Politics in Europe*; and Mario Telo (ed.), *Vers une nouvelle Europe? Towards a New Europe?* (Bruxelles: Editions de l'Université de Bruxelles, coll. de l'Institut d'études européennes, 1992).

10. Jean-Paul Fitoussi, et al., *Competitive Disinflation, the Mark and Budgetary Politics in Europe*, First Report of the International Policy Group of OFCE (Oxford: Oxford University Press, 1993).

6

France and Global Competition

William James Adams

"Global competition" is one of those fashionable phrases that is invoked more often than it is defined. Yet the particulars of its definition will affect any appraisal of its impact on a national economy. This analysis of France and global competition begins, therefore, with a discussion of possible meanings of the term.

Global competition might simply signify that national borders are highly permeable to flows of goods, services, capital, and workers.[1] In this view, global competition impinges on a national economy insofar as that economy exports a large fraction of what it produces and imports a large fraction of what it consumes. In effect, this view equates exposure to global competition with participation in an open economy.

A second possible definition of the term emphasizes the ability of a country to sell its products (or the products of enterprises based within its borders[2]) in the global marketplace. In this view, global competition relates less to the concept of openness than to the concept of competitiveness. A country deals satisfactorily with global competition if and only if it sells "satisfactorily" abroad. Frequently, this ability to sell satisfactorily abroad is thought to derive from a firm's ability to use its muscle in a no-holds-barred economic environment pockmarked by market imperfection.

A third possible interpretation of global competition focuses on the response of domestic producers to the exigencies of vigorous foreign competition. In other words, unlike its incarnation as competitiveness, this definition emphasizes the purifying effect of global market forces on domestic competition -- the degree to which foreign enterprises fortify anemic domestic competition to the point where domestic firms must improve their products, lower their costs, or, at the very least, lower their prices in order to survive. In this view, then, global competition impinges on a country to the extent that it obliges domestic firms to compete in the Schumpeterian or the neoclassical manner.

In the next three sections of this chapter each of these conceptions of global competition will be applied in turn to the French economy since World War II. The discussion will demonstrate why the three are not equivalent. At the same time, however, it will demonstrate that by using any of the three definitions, global competition has impinged fundamentally and pervasively on the contemporary French economy.

In the last section of the chapter, the durability of France's commitment to and involvement in global competition will be examined. Experiencing an unemployment rate of 12 percent, and finding no convincing sign that the shortage of jobs will abate soon, the French government might find it difficult to resist calls for protectionism.[3] Tentatively and unorthodoxly, this chapter argues that France cannot withdraw only slightly from global competition and that a radical withdrawal would entail too high a price in foreign-policy and security terms to be attractive. As a result, at the level of action as opposed to rhetoric, France may be expected to remain chained to the global economy for the foreseeable future -- however uncomfortable economically, socially, and (therefore) politically the link proves to be.

The Openness of the French Economy

France today exports a considerable fraction of what it produces and imports a considerable fraction of what it consumes. In the economy as a whole, in 1990, exports accounted for 23 percent of production and imports accounted for an equal percentage of consumption (Table 6.1). On these measures, France is twice as open as Japan and the United States, slightly more open than Italy and Spain, slightly less open than the United Kingdom, two-thirds as open as Germany, and one-third as open as Belgium.

A given level of aggregate openness can be achieved in various ways. One way consists of tremendous openness in a small number of economic sectors, coupled with minimal openness in the rest. Another consists of moderate and (roughly) uniform openness across economic sectors. Arguably, a country exhibiting high propensities to export and import across the full spectrum of economic activity is more affected by global competition than is a country in which the cross-activity variance of such propensities is large. Sector-specific measures of the propensity to trade will help indicate which type of openness characterizes the French economy.[4]

In 1990, very few goods sectors displayed low propensities to import (Table 6.2) or low propensities to export (Table 6.3). In only two of twenty-four goods sectors was the ratio of imports to domestic consumption below 10 percent. In

TABLE 6.1 Importance of International Trade, Selected Countries, Selected Years

	1960	*1970*	*1980*	*1990*
	Ratio of Exports to GDP (%)			
France	14.5	15.8	21.5	22.6
Germany	19.0	21.2	26.4	32.2
Italy	13.0	16.4	21.9	20.9
United Kingdom	20.9	23.1	27.3	24.5
Spain	9.9	12.9	15.4	17.1
Belgium	38.4	51.9	62.9	73.9
Japan	10.7	10.8	13.7	10.8
United States	5.2	5.8	10.2	10.0
	Ratio of Imports to AHC (%)			
France	12.7	15.4	22.5	22.6
Germany	16.9	19.5	26.8	27.9
Italy	13.5	16.4	24.0	20.8
United Kingdom	22.0	22.4	25.6	26.4
Spain	7.4	13.8	17.4	19.8
Belgium	38.9	50.7	63.8	73.2
Japan	10.3	9.6	14.5	10.1
United States	4.5	5.5	10.8	11.3

Note: AHC denotes apparent home consumption (GDP+imports-exports). GDP, exports, and imports are measured in current prices at purchasers' values.

Source: Organisation for Economic Cooperation and Development, *National Accounts*, volume 1: *Main Aggregates, 1960-1991* (Paris: OECD, 1993).

sixteen of the twenty-four, that ratio exceeded 25 percent. Meanwhile, the ratio of exports to output was above 10 percent in all but four of the twenty-four sectors. Thirteen of the twenty-four sectors sent more than one-quarter of their output abroad. The very nature of the relatively closed sectors betrays the breadth of today's openness. Two of the sectors displaying low propensities to export (coal; petroleum/natural gas) involve natural resources that France lacks. The other two sectors displaying low propensities to export (electricity/manufactured gas/municipal water; printing/publishing) displayed low propensities to import as well. Both are sectors in which the "natural" barriers to trade are large -- in the one case due to transport costs, in the other due to linguistic and cultural differentiation.

TABLE 6.2 Propensity to Import, by Industry, 1960 and 1990

Industry (NAP-T)

	Goods	*1990*	*1960*	*Change*
6	Electricity, other gas, water	1.1	0.8	0.3
22	Printing and publishing	8.7	3.4	5.3
2	Meat and dairy products	11.5	3.7	7.8
1	Agriculture	12.5	13.6	-1.1
13	Metallic products	13.3	2.5	10.8
9	Building materials/nonmetal minerals	14.3	11.0	3.3
3	Other food products, tobacco	18.0	7.6	10.4
12	Drugs, personal & home care products	22.9	3.9	19.0
23	Rubber and plastics	28.1	9.5	18.6
20	Wood, incl. furniture; misc. mfg.	29.7	8.6	21.1
10	Glass	32.8	4.1	28.7
21	Paper	33.3	12.7	20.6
5	Petroleum, natural gas	34.6	23.7	10.9
15A	Electrical/electronic eq., business	36.6	9.0	27.6
17	Ships, aerospace eq., military prods.	38.9	13.5	25.4
7	Iron ore, iron, basic steel	39.1	12.3	26.8
18	Textiles and apparel	39.3	4.6	34.7
4	Coal	40.1	21.3	18.8
16	Ground transport equipment	40.1	4.5	35.6
14	Mechanical equipment	41.7	16.2	25.5
19	Leather, including shoes	51.7	5.1	46.6
8	Basic nonferrous metals and ores	51.9	33.2	18.7
11	Bulk chemicals, manmade fibers	56.1	20.1	36.0
15B	Electrical/electronic eq., household	64.4	7.3	57.1
				continues

Tables 6.2 and 6.3 also reveal the degree of openness in the service sectors of the economy. Seven of the twelve sectors were completely unaffected by international trade. Three of the remaining five displayed propensities to import and export of at least 5 percent. The pattern is quite consistent with plausible a priori expectations regarding which services are subject to "natural" barriers to trade.

The broad-based openness of the French economy today is hardly surprising. Institutional developments at the European and global levels help explain the economic openness of contemporary France. During the 1950s, France joined five other European countries in forming the European Community (EC). Although different in important respects, each of these countries eliminated virtually all tariffs and quotas on the free movement of relevant goods and services between member states. Relying occasionally on judicial activism and occasion-

TABLE 6.2 (continued)

Industry (NAP-T)

	Services	*1990*	*1960*	*Change*
24	Construction	0.0	0.0	0.0
25-8	Wholesale, retail trade	0.0	0.0	0.0
29	Sale, repair of automobiles	0.0	0.0	0.0
30	Hotels, cafés, restaurants	0.0	0.0	0.0
34	Consumer services	0.0	0.0	0.0
35	Rental of buildings	0.0	0.0	0.0
38	Government services	0.0	0.0	0.0
32	Telecommunications, incl. mail	0.7	0.9	-0.2
36	Insurance	3.9	3.3	0.6
33	Business services	5.0	5.0	0.0
37	Financial services	5.9	2.3	3.6
31	Transport services	8.7	8.1	0.6

Note: Propensity to import is imports (cif) expressed as a percentage of apparent home consumption (domestic production-exports+imports).

Sources: 1990: French national income accounts and input-output tables. 1960: Institut National de la Statistique et des Etudes Economiques, *Rétropolation 1959-1969 de Comptes Détaillés des Biens et des Services*, Archives et Documents No. 164 (Paris: INSEE, 1986).

ally on legislative initiative, the EC has gone well beyond commercial disarmament toward the construction of community-wide markets for goods and services.[5] Once the United Kingdom joined the EC in 1973, the Community signed a series of bilateral treaties with the new and remaining members of the European Free Trade Association (EFTA) -- treaties that established free-trade in industrial products between the EC and each EFTA country. Meanwhile, within the framework of the General Agreement on Tariffs and Trade (GATT), the EC negotiated with the rest of the world a series of reductions in tariffs. Once the Dillon, Kennedy, and Tokyo rounds of negotiations had been completed, relatively few products continued to receive great tariff protection.

These profound institutional changes are associated with equally profound changes in the openness of the French economy. In the economy as a whole, the propensity to export was 56 percent larger in 1990 than it had been in 1960, while the exposure to imports was 78 percent larger in 1990 than it had been in 1960 (Table 6.1). The percentage growth in the propensity to trade internationally was roughly comparable in France to what it was during this period in Germany, Italy, and Spain; it was well below the growth registered in Belgium and the United States,[6] and well above that exhibited by Japan and the United Kingdom.

The change in aggregate openness reflects the broadening of openness from just a few sectors in 1960 to the overwhelming majority of goods sectors in 1990.

TABLE 6.3 Propensity to Export, by Industry, 1960 and 1990

Industry (NAP-T)	Goods	1990	1960	Change
6	Electricity, other gas, water	5.1	0.7	4.4
22	Printing and publishing	6.4	6.9	-0.5
4	Coal	6.4	2.2	4.2
5	Petroleum, natural gas	8.1	8.3	-0.2
9	Building materials/nonmetal minerals	11.2	12.2	-1.0
13	Metallic products	11.7	5.6	6.1
2	Meat and dairy products	14.4	4.2	10.2
1	Agriculture	19.3	3.8	15.5
3	Other food products, tobacco	19.8	7.5	12.3
20	Wood, incl. furniture; misc. mfg.	22.5	18.4	4.1
21	Paper	22.9	7.5	15.4
23	Rubber and plastics	26.2	13.4	12.8
12	Drugs, personal & home care products	30.5	14.9	15.6
18	Textiles and apparel	32.2	17.5	14.7
15A	Electrical/electronic eq., business	32.8	14.0	18.8
19	Leather, including shoes	37.8	15.1	22.7
1	Mechanical equipment	38.1	19.6	18.5
10	Glass	38.5	18.5	20.0
7	Iron ore, iron, basic steel	40.6	24.7	15.9
8	Basic nonferrous metals and ores	43.2	16.5	26.7
16	Ground transport equipment	44.4	25.9	18.5
15B	Electrical/electronic eq., household	51.3	9.6	41.7
11	Bulk chemicals, manmade fibers	54.9	21.5	33.4
17	Ships, aerospace eq., military prods.	56.0	15.4	40.6
	Services			
24	Construction	0.0	0.0	0.0
25-8	Wholesale, retail trade	0.0	0.0	0.0
29	Sale, repair of automobiles	0.0	0.0	0.0
30	Hotels, cafés, restaurants	0.0	0.0	0.0
34	Consumer services	0.0	0.0	0.0
35	Rental of buildings	0.0	0.0	0.0
38	Government services	0.0	0.0	0.0
32	Telecommunications, incl. mail	0.7	2.2	-1.5
36	Insurance	1.7	3.7	-2.0
37	Financial services	5.7	2.9	2.8
33	Business services	8.2	10.3	-2.1
31	Transport services	14.0	25.4	-11.4

Note: Propensity to export is exports expressed as a percentage of domestic production.

Sources: 1990: French national income accounts and input-output tables. 1960: Institut National de la Statistique et des Etudes Economiques, *Rétropolation 1959-1969 de Comptes Détaillés des Biens et des Services*, Archives et Documents No. 164 (Paris: INSEE, 1986).

In 1960, fourteen of the twenty-four goods sectors displayed propensities to import of less than 10 percent, and only one of the twenty-four displayed a propensity in excess of 25 percent (Table 6.2). Meanwhile, ten of the goods sectors exported less than 10 percent of their output, and only one exported as much as 25 percent of its production (Table 6.3). In contrast, in most service sectors, the propensities to import and export were identical in 1960 and 1990: at both points in time, most service sectors were uninvolved in international trade. In those service sectors that are susceptible to international trade, despite the incipient deregulation already occurring within the framework of the 1992 program, the propensity to export tended to decline between 1960 and 1990. In transport services, the decline exceeded 10 percentage points.

The period between 1960 and 1990 is often divided into two subperiods. The first, expiring around 1974, is considered part of the *trente glorieuses* -- the period of rapid economic growth and the formation of the EC. The second, from 1974 onward, is considered part of the *crise* -- the period of slow growth, high unemployment, and (alleged) eurosclerosis that followed the first explosion of oil prices. It is interesting, therefore, to examine the degree to which the opening that occurred between 1960 and 1990 displays a different rhythm during different decades of this thirty-year period.

In the economy as a whole, the propensities to import and export increased more between 1970 and 1980 than they did between 1960 and 1970 and between 1980 and 1990 (Table 6.1). Even so, openness increased monotonically over the three decades. At the sectoral level, the propensities to import and export tended to increase throughout the thirty-year period: among goods sectors, the propensity to import tended to be greater in 1970 than in 1960, greater in 1980 than in 1970, and greater in 1990 than in 1980.[7] Only five goods sectors ever experienced a drop in import-propensity from the beginning of one decade to its end. All but one of these declines (petroleum/natural gas from 1980 to 1990) amounted to less than 3 percentage points. Similarly, among goods sectors, the propensity to export tended to be greater in 1970 than in 1960, greater in 1980 than in 1970, and greater in 1990 than in 1980.[8] Other than the decline of the propensity to export wood between 1960 and 1970 (by 6.5 percentage points), no goods sector displays a decline of export propensity that exceeded 4 percentage points during any of the three decades. The number of goods sectors that display a drop in export-propensity from the beginning of one decade to its end never exceeded five.

More surprisingly, perhaps, the increases in trade propensities tended to be fairly steady over time: statistically speaking, the mean increase in the propensity to import during the period 1960-1970 was indistinguishable from the mean increase in the propensity to import during the period 1970-1980 (Table 6.4).[9] It was also indistinguishable from the mean increase in the propensity to import during the period 1980-1990. Similarly, the mean increase in the propensity to import during the period 1970-1980 was indistinguishable from the mean in-

TABLE 6.4 The Pace of Opening, 1960-1990

Decade 1			Decade 2			Mean Difference	
Years	DIM	DEX	Years	DIM	DEX	DIM	DEX
1960-70	7.3	3.8	1970-80	7.7	6.6	0.5	2.8**
1960-70	7.3	3.8	1980-90	6.2	5.0	-1.1	1.1
1970-80	7.7	6.6	1980-90	6.2	5.0	-1.5	-1.6

Note: DIM denotes the mean change in import-propensity between the first and the last years of the decade. The mean is calculated over the 24 goods industries defined according to NAP-T. Import-propensity is measured as in Table 6.2. DEX denotes the mean change in export-propensity between the first and the last years of the decade. The mean is calculated over the 24 goods industries defined according to NAP-T. Export propensity is measured as in Table 6.3. Unless followed by an asterisk, the mean change in DIM or DEX between decade 1 and decade 2 fails to differ significantly from 0 in a two-tail t-test. Two stars denotes statistical significance at the .05 level.

Sources: 1960 and 1970: Institut National de la Statistique et des Etudes Economiques, *Rétropolation 1959-1969 de Comptes Détaillés des Biens et des Services*, Archives et Documents No. 164 (Paris: INSEE, 1986). 1980 and 1990: French national income accounts and input-output tables.

crease in the propensity to import during the period 1980-1990. Regarding exports, the propensity to export tended to increase more between 1970 and 1980 than it did between 1960 and 1970. Otherwise, pairwise comparisons of decades fail to reveal any statistically significant differences in the tendency for export-propensity to grow. In short, it would be difficult to argue that the opening process stopped or reversed direction once the blush of common market and rapid growth had begun to fade.

Although the opening of the French economy proceeded steadily over the entire thirty-year period, one feature of its timing does warrant mention. During the early years of the European Economic Community (EEC) (i.e., during the first of the decades under examination here), at the sectoral level, the propensity to import tended to rise more than the propensity to export.[10] Thereafter, one cannot reject the hypothesis that the two rose at the same rate.

The opening of the French economy since World War II should be evaluated in a larger historical context. Such an evaluation permits a determination of whether the postwar opening, observed in Tables 6.1, 6.2, and 6.3, merely represents a reversal of the closure associated with depression in the 1930s and war in the 1940s or whether it represents instead the creation of the most open economy France has known during its industrial life. An historical approach of this type entails an examination of the evolution of France's exposure to international trade back to the early years of the Third Republic. Rather than delve deeply into the

TABLE 6.5 Ratio of Terminal to Initial GDP and Exports, Selected Countries, Selected Intervals

| | 1900 | 1929 | 1959 | 1989 |
	1870	1899	1929	1959
France				
GDP	1.56	1.65	1.66	3.07
Exports	1.98	2.31	1.75	7.37
Ratio	1.27	1.40	1.05	2.40
Germany				
GDP	2.25	2.05	2.63	2.63
Exports	2.53	2.18	1.47	7.83
Ratio	1.12	1.06	0.56	2.98
Italy				
GDP	1.44	2.20	2.25	3.28
Exports	1.66	1.76	2.47	11.08
Ratio	1.15	0.80	1.10	3.38
United Kingdom				
GDP	1.85	1.35	1.80	2.16
Exports	1.88	1.33	1.42	5.80
Ratio	1.02	0.99	0.79	2.69

Note: For each country, the number in row three, column j is the ratio of the number in row two, column j to the number in row 1, column j.

Source: Calculations from index-number data in Angus Maddison, *Dynamic Forces in Capitalist Development: A Long-Run Comparative View* (Oxford: Oxford University Press, 1991).

historical literature on French national income and its components, this analysis relies on information collected by Angus Maddison[11] to provide a rough idea of the opening process during the last quarter of the nineteenth century and the first half of the twentieth century.

Maddison presents index numbers representing the annual growth of GDP, of imports, and of exports from 1870 to 1989. This information is used here as follows: first, Maddison's entire period of 120 years is decomposed into 30-year subperiods. Next, for each subperiod, the percentage growth of GDP and the percentage growth of exports is calculated. Finally, the two rates of growth are compared: if exports are growing faster than GDP, we may conclude that the economy is opening; if GDP is growing faster than exports, we may conclude that the economy is closing. The larger the ratio of growth of exports to growth of GDP, the greater the degree of opening. Repeating this entire procedure separately for Germany, Italy, and the United Kingdom, the opening process in France may be compared with that in the other large countries of Europe.

The results appear in Table 6.5. During each of the thirty-year intervals, French exports grew more rapidly than did French GDP. The rate of opening was slightly greater during the first third of the twentieth century than it was at the end of the nineteenth century or in the middle of the twentieth century. The most important difference in the rate opening, however, is that between the interval since formation of the EEC and those that precede it. During the thirty years starting in 1959, French GDP tripled, but French exports increased by 637 percent.

Despite the fact that French exports grew virtually as rapidly as those of Italy, and appreciably more rapidly than those of the United Kingdom, France appears to have opened less during the EEC period than did the other large countries of Europe. Alternately, France is the only one of the four in which exports grew more rapidly than GDP during each of the four intervals. Thus, in the aggregate, not only is the French economy today about as open as are its large European cousins, but it is also more open today than at any time in its industrialized life.

The Competitiveness of the French Economy

In popular parlance, a competitive economy is one in which domestic producers can outsell foreign rivals in the world marketplace. For a variety of reasons, the openness of an economy does not reflect perfectly its competitiveness. Two of these warrant discussion here.

First, a high propensity to export might be achieved via sales in sheltered foreign markets -- markets in which an exporting country enjoys artificial or natural advantages over other potential exporters. Historically speaking, colonial (and quasi-colonial) relationships have been important sources of artificial advantage, while geographic proximity (in transport-cost terms) has been an important source of natural advantage. In the French context, European geography precludes enjoyment of much natural advantage; but the colonial past opens the possibility of artificial advantage.

To explore the lingering commercial effects of empire, the shares of French exports that are destined to two distinct groupings of countries were calculated: those that belonged to the French Overseas Union (FOU) as of 1952 and those that currently belong to the Organization for Economic Cooperation and Development (OECD).[12] Such calculations were performed for the years 1952 through 1992.[13] At the beginning of this period, France sent 42 percent of its exports to the FOU and 43 percent of its exports to the OECD. Forty years later, it sent 7 percent of its exports to the FOU and 78 percent of its exports to the OECD. In other words, the role of quasi-colonial markets has declined radically. It cannot be said that the dramatic and pervasive increase in France's propensity to export has been achieved via recourse to quasi-colonial advantage.[14]

A second reason why the openness of an economy does not necessarily reflect its competitiveness is more fundamental. By virtue of the law of comparative advantage no country can be a net exporter of all products. As a result, each country can be expected to account for a share of the world's exports that is larger in some lines of business than in others. At the sectoral level, then, competitiveness is usually associated with achieving shares of world exports that are especially large in the especially desirable sectors.

An appraisal of France's ability to account for shares of world exports that are especially large in the especially "desirable" sectors is best accomplished in two steps. The first involves a determination of France's share of world exports in each particular economic sector. The second involves a determination of which sectors are desirable. Pursuant to the first step of the exercise, the calculation

$$(100)(XF_i)/(XOECD_i)$$

was made for each division of the Standard International Trade Classification (SITC),[15] where XF_i denotes French exports of goods assigned to division i and $XOECD_i$ denotes exports from all OECD countries of goods assigned to division i. To chart the evolution of France's competitiveness, such calculations were performed for both 1990 and 1970.[16] Moreover, to compare France's pattern of exports with those of "rival" countries, both sets of calculations were performed for Germany, Italy, and the United Kingdom as well.

Looking first at central tendencies, in 1990, across the sixty-four divisions, the (unweighted) mean French share of OECD exports was 10.3 percent (Table 6.6). Germany's mean share was one-third larger, while those of Italy and the United Kingdom were roughly two-thirds as large. When each division is weighted in proportion to its contribution to total OECD exports, the mean French share declines somewhat, implying that France's ability to export is relatively large in SITC divisions accounting for relatively small shares of total OECD exports. Between 1970 and 1990, according to both the unweighted and the weighted measures, the mean share of OECD exports rose slightly in three of the four countries examined; in the United Kingdom, it fell comparably slightly.

At the level of particular sectors, of course, export ability can depart considerably from the economy-wide mean.[17] In which divisions does France account for an especially large share of OECD exports? Table 6.7 identifies the ten SITC divisions in which France accounted for the largest shares of OECD exports during 1990; Table 6.8 performs the same function for 1970. In 1990, six of the ten divisions covered were raw or processed foods, another involved a non-food raw material re-exported from France, and still another involved primary energy. The remaining two divisions (travel goods, handbags, and similar products; essential

TABLE 6.6 Export Ability, Selected Countries, 1970 and 1990

| | Unweighted | | Weighted | |
	1970	1990	1970	1990
France	8.9	10.3	8.3	8.7
Germany	12.7	13.9	15.9	16.4
Italy	6.2	7.3	6.3	6.9
United Kingdom	8.0	6.7	8.9	7.7

Note: In the weighted averages, each SITC division's contribution to the mean is weighted in proportion to the division's contribution to the total value of exports from OECD countries. The 1970 data are reported according to SITC Revision 1; means relate to 55 divisions from SITC sections 0 through 8, plus SITC section 9 (N=56); data on electric current (SITC division 35) are unavailable for Germany and Italy: For them, N=55. The 1990 data are reported according to SITC Revision 3; means relate to 63 divisions from SITC sections 0 through 8, plus SITC section 9 (N=64); data on electric current are unavailable for Italy: For it, N=63.

Sources: 1970: Organization for Economic Cooperation and Development, *Statistics of Foreign Trade*, Series C: *Trade by Commodities, Market Summaries: Exports* (Paris: OECD, 1972). 1990: Organization for Economic Cooperation and Development, *Foreign Trade by Commodities, 1991*, Series C, vol. 1 (Paris: OECD, 1992).

TABLE 6.7 French Competitive Advantage, 1990

SITC	Division	French Share
23	Crude rubber	16.6
02	Dairy products	17.5
22	Oil seeds and oleaginous fruits	17.6
04	Cereals and cereal preparations	20.2
83	Travel goods, handbags, similar	23.6
00	Live animals	24.9
55	Perfume materials; toilet, polishing, cleaning preparations	25.4
06	Sugars, sugar preparations, honey	30.2
11	Beverages	36.4
35	Electric current	41.6

Note: The 10 SITC divisions in which the French share of OECD exports is largest. SITC divisions as defined in revision 3.

Source: Organization for Economic Cooperation and Development, *Foreign Trade by Commodities, 1991*, Series C, vol. 1 (Paris: OECD, 1992).

oils/perfume materials/toilet, polishing, and cleaning preparations), are densely populated with luxury consumer goods. The pattern in 1970 was quite similar to that in 1990: France's competitiveness in product terms was especially developed in raw and processed foods; elsewhere in manufacturing, it tended to reside in luxury consumer goods.

At the other end of the competitiveness spectrum, in 1990, the French share of OECD exports in ten divisions was less than 5 percent.[18] With the exception of metal-working machinery, most of these involve production of, or heavy reliance on, raw materials not produced abundantly in France. The corresponding number of divisions in 1970 was twelve.[19] The divisional composition of the list is rather similar to that in 1990.[20]

The big question, of course, is the degree to which the French pattern of competitiveness is desirable. But which products are desirable? The most sensible answer to that question is straightforward: "Desirable products are those that assure the nation a high and rising standard of living."[21] The particular products that contribute best to high and rising standards of living can vary from one country to another. Hence the difficulty of identifying them with assurance in the absence of extended economic analysis. Rather than attempt such analysis here, this chapter shall simply examine the pattern of French competitiveness with two criteria in mind: how similar is the French pattern to those of Germany, Italy, and the United Kingdom; and is the French pattern conducive to a high aggregate share of OECD exports in the future, given the variation across divisions in the rate of growth of OECD exports?

To gauge the similarity of the French pattern of competitiveness to those of Germany, Italy, and the United Kingdom, the (Pearson) correlation coefficient linking variations across divisions in one country's share of OECD exports with the corresponding variations in each other country's share (Table 6.9) was calculated.[22] In 1990, as in 1970, France's pattern of competitiveness bore most resemblance to that of the United Kingdom. For no other pairing of the four countries could one reject the hypothesis in 1990 that competitiveness in the one was uncorrelated with competitiveness in the other. In 1970, the German and UK patterns had borne some similarity, but not as much as that between the UK and French patterns.

France's export shares in divisions at the head of Germany's competitiveness list in 1990 (Table 6.10) and in 1970 (Table 6.11) were also examined, comparing the French position in those sectors to the positions of Italy and the United Kingdom. Germany's competitive advantage is heavily concentrated in the machinery and chemicals sections of the SITC, together with manufactures of metals. In seven of Germany's top ten divisions (in terms of competitiveness in 1990), the combined export share of France, Italy, and the United Kingdom was smaller than was the German share on its own. In none of the ten divisions did France alone account for as much as half of Germany's export share. France does not display much competitiveness where Germany is strong.

TABLE 6.8 French Competitive Advantage, 1970

SITC	Division	French Share
23	Crude rubber	12.4
35	Electric energy	12.7
61	Leather, leather manufactures	14.0
04	Cereals, cereal preparations	15.1
62	Rubber manufactures	17.1
00	Live animals	17.9
02	Dairy products and eggs	19.8
55	Perfumes; toilet, polishing, cleansing preparations	22.1
11	Beverages	27.5
06	Sugar, sugar preparations, honey	36.0

Note: The 10 SITC divisions in which the French share of OECD exports is largest. SITC divisions as defined in revision 1.

Source: Organization for Economic Cooperation and Development, *Statistics of Foreign Trade*, Series C: *Trade by Commodities, Market Summaries: Exports* (Paris: OECD, 1972).

TABLE 6.9 Cross-Industry Correlations of Export Ability Between Large EC Countries

Countries	1970	1990
France and Germany	-0.03	-0.03
France and Italy	0.11	0.06
France and UK	0.44**	0.30*
Germany and Italy	0.04	0.11
Germany and UK	0.30*	0.22
Italy and UK	0.08	-0.07

Note: In column 1, N=55; in column 2, N=63 (Division 35, electric current, is excluded). One and two asterisks denote statistical significance at the .05 and .01 levels, respectively, in two-tail t-tests.

Sources: 1970: Organization for Economic Cooperation and Development, *Statistics of Foreign Trade*, Series C: *Trade by Commodities, Market Summaries: Exports* (Paris: OECD, 1972). 1990: Organization for Economic Cooperation and Development, *Foreign Trade by Commodities, 1991*, Series C, vol. 1 (Paris: OECD, 1992).

TABLE 6.10 German Competitive Advantage, 1990

SITC	Division	Share of OECD Exports			
		D	F	I	UK
57	Plastics, primary	21.6	10.3	4.3	5.6
69	Manufactures of metals n.e.s.	22.6	8.7	11.1	6.6
59	Chemicals n.e.s.	22.9	11.3	4.1	11.4
78	Road vehicles	23.2	8.6	4.7	4.5
74	General industrial machinery	23.9	7.7	10.5	7.0
58	Plastics, non-primary	24.2	5.7	8.8	7.1
72	Specialized machinery	24.5	5.9	11.5	7.0
73	Metal working machinery	25.4	4.1	10.3	5.8
43	Animal/vegetable fats/oils, processed	28.7	3.4	4.5	4.8
53	Dyeing,tanning,coloring materials	29.2	7.2	3.7	11.8

Note: The 10 SITC divisions in which the German share of OECD exports is largest. SITC divisions as defined in revision 3. D=Germany, F=France, I=Italy, UK=United Kingdom. N.e.s. denotes not elsewhere specified.

Source: Organization for Economic Cooperation and Development, *Foreign Trade by Commodities, 1991*, Series C, vol. 1 (Paris: OECD, 1992).

TABLE 6.11 German Competitive Advantage, 1970

SITC	Division	Share of OECD Exports			
		D	F	I	UK
54	Pharmaceutical prods.	20.0	9.4	6.3	13.7
69	Manufactures of metal n.e.s.	21.4	8.3	7.9	11.0
71	Machinery except electric	22.9	6.8	7.5	11.9
43	Animal/vegetable oils/fats, processed	22.9	3.1	1.2	6.6
59	Chemical materials/prods n.e.s.	23.4	9.4	3.4	12.9
58	Plastic materials	24.6	7.3	6.4	8.9
81	Sanitary,plumbing,heating, lighting fixtures	25.9	7.8	9.8	7.6
82	Furniture	26.9	6.3	11.9	6.0
32	Coal,coke,briquettes	32.8	3.0	0.7	3.4
53	Dyeing,tanning,coloring materials	35.7	6.5	1.9	13.0

Note: The 10 SITC divisions in which the German share of OECD exports is largest. SITC divisions as defined in revision 1. D=Germany, F=France, I=Italy, UK=United Kingdom.

Source: Organization for Economic Cooperation and Development, *Statistics of Foreign Trade*, Series C: *Trade by Commodities, Market Summaries: Exports* (Paris: OECD, 1972).

What about the future? Do France's strengths occur in divisions exhibiting rapid export growth? Using the ratio of OECD exports in 1990 to OECD exports in 1980 as the measure of a sector's growth potential, a weak positive correlation exists between export growth in the division and the share of the division's exports attributable in 1990 to Germany.[23] Similarly weak positive correlations exist between export growth on the one hand and Italian and UK competitiveness on the other.[24] Of the four large European countries studied here, only France fails to display a tendency toward competitiveness in divisions characterized by relatively rapid export growth.[25] For this reason, France might find it relatively difficult to maintain in the aggregate its share of OECD exports.

Competition in the French Economy

The previous section suggested that competitiveness is especially valuable to a country in those sectors that assure it a high and rising standard of living. In no sector can firms provide such assurance unless they act relentlessly to lower costs, improve products, and set prices in an (allocatively) efficient manner. The third dimension of global competition, then, concerns the degree to which the dramatic opening of the French economy since World War II has altered the state of competition in French markets. Has opening served to fortify competition, and has competition served to stimulate static and dynamic efficiency?

Large propensities to import do not guarantee a competitive domestic market. Foreign exporters might be owned by the same parent companies as are the domestic importers. If so, international trade becomes nothing more than intramural transactions of multinational firms. It does not increase the number of (independent) sellers in the domestic market and is thus unlikely to invigorate competition there.[26] Even when foreign exporters are not controlled in common with domestic importers, a high propensity to import does not guarantee competition in the home market. In a world of national oligopolies and cartels, all firms might readily adopt the strategy of allowing each national oligopoly or cartel to play a leadership role in its domestic market, with foreigners simply and automatically matching the pricing and other behavior of their domestic counterparts. If this happens, then imports cannot be relied upon to augment domestic competition.

These qualifications to the presumed relationship between imports and competition are not merely hypothetical possibilities. The records of antitrust proceedings before the Court of Justice of the European Communities demonstrate how international trade within the EC has been used (on occasion) actually to reduce the likelihood of genuine international competition.[27]

Suppose, however, that imports do intensify competition in domestic markets. Does the extra competition improve the economic performance of domestic producers? According to one line of thought, traceable to Adam Smith, competition is highly likely to improve performance in all its dimensions. According to another line of thought, however, one associated with Joseph Schumpeter, the effects of competition are not always salutary. Although Smithians and Schumpeterians would probably agree that greater import competition results in closer conformity of domestic prices to domestic costs of production, the Schumpeterians would argue that competition can jeopardize domestic innovation.

How, then, has import competition affected prices in the French economy? One way to answer this question is to examine the degree to which variations over time in the rate of inflation are explained (negatively) by corresponding variations in the propensity to import. Using data for the period 1959-1979, INSEE has performed calculations of this sort at the sectoral level.[28] Controlling for variations over time in the prices of intermediate inputs and in unit labor costs, it found a large negative relationship between changes in price and changes in the propensity to import, leading it to conclude that international competition "is now an important element in price-determination."[29]

A second way to analyze the relationship between imports and inflation is to determine the degree to which variations in inflation across sectors correlate negatively with corresponding variations in the propensity to import. Toward this end, INSEE has published a graph in which a sector's (average annual) rate of inflation between 1959 and 1979 is plotted against its exposure to international competition during that period. It concludes that "anomalies aside, exposure to foreign competition seems to play a significant role in the evolution of prices -- and this despite the fact that the sectors studied here are extremely diverse and subject to very different rates of increase in their costs."[30] This finding accords with Auquier's observation of a negative correlation (*ceteris paribus*) across economic sectors between price-cost margin and the propensity to import,[31] and with my own finding of negative correlations across economic sectors between the rate of increase in prices and the change in the propensity to import during the first five and first ten years of the EEC.[32]

One especially interesting way to determine the impact of international competition on the pricing of French producers would make use of the following line of thought. If foreign competition fails to impinge strongly on French producers, then we would expect their market power to depend heavily on the domestic elements of their market structures. As a result, in a cross section of economic sectors, we might expect the price-cost margins or profitability of leading producers to depend positively on the concentration of domestic production. Alternately, if international competition has become so important that the relevant market for French producers has become meta-national in scope -- coextensive, say, with the borders of the EC -- then we would expect the price-cost margins and profitability of French producers to depend on concentration at the EC, not the French, level. Over time, as the geographic boundaries of meaningful markets evolved from national to EC configurations, we would expect national concentration to lose its significance and EC concentration to acquire it. Unfortunately, the empirical literature contains few studies based on this line of thought.[33] We know that national levels of concentration did affect price-cost margins and profitability during the early years of the EC;[34] but a paucity of data has prevented a determination of the effect of concentration at the EC level on today's price-cost margins and profitability.

But what of the Schumpeterian questions? How do changes in the state of competition affect the creative behavior of market participants? In sectors that had been closed to import competition and then are opened to it, do producers respond with relatively large increases in inventive activity and relatively large increases in spending on plant and equipment?[35] Do such responses result in relatively large subsequent increases in productivity and ability to export? Answers to such questions are being sought in the U.S. setting;[36] but in the French context much of the required statistical work remains to be done.

In sum, the vigor of competition in French product markets is considerably greater today than it was at the end of World War II. Although market power has not disappeared from the French scene, French firms are not as immune to competitive forces as they were earlier in the century. The rise of competition has many causes, including the vigilance of antitrust authorities and the deregulation of important markets, at both the national and the EC levels. In no small measure, however, the rise of competition in France is attributable to the increasing importance of imports. Whether the increase in import competition has contributed to French social welfare in Schumpeterian as well as neoclassical ways remains an open question. Judging, however, from the evidence gathered in other national settings, it probably has.

Whither France's Commitment to Global Competition?

The second half of the twentieth century is not the first period during which France has submitted itself willingly to global competition. Starting in 1860, it signed commercial treaties with several European countries, curtailing sharply the insulation of domestic industries from the rest of the world. Before the end of the nineteenth century, however, these treaties had been abrogated, demonstrating the all-too-reversible nature of global involvement. Is there any reason to expect France to resist protectionism more successfully today than it did a century ago?

Symptoms and causes of a coming protectionism are certainly not hard to find.[37] The most prominent recent symptom, perhaps, were the positions France took in the Uruguay round of trade negotiations in order to insulate French farmers from global competition.[38] The most important cause, however, is the current mediocrity of economic conditions in France. The standard of living is growing very slowly by postwar standards. More than three million people -- 12 percent of the labor force -- are unemployed, and most observers predict that the situation will deteriorate further before it improves. Technological change is imposing a radical restructuring of the labor force; it is also underscoring the importance to rich countries of goods that France has not been historically adept at exporting. Ominously, slow growth, high unemployment, and technological revolution also characterized the nineteenth-century moment when France foresook free trade.[39]

Despite these and other harbingers of protectionism, though, this analysis suggests that France will remain committed to global competition for the foreseeable future. However alluring protectionism might be, to government officials and ordinary citizens alike, it is simply not a viable option for a country in France's position. This is certainly the case if protection entails insulation of France from all other countries, including those in Western Europe; it is even the case, probably, if protection consists of divorcing the EC (now called the European Union, or EU) as a whole from the rest of the world.

A retreat from global competition can take many forms. Suppose first that it consists of nothing more than curbing the inflow of foreign goods, services, and (possibly) investment. If "foreign" means "non-French," then the imposition of such restraints would oblige France to withdraw from the EU. Such withdrawal would lower France's standard of living dramatically.[40] Moreover, whether directly as a result of French inflow barriers or indirectly as a result of outflow barriers erected in retaliation by other countries, it might deprive France of raw materials and/or finished products that are vital to military security. Most importantly, however, withdrawal from the EU would amount to removal of the plinth underlying French foreign policy. Ever since World War II, France has based its foreign policy on the weaving of entangling arrangements with and around Germany. To withdraw from the EU would be to unravel those arrangements in a period of dangerously resurgent European nationalism.

Sophisticated proponents of retreat from global competition take "foreign" to mean "non-EU" rather than "non-French." In so doing, they reduce the degree to which protectionism would lower the French standard of living and deprive France of military products. To the extent that other EU countries can be persuaded to embrace protectionism enthusiastically, it also eliminates the need to redesign French foreign policy.

Although protectionism appeals to many social groups in the EU -- not all of them French -- and although current economic conditions throughout the Union, together with today's fashionable talk of a global marketplace carved tidily into regional trading blocs, make protectionism especially alluring at this time, it is unlikely even today that France could persuade (enough) other member states to endorse a sharp reorientation of EU policy in the protectionist direction. Even if it could, however, protectionism at the EU level would confront a fundamental contradiction: on the one hand, if other EU countries are important sources of the world's "best" products and production methods, then protection at the EU's borders will not insulate French producers from the rigors of global competition; on the other hand, if other EU countries are not important sources of such products and methods, then France's standard of living and access to military products would decline appreciably.

To gauge the degree to which protection at the EU level would shield French producers from global competition, the share of France's total imports that originates within the EU was calculated for each SITC division. Table 6.12 identifies the twenty-two (of sixty-four) divisions in which EU countries supply at least 75 percent of French imports. This group of twenty-two includes such important traditional sectors as iron and steel and road vehicles. Table 6.13 identifies the twenty-one (of sixty-four) divisions in which EU countries supply less than half of French imports. Of the products that France imports primarily from outside the EU, most are raw and waste materials that are not produced abundantly in the EU. Only eight of these twenty-one divisions, most of them containing various kinds of machinery, involve manufactured products.[41] Moreover, even in these divisions, the EU remains the source of one-third or more of France's imports. Thus protectionism at the EU level would fail to insulate most French industries from the rigors of global competition.

The retreat from global competition need not consist exclusively of protectionism. It may also include a dollop of industrial policy. If so, the need for protection might be temporary; so might any decline in living standards and access to state-of-the-art military products. Arguably, in the long run, global competition would be reinforced rather than diminished, as global oligopolies became obliged to welcome new French (and other EU) members to their ranks. Protection would be less a bulwark of the status quo than the spearhead of a new industrial structure chosen deliberately for its social utility.

France has a long tradition of industrial policy (even if the continuity of interventionism since Colbert is often exaggerated).[42] Since World War II, French industrial policy has consisted primarily of the mobilization and allocation of financial resources in regulated and segmented capital markets, the granting of subsidies to industrial enterprises, and the use of government procurement to create demand for (certain kinds of) domestically produced goods. Public enterprises, financial and industrial, have played important roles on both the supply and the demand sides of various markets. In the hopes of creating formidable national champions, capable of defending French interests in global competition, the government has employed both carrots and sticks to merge and restructure enterprises in several industries.

However successful it may have been in the past, an industrial policy conducted unilaterally by France is unlikely to be feasible at this time. One reason is the degree to which the EU now inhibits individual member states from promoting their domestic industries. The EU's strictures are embodied in the EEC and ECSC treaties, in the secondary legislation flowing from those treaties, and, most importantly perhaps, in the propensities of the commission and the Court of Justice

TABLE 6.12 Products Imported Primarily from the Rest of the EC, 1990

MEC/M	SITC	Division
92.7	2	Dairy products
90.3	35	Electric current
89.8	12	Tobacco and manufactures thereof
88.1	11	Beverages
87.8	9	Miscellaneous edible products
86.5	81	Prefab buildings; sanitary fixtures
86.4	43	Animal or vegetable fats and oils, processed
85.1	1	Meat and meat preparations
84.6	00	Live animals
84.6	58	Plastics in non-primary forms
84.3	67	Iron and steel
84.0	82	Furniture and parts thereof
83.9	78	Road vehicles
82.4	41	Animal oils and fats
81.1	57	Plastics in primary forms
80.7	66	Non-metallic mineral manufactures n.e.s.
80.1	62	Rubber manufactures, n.e.s.
79.0	29	Crude animal and vegetable materials, n.e.s.
77.8	69	Manufactures of metal n.e.s.
77.6	4	Cereals and cereal preparations
76.7	55	Perfumes; toilet/polishing/cleaning preparations
75.9	53	Dyeing, tanning and coloring materials

Note: SITC divisions in which imports from the rest of the EC account for at least 75 percent of total French imports. SITC divisions as defined in revision 3. N.e.s. denotes not elsewhere specified. MEC=imports from the rest of the EC during 1990. M=total imports during 1990.

Source: Organization for Economic Cooperation and Development, *Foreign Trade by Commodities*, 1991, Series C, vol. 1 (Paris: OECD, 1992).

to enforce the rules guaranteeing undistorted competition in the Union. Substantively, these rules affect the whole gamut of governmental intervention, including the granting of subsidies to public and private enterprises, the regulation of financial markets, the practice of government procurement, and the promotion of mergers and acquisitions.

Subsidies are curbed in several ways -- by defining the concept of subsidy broadly and the concept of acceptable subsidy narrowly, by forcing national governments to recover subsidies granted in violation of Union rules, and by facilitating the lawsuits of those seeking damages from governments guilty of granting illegal subsidies.[43] The commission's handling of France's financial contributions to Renault during the mid-1980s reveals its willingness to challenge the

TABLE 6.13 Products Imported Primarily from Outside the EC, 1990

MEC/M	SITC	Division
15.3	34	Gas, natural and manufactured
16.5	24	Cork and wood
19.8	25	Pulp and waste paper
22.8	33	Petroleum, petroleum products, and related
27.7	8	Feeding stuff for animals
31.7	21	Hides, skins, and furskins, raw
32.0	28	Metalliferous ores and metal scrap
32.6	75	Office and automatic data processing machines
33.8	76	Telecommunications and sound equipment
35.0	26	Textile fibres and their wastes
35.1	22	Oil seeds and oleaginous fruits
37.5	83	Travel goods, handbags, and similar
38.2	3	Fish
39.8	79	Transport equipment other than road vehicles
41.8	88	Photographic apparatus; watches and clocks
43.8	84	Apparel and clothing accessories
46.0	27	Crude fertilizers
48.1	71	Power generating equipment
48.3	23	Crude rubber (including synthetic and reclaimed)
48.6	6	Sugars, sugar preparations, and honey
49.0	7	Coffee, tea, cocoa, spices; manufactures thereof

Note: SITC divisions in which imports from the the rest of the EC account for a minority of total French imports. SITC divisions as defined in revision 3. MEC=imports from other members of the EC during 1990. M=total imports during 1990.

Source: Organization for Economic Cooperation and Development, *Foreign Trade by Commodities, 1991*, Series C, vol. 1 (Paris: OECD, 1992).

subsidy behavior of member states even when the challenge carries with it, due to the symbolic and economic significance of the subsidized enterprise, the risk of serious confrontation with the member state concerned.[44]

EU-imposed deregulation of national financial markets is, arguably, the most significant feature of the 1992 program. Even before 1 January 1993, France had relinquished most of its power to segment national financial markets. In striking down the barriers that prevented foreign banks from serving domestic markets, whether by local establishment or by the export of services, and in preventing recourse to foreign exchange controls under any but temporary circumstances, the EU made it very difficult for any member state, including France, to orient the allocation of savings according to governmental preferences.[45]

The 1992 program also curtails the ability of governments engaging in public procurement to discriminate against enterprises resident in other member states. Not only is procurement defined broadly to include all but small purchases of both goods and services, but government is defined to include national governments, local governments, and even public utilities -- whether or not they are state-owned. Foreign firms that believe they have suffered discrimination must be given the right to sue the alleged discriminator in court.

A final example of how the *acquis communautaire* constrains national industrial policies relates to mergers and acquisitions. An enduring theme of those who advocate industrial policy in France is the feeble size of French firms. In one version of the argument, emphasis is placed on the failure of small French firms to realize all available economies of scale, in research and production alike. In another version of the argument, success in global competition is said to require possession of no less market power than is exercised by foreign rivals, the assumption being that market power is positively associated with firm size. In both versions of the diagnosis, the large numbers of small firms that make up French industries must be consolidated to form one or two national champions per sector. The best way to ensure that the process of consolidation proceeds in the public interest is for the national government to arrange the mergers.

The EEC treaty, unlike its ECSC counterpart, does not confer on the EU any explicit power to regulate mergers. In 1973, however, the Court of Justice ruled that certain mergers and joint ventures might run afoul of the treaty's antitrust provisions.[46] Sixteen years later, the Council adopted legislation introducing explicit regulation of mergers at the EU level.[47] The commission has used this regulatory power more to compel merging firms to modify the details of their plans than to prevent mergers outright.[48] Nevertheless, the commission has not approved every merger subject to its control. For example, it prevented a European consortium including Aérospatiale, an enterprise owned by the French state and an important national champion in a most strategic industry, from acquiring a Boeing subsidiary engaged in the manufacture of small commercial jet aircraft.[49] In so doing, the commission signaled its willingness to restrict the freedom of member states to engage in industrial policy via the promotion of mergers.

In these and other[50] ways, then, the EU inhibits industrial policy at the national level. The inhibitions are imperfect, of course, in the sense that member states enjoy no small latitude, within and beyond the letter of EU law, to engage in the promotion of domestic industry. Nevertheless, feeling the ever-growing weight of the *acquis communautaire*, realistically, France would have to withdraw from the EU in order to conduct an industrial policy worthy of the name. The implausibility of such withdrawal has already been discussed above.

Suppose for a moment, though, that France did take the drastic step of exiting the Union. In all probability, the legal freedom to engage in industrial policy would quickly prove to be economically illusory. The fundamental constraint on France's ability to pursue successful industrial policies unilaterally is their cost. The financial resources required to develop a globally competitive industrial sector are too large for the government of a medium-size economy to mobilize without encountering fatal political problems. Whatever the government's taste for industrial policy, its budget constraint renders pervasive promotional activity infeasible. Government budget constraints bind especially tightly in periods, such as this, during which high levels of unemployment and a rapidly aging population compel a choice between a welfare state for individuals and a welfare state for enterprises.[51]

If protection-cum-industrial policy were adopted at the EU, rather than the French, level, both the legal and the financial impediments to industrial policy would abate. The *acquis communautaire* does not inhibit Union-level industrial policy, and, theoretically at least, the resources available to the Union as a whole exceed those available to any single member state. Once again, however, it is by no means obvious that France could convince enough other member states to embrace a pervasive industrial policy at the Union level. Even if it could, the Union itself might encounter a budget constraint well before it was able to implement its intended industrial structure. The Union's agricultural experience is relevant in this regard. Although agriculture constitutes just one sector of the economy, accounting for small fractions of output and employment alike, the financial requirements of the common agricultural policy (CAP) have paralyzed meaningful Union initiatives in other sectors of the economy. Internal pressure from budget constraint, no less than external pressure from the Cairns group of agricultural exporters and the United States, explains the EU's efforts, before as well as during the Uruguay round, to cap CAP. As a result, there is hardly more reason to believe that an industrial policy would succeed at the EU level than that it would succeed at the national level -- or that the recourse to protection would be temporary.

Conclusion

After World War II, France decided to participate actively in the global economy. Having chosen a global perspective primarily to guarantee national security, rather than economic prosperity, its commitment to global competition has remained intact despite the mediocrity of domestic economic conditions since the late 1970s. Meanwhile, its prolonged experience of openness has resulted in a remarkably broad recognition that protectionism-cum-industrial policy is not a viable policy for a medium-size economic country; it might not even be such for a regional trading bloc. The breadth of the recognition of this truth within French society helps to explain the tweedle-dum, tweedle-dee politics of current French economic policy making. The harsh realities of high unemployment and the postponement of economic and monetary union might result in some backsliding toward protectionism. Nevertheless, however reluctant it may be, France's commitment to global competition is likely to endure.

Notes

1. In the interest of brevity, I shall focus in this chapter on imports and exports of goods and services.

2. The importance of the location of a firm's headquarters, as distinct from the location of its production facilities, is stressed in Irving B. Kravis and Robert E. Lipsey, "Sources of Competitiveness of the United States and of Its Multinational Firms," *Review of Economics and Statistics,* 74 (May 1992), 193-201.

3. See in particular the chapter by Suzanne Berger in this volume.

4. Calculations of propensities to import and export require information on output as well as on trade. Rarely is such information published according to a common scheme of industrial classification. The best published information of a compatible nature extends back to 1959 and divides the economy into 36 sectors of activity. The industrial classification is known as the level-T disaggregation of the *Nomenclature d'Activités et de Produits (NAP)*, as used in the national income accounts.

5. See William James Adams, ed., *Singular Europe: Economy and Polity of the European Community after 1992* (Ann Arbor: The University of Michigan Press, 1992); and Dennis Swann, ed., *The Single European Market and Beyond: A Study of the Wider Implications of the Single European Act* (London: Routledge, 1992).

6. Interestingly, Belgium and the United States lie at the opposite extremes of exposure to trade at the beginning of this period.

7. These tendencies amount to (separate) rejections of the three null hypotheses that the propensity to import at the end of the decade fails to differ from the propensity to import at the beginning of the decade. The test is a two-tail t-test at the .001 level of statistical significance (N=24).

8. These tendencies amount to (separate) rejections of the three null hypotheses that the propensity to export at the end of the decade fails to differ from the propensity to export at the beginning of the decade. The test is a two-tail t-test at the .01 level (1960 to 1970) or the .001 level (1970 to 1980, 1980 to 1990) of statistical significance (N=24).

9. In other words, in a two-tail t-test at the .05 level of statistical significance (N=24), it is impossible to reject the hypothesis that the two means are equal.

10. The mean increase in the propensity to import was 7.3 percentage points; the mean increase in the propensity to export was 3.8 percentage points. The difference between these means differs significantly from 0 in a two-tail t-test at the .01 level of statistical significance (t=3.6, N=24).

11. Angus Maddison, *Dynamic Forces in Capitalist Development: A Long-Run Comparative View* (Oxford: Oxford University Press, 1991).

12. Note that the countries belonging to each group do not change over time. Thus, although Algeria does not belong to today's Franc Zone, French exports to Algeria in 1992 are included in the FOU total. Similarly, although Japan did not belong to the OECD in 1952 (in fact, the OECD did not yet exist), French exports to Japan in 1952 are included in the OECD total. Members of the FOU are identified in William James Adams, *Restructuring the French Economy: Government and the Rise of Market Competition since World War II* (Washington: The Brookings Institution, 1989), p. 354.

13. For annual information covering the period 1952-1984, see Adams, *Restructur-*

ing the French Economy: table 22, p. 178. The data used in the 1992 calculation are taken from International Monetary Fund, *Direction of Trade Statistics Yearbook, 1986-1992* (Washington: International Monetary Fund, 1993).

14. It should be pointed out, however, that after 1974, France attempted to cultivate export markets in OPEC countries. This cultivation often took the form of government-to-government contracts specifying French performance of large construction contracts (inclusive of the necessary equipment) in return for supplies of petroleum. Such contracts create quasi-colonial patterns of trade. See Benjamin Camus et al., *La Crise du Système Productif* (Paris: Institut National de la Statistique et des Etudes Economiques, 1981), esp. pp. 186-187.

15. In its current form (i.e., in Revision 3), the SITC divides product space into ten sections; the ten sections are then subdivided into 67 divisions. The OECD reports trade information for each of the 63 divisions of sections 0 through 8 of the SITC Revision 3. Regarding section 9, it reports trade only for the section as a whole. As a result, I treat Section 9 as a single division, resulting in a data set of 64 industries. Italian exports of electric current (Division 35) are not reported, so the Italian sample consists of 63 industries.

16. Unfortunately, the OECD reports its 1970 data according to Revision 1 of the SITC. Most divisions are defined quasi-identically in the two classifications. The major differences concern Section 5 (chemicals) and Section 7 (machinery). The OECD provides data for each of the 55 divisions of sections 0 through 8, and for Section 9 as a whole, of the SITC Revision 1. Treating Section 9 as a single division, my data set for 1970 thus comprises 56 industries. German and Italian exports of electric current (Division 35) are not reported, so the German and Italian samples consist of 55 industries.

17. In 1990, the coefficient of variation in export ability, across industries, was 0.76 in France, 0.48 in Germany, 1.19 in Italy, and 0.59 in the United Kingdom. The corresponding coefficients of variation in 1970 were 0.71 in France, 0.65 in Germany, 1.26 in Italy, and 0.76 in the United Kingdom.

18. In ascending order of French share: miscellaneous edible products and preparations; coal, coke and briquettes; tobacco and tobacco manufactures; gas, natural and manufactured; pulp and waste paper; animal or vegetable fats and oils, processed; fertilizers; petroleum and petroleum products; metal-working machinery; cork and wood.

19. In ascending order of French share: tobacco and tobacco manufactures; pulp and paper; oil seeds, oil nuts and oil kernels; fish and fish preparations; mineral tar and crude chemicals from coal, petroleum, and natural gas; animal oils and fats; gas, natural and manufactured; coal, coke and briquettes; animal and vegetable oils and fats, processed; coffee, tea, cocoa, spices, and manufactures thereof; wood, lumber, and cork; paper, paperboard and manufactures thereof.

20. Nothing should be inferred from the absence of "metal-working machinery" from the 1970 list; such a division did not exist in Revision 1 of the SITC.

21. This view is developed carefully in Michael E. Porter, *The Competitive Advantage of Nations* (New York: The Free Press, 1990), esp. circa p. 6. Granted, account must be taken of national security and economic viability during military emergencies; but these can be and have been overplayed relative to standard of living.

22. Note that the correlation between one country's share of OECD exports and another country's share of OECD exports is necessarily negative if the two together account for a very large fraction of the OECD's exports.

23. The correlation coefficient differs from 0 at the .10 level of statistical significance in a two-tail t-test (r=.28, N=63).

24. The correlation coefficient differs from 0 in a two-tail t-test--at the .10 level of statistical significance in Italy (r=.25, N=63) and at the .05 level of statistical significance in the United Kingdom (r=.26, N=63).

25. The French correlation coefficient fails to differ from 0 at the .10 level of statistical significance in a two-tail t-test (r=-.01, N=63).

26. In the Australian context, for example, foreign control of Australian productive capacity serves to reduce the sensitivity of Australian prices to import competition. See Peter J. Williamson, "Import Penetration in Imperfectly Competitive Markets: A Study of Firm and Industry Behaviour Under Import Threat," Ph.D. Dissertation, Harvard University, 1984.

27. See, for example, *Re the European Sugar Cartel*, [1973] CMLR D65; and *Coöperatieve Vereniging 'Suiker Unie' and Others v. EC Commission*, Joined Cases 40-48/73, 50/73, 54-56/73, 111/73, and 113-114/73, [1976] 1 CMLR 295. Alternately, Auquier has found that price-cost margins in French manufacturing industries are influenced more by imports from EC countries than by imports from the rest of the world. See Antoine Auquier, "Industrial Organization in an Open Economy: French Industry and the Formation of the European Common Market," Ph.D. Dissertation, Harvard University, 1977, chap. 3.

28. The level of sectoral detail used by INSEE was the same as that used here: NAPT. The explanatory variable used by INSEE was designed to measure exposure to international competition in export as well as import markets.

29. Benjamin Camus et al., *La Crise du Système Productif* (Paris: Institut National de la Statistique et des Etudes Economiques, 1981), p. 293.

30. Camus et al., *La Crise du Système Productif*, p. 288.

31. Auquier, "Industrial Organization in an Open Economy: chap. 3.

32. See Adams, *Restructuring the French Economy:* p. 172.

33. See, however, Leo Sleuwaegen and Hideki Yamawaki, "Formation of the European Common Market and Changes in Market Structure and Performance," *European Economic Review*, 32 (September 1988), 1451-1475.

34. Frédéric Jenny and André-Paul Weber, *Concentration et Politique des Structures Industrielles* (Paris: La Documentation Française, 1974), examines the correlation across economic sectors (44 two-digit industries defined according to the NAE classification scheme) between the rate of return on assets (during the period 1967-1969) and a variety of structural variables, including the share of domestic production attributable to the four largest producers (in 1967). The partial effect of concentration differs positively from 0 at the .05 level of statistical significance.

35. In principle, "relatively" means "in relation to what otherwise would have been the case." In practice, "relatively" might mean either "in relation to sectoral trends" or "in relation to contemporaneous developments in sectors not experiencing increases in competition from imports."

36. For example, using a sample of 308 manufacturers of high-tech products in the United States during the period 1971-1987, Scherer and Huh have analyzed the changes in expenditure on R&D that follow increases in import competition in their domestic markets and reductions in net exports from their domestic industries. In the sample as a whole, in the short run, increases in competition from imports tended to provoke decreases

in expenditure on R&D. However, attempts by government to shield domestic producers artificially from foreign competition tended to reduce R&D expenditure still further. Moreover, in the long run, R&D may have tended to increase in response to international competition. In both runs, however, the R&D response to international competition varies greatly from one firm to the next. See F.M. Scherer and Keun Huh, "R&D Reactions to High-Technology Import Competition," *Review of Economics and Statistics*, 74 (May 1992), pp. 202-212.

37. See also the contribution of Suzanne Berger to this volume.

38. At the time this chapter was written, the Uruguay round of trade negotiations was still in process. As a result, it would have been foolhardy indeed to attempt a final verdict here on the gamesmanship, international and domestic, of 1992-1993. For example, it is inappropriate at the moment of this writing to conclude from its stated positions that France had turned protectionist. What France was holding out for -- whether, even, it was protection of French agriculture -- is still a matter of speculation.

39. On slow growth in the late nineteenth century, see Jean-Jacques Carré, Paul Dubois, and Edmond Malinvaud, *La Croissance Française: Un Essai d'Analyse Economique Causale de l'Après-Guerre* (Paris: Editions du Seuil, 1972), p. 23.

40. See Jean-Marcel Jeanneney, *Pour un Nouveau Protectionnisme* (Paris: Editions du Seuil, 1978), p. 82.

41. Although small in number, however, these eight account for a disproportionately large fraction of international trade -- at both the French and the OECD levels.

42. On the scope and method of French industrial policy, see William James Adams and Christian Stoffaës, eds., *French Industrial Policy* (Washington: The Brookings Institution, 1986); and Adams, *Restructuring the French Economy:* chap. 3.

43. On recent developments regarding damage suits, see "Subsidy Ruling Threatens Coal and Steel Jobs," *The European*, 5-11 November 1993, p. 1.

44. See Commission Decision of 29 March 1988 concerning aid provided by the French Government to the Renault group (88/454/EEC), Official Journal of the European Communities No L 220/30 (11 August 1988). See also "Renault and the EC: Victory for All," *The Economist*, 26 May 1990, p. 73.

45. Why did France, a country that relied heavily on financial regulation to effect its industrial policies, embrace enthusiastically the EC's program of financial deregulation? To an outsider, the most plausible explanation involves the relationship between financial deregulation on the one hand and economic and monetary union (EMU) on the other. After President Mitterrand's decision, early in 1983, to abandon reflation and embrace austerity, French policy makers realized that EMU constituted France's best hope for reducing the high unemployment associated with the deflationary bias of the European Monetary System. They also realized, moreover, that EMU would not be implemented before a pan-EC market was created for financial capital. In effect, then, in endorsing deregulation of EC financial markets, France was paying in advance for EMU. Given the collapse of optimism regarding EMU, following the difficulties associated with ratification of the Maastricht Treaty and the (consequent) perturbations of currency markets during September 1992 and August 1993, one is tempted to wonder whether French enthusiasm for deregulated financial markets will endure. If it does not, then considerable backsliding on this aspect of the 1992 program might occur, restoring some modicum of feasibility to national industrial policy.

46. *Europemballage and Continental Can v Commission of the European Communi-*

ties, Case 6/72, 1973 ECR 215.

47. Council Regulation (EEC) No 4064/89 of 21 December 1989 on the control of concentrations between undertakings. Official Journal of the European Communities No. L 395/1 (30 December 1989).

48. During 1992, for example, the commission approved 47 and rejected 0 mergers during the course of a preliminary (i.e., Phase I) examination. Four of the 47 mergers were approved only after the parties agreed to modify their original plans. The commission also approved 4 and rejected 0 mergers during the course of an in-depth (i.e., Phase II) examination. In three of these four approvals, however, the parties were obliged to modify their original plans. In a 52nd case resolved during 1992, the parties decided to drop their proposed merger once the commission chose to investigate it. See Commission of the European Communities, *Twenty-Second Report on Competition Policy 1992* (Luxembourg: Office for Official Publications of the European Communities, 1993), point 244, p. 137.

49. Commission Decision of 2 October 1991, Aérospatiale-Alenia/de Havilland (91/619/EEC), Official Journal of the European Communities No. L 334/42 (5 December 1991).

50. I have not discussed several other constraints the EC places on the interventionist behavior of member states. These constraints apply to internal taxes, indirect and direct, that discriminate against foreign goods and services; to exclusive privileges granted to state monopolies of a commercial character; and to the practice of rubber-stamping private cartel behavior so as to protect it from the reach of antitrust law. Examples of Court-of-Justice pronouncements on these issues, all relating to the behavior of the French government, are: *Seguela and Lachkar and Others v. Administration des Impôts*, Joined Cases 76, 86 to 89 and 149/87, 1988 ECR 2397 [internal indirect taxes]; *Grandes Distilleries Peureux v Directeur des Services Fiscaux*, Case 86/78, 1979 ECR 897, and *Grandes Distilleries Peureux v. Directeur des Services Fiscaux*, Case 119/78, 1979 ECR 975 [behavior of state monopolies]; *Bureau National Interprofessionnel du Cognac v. Clair*, Case 123/83, 1985 ECR 391, and *Bureau National Interprofessionnel du Cognac v. Aubert*, Case 136/86, 1987 ECR 4789 [governmental rubber-stamping of cartel decisions].

51. The situation is not unlike that in markets for foreign exchange. From the late 1970s to the early 1990s, the French government has expressed a strong desire to stabilize the value of the franc at a relatively high level against other currencies. Given, however, the amount of private money engaged in arbitrage, it has occasionally found itself unable to achieve the desired stabilization. Such was the case in August 1993. See the contributions of David Cameron and Jacques Le Cacheux to this volume.

7

From Barre to Balladur: Economic Policy in the Era of the EMS

David Ross Cameron

In speaking of France since the election of François Mitterrand in 1981, Stanley Hoffmann has said "the most salient fact throughout the period was the rise of unemployment, which none of the six governments -- five Socialist and one conservative -- had been able to stop between 1983 and 1993."[1] As Mitterrand's second *septennat* draws to a close, the rate of unemployment hovers between 12 and 13 percent, roughly 5 percentage points above the level when Mitterrand first took office and one of the highest in the European Union.[2] Even after the economy had begun to recover in early 1994 from the worst recession in the post-World War II era, the unemployment rate remained over 12 percent, and it was apparent that a very large portion of the unemployment was structural, rather than cyclical, and would endure in the future, rather than be alleviated by the recovery.[3]

While France became, over the course of the Mitterrand presidency, a country of high unemployment, it also became a country that, by the late 1980s and early 1990s, enjoyed a high degree of price stability, a large trade surplus, and a strong currency. Thus, the rate of inflation never exceeded 4 percent after 1986, and since the end of 1992, it has been at or below 2 percent, considerably below the rate in most of its neighbors -- including inflation-averse Germany.[4] In 1993, the country enjoyed a trade surplus of 88 billion francs, and in the first half of 1994, the cumulative trade surplus exceeded 30 billion francs and the government was predicting a surplus for the year of 100 billion francs.[5] This occurred despite the government's refusal to devalue the franc after early 1987 -- and de-

117

spite the fact that several of France's most important trading partners devalued or floated their currencies on several occasions after that date.[6]

What lends special irony to the performance of the French economy over the past dozen years, of course, is the atypical mix of government partisanship and macroeconomic policy. Figure 7.1 presents the rates of inflation and unemployment in France and its major trading partners in the European Union over the period since 1979.[7] If one knew nothing about the domestic politics and partisanship of the government and simply assumed, following Kirschen and many others,[8] that governments controlled by leftist parties typically pursue full employment, even at the cost of accelerating inflation, while conservative parties typically pursue price stability, even at the cost of high unemployment, one could be excused for imagining that conservative parties had governed in France throughout the period. In the period between 1981 and 1986, for example, France experienced a considerably sharper deceleration in the rate of change in prices than its neighbors. And in the more recent period, after 1986-1987, it appears to have experienced a systematically higher rate of unemployment and lower rate of inflation. This despite the fact that, as Hoffmann notes, five of the now seven governments since 1981 -- in office for ten of the fourteen years -- were controlled

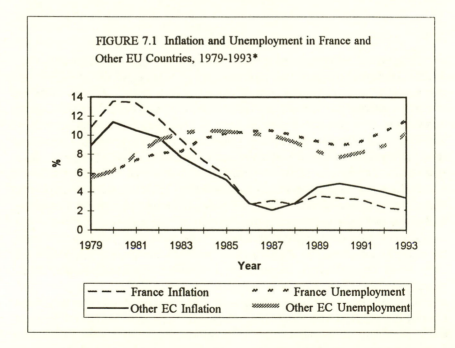

FIGURE 7.1 Inflation and Unemployment in France and Other EU Countries, 1979-1993*

*Other EU includes Germany, Belgium, Netherlands, Luxembourg, Italy, the United Kingdom, and Spain.

by the Socialist Party and its allies. And throughout the period, of course, the Elysée was occupied by the successful presidential candidate of that party.[9]

This chapter considers why -- despite predominant control of government by the Socialists -- France pursued a policy that sacrificed employment (and growth) for price stability (and external balance and a strong currency). It analyzes in turn the constraints within which French governments operated in the domain of macroeconomic policy, the choices they made in that domain in the face of those constraints, and the consequences of those choices. In regard to constraints, the chapter emphasizes those emanating from the international political and economic context within which France is located -- first and foremost, those deriving from its membership in the European Union and its relationships with the other members of the Union. In regard to policy choices, it demonstrates how the choices made in the realm of macroeconomic policy were themselves the inexorable by-product of choices made in the realm of international financial policy -- in particular, exchange rate policy in Europe. And finally, the chapter examines the impact of these choices on several key dimensions of economic performance, as well as their political consequences -- in particular, their impact on support for the parties that formed the governments that made the choices and for the European Union from which the constraints emanated.

European Constraints

If there is one lesson to be learned from the experience of the Mitterrand presidency, it is that French macroeconomic policy is constrained by the country's international economic environment. Above all, it is constrained by the country's membership in the European Community (now Union) and the economic and financial relations with the other member states that derive from membership. This is not to say that the international context dictates a particular domestic policy and that the government can exercise no choice with regard to domestic economic policy; indeed, the nature and extent of the constraint depend largely on the policy choices that are made with respect to that context. Nevertheless, to the extent that the French economy is relatively "open" and embedded in a larger international economy, domestic economic policy inevitably is constrained, to some degree at least, by that larger context.

Domestic macroeconomic policy and international economic policy are often regarded as two separate and distinct domains of policy. As plausible as the separation may be for economies that are relatively "closed," in terms of their dependence (or lack thereof) on external producers and consumers, it is less meaningful for economies that are relatively open and dependent on such producers and consumers for a significant portion of the goods and services that are consumed and produced in the country. In such economies, more so than in closed ones, policy in one domain inevitably has a consequence for policy in the other.

Thus, in a relatively open economy, international policy -- for example, the exchange rate of the nation's currency vis-à-vis those of its major trading partners -- will critically influence the price, and hence external demand and domestic production, of goods for export markets as well as the price, and hence *domestic* demand and consumption, of imported goods. In so doing, it thus affects domestic income, employment, and profits. Similarly, domestic macroeconomic policy -- for example, policy involving interest rates -- affects domestic demand, production, employment, and, in turn, wages and prices, which, in turn, affect the competitiveness of exports, the consumption of imports, and the balance of trade.

Because domestic and international economic policy are, to some degree at least, interdependent and intertwined in open economies, policy in one domain can, and often does, constrain policy in the other. That is, choosing a particular policy and opting for a particular outcome in either domain may necessarily limit the policy choices available in the other domain, insofar as the choice in one affects performance in the other. To cite but one example that will reappear later, to maintain a country's currency within a target range, in terms of its exchange rate with the currencies of its trading partners, may, depending upon the relative performance of the economies, require particular fiscal and monetary policies that, in turn, have an impact on domestic production, income, and employment. Conversely, to achieve a particular targeted rate of growth and employment may require, insofar as they depend on the performance of the traded goods sector, a particular exchange rate of the nation's currency vis-à-vis those of its trading partners. In short, choosing a target in one domain -- either domain -- may constrain policy in the other.

Compared with the U.S. and Japanese economies, the French economy -- like those of most members of the European Union (above all, the smaller members of the Union) -- is relatively open. Like the economies of the other members, it has become markedly *more* open over the past several decades. And as that has happened, it has become more dependent, especially, on trade with the other member states of the Union. Table 7.1 presents several measures of the magnitude and relative importance of exports and imports in the French economy. The data indicate that, by the early 1990s, exports and imports each constituted between one-fifth and one-quarter of total Gross Domestic Product, roughly twice as much as they had in the early 1960s. The data also indicate an increasing concentration of French trade within the Community; thus, whereas trade with other member states constituted about one-third of all French trade in the early 1960s and about one-half of all trade in the mid-to-late 1970s, by 1992 more than 60 percent of all French exports were sold in other member states of the Community and about the same proportion of all French imports came from those member states.

Taking the two measures of trade dependence together -- that is, the magnitude of trade relative to G.D.P. and the extent of trade concentration within the EC -- provides a measure of the extent to which France is economically depen-

TABLE 7.1 Trade Dependence of the French Economy, 1962-1992

	Trade Dependence (Exports/Imports as % of G.D.P.)		Trade Concentration Within EC (Exports to/Imports from EC as % of all Exports/Imports)		Economic Dependence on Intra-EC Trade (Exports to/Imports from EC as % of G.D.P.)	
	Exports	*Imports*	*Exports*	*Imports*	*Exports*	*Imports*
1962	12.3	11.0	36.8	33.6	4.5	3.7
1968	12.8	12.6	43.0	47.4	5.5	6.0
1974	20.1	21.6	53.6	47.8	10.8	10.3
1980	21.5	22.7	53.3	49.6	11.5	11.3
1986	21.2	20.2	55.3	59.4	11.7	12.0
1992	23.0	21.8	61.7	59.5	14.2	13.0

Source: International Monetary Fund, *International Financial Statistics Yearbook, 1993* (Washington, D.C.: I.M.F., 1993), and earlier volumes; International Monetary Fund, *Direction of Trade Statistics, 1992* (Washington, D.C.: I.M.F., 1993), and earlier volumes.

dent on intra-EC trade. The data in Table 7.1 suggest that by the early 1990s exports to, and imports from, other member states of the European Community amounted to roughly 13 to 14 percent of G.D.P. Compared with the figures for 1962, early in the life of the European Economic Community and at a time when it consisted only of the six original members, the figures for 1992 suggest that France's economic dependence on the Community has increased more than *three-fold* over the past three decades.

As the French economy has become increasingly dependent on trade -- especially on trade within the European Community -- domestic macroeconomic policy has become increasingly intertwined with, and dependent upon, international economic policy, and vice versa. Increasingly, policy in *either* domain affected the performance of the economy, and hence policy, in the other, and as that occurred, it became increasingly likely that policy in one domain would *constrain* policy in the other. For example, as the economy became increasingly dependent on trade in general, and trade within the EC in particular, it became increasingly sensitive to comparative prices within the EC -- the prices of its domestically produced goods for export relative to those of goods produced in the countries to which it was exporting, as well as the prices of its domestically produced, import-competing goods vis-à-vis those of goods imported from abroad. Those relative prices could be affected, of course, either by domestic policy -- for example, by the impact of fiscal and monetary policy on domestic demand, unemployment, wages, and prices -- or by international policy -- for example, by changes in the exchange rate between the franc and the currencies of France's trading partners.

If the sensitivity of the French economy to relative prices of exports and imports increased as the traded goods sector increased in size, that sensitivity was greatly accentuated by the creation in 1979 of the European Monetary System and its evolution over time into an increasingly stable exchange rate regime. Proposed as a remedy for the several defects of the "snake" that had existed since 1972, the EMS was designed to create a "zone of monetary stability" in Europe.[10] The founders of the EMS -- Helmut Schmidt, Valéry Giscard d'Estaing, Roy Jenkins, and a few others -- did not intend to create a stable exchange-rate regime in which currencies were seldom realigned. But as it evolved, the EMS in fact became a stable exchange-rate regime -- so much so, in fact, that by the late 1980s it was as stable, in terms of the infrequency of realignments, as the old Bretton Woods regime had been in its heyday in the early 1960s.

Table 7.2 provides a summary of the realignments that occurred in the EMS from its advent in 1979 to September 1992.[11] The data indicate that the frequency and magnitude of realignments decreased sharply over time, to such an extent that by the late 1980s the EMS appeared to have evolved into a quasi-fixed exchange-rate regime. Thus, while seven realignments occurred in the first four years of the EMS, through March 1983, of which five involved two or more currencies and four involved the franc and/or the mark, in its next four years, from April 1983 through April 1987, there were only four realignments, only three that involved two or more currencies, and only two involved the franc and/or the mark. And in the five and one-half years from April 1987 until September 1992, there was only *one* realignment, and it involved only one currency.[12]

The development of the EMS into a highly and increasingly stable exchange-rate regime throughout the 1980s and early 1990s had a profound effect on the open and trade-dependent economies of the EC. In particular, the greater sta-

TABLE 7.2 Summary of Realignments in the European Monetary System
March 1979-August 1992

	Number of Realignments	Number of Realignments Involving Two or More Currencies	Number of Franc-Mark Realignments	Cumulative Change in Value of Franc vis-à-vis Mark
March 1979-March 1983	7	5	4	28%
April 1983-April 1987	4	3	2	9%
May 1987-August 1992	1	0	0	0%

bility over time in exchange rates within the EMS greatly increased the extent to which the combined effects of trade dependence and trade concentration constrained macroeconomic policy in the member states of the EC. To the extent that currencies remained in the EMS and within their narrow bands at their existing valuations, the relative prices of their exports and the imports from others became less susceptible to change through realignment as the EMS became increasingly stable. As that happened, the burden of adjustment of relative prices was shifted to domestic policy. Thus, for example, EMS stability caused the currencies of the members with relatively high rates of inflation to appreciate over time and become overvalued. In a world of flexible exchange rates, that overvaluation -- typically associated not only with a high rate of inflation but a trade deficit, as exports became less competitive and imports became less costly -- could be corrected by devaluation or depreciation of the currency. But as exchange rates became increasingly stable in the EMS, they were less responsive to overvaluations (and undervaluations as well). As a result, to a greater extent than would have been the case had the EMS remained as prone to realignment as it was in its early years, countries with relatively high rates of inflation and recurring trade deficits with their EC partners were forced to adjust relative prices downward by contracting domestic demand, through some combination of tight fiscal policy and high interest rates.

To say that the increasing stability of exchange rates in the EMS increasingly placed the burden for adjustment of relative prices on domestic macroeconomic policy, and that EMS members with weak and overvalued currencies increasingly found themselves forced to adjust relative prices through contractionary fiscal and monetary policy, is not to suggest that such countries had no choice in policy in the face of such constraint. But it *does* suggest that the choice in policy, for EMS members with open economies, revolved around the issue of EMS membership and the value of the currency within it. To remain within an EMS that was becoming increasingly stable meant adjusting relative prices through macroeconomic policy -- in the case of countries with weak and overvalued currencies, through *contractionary* macroeconomic policy. To avoid that constraint, and that contractionary policy, required either that a country devalue frequently if it remained in the EMS -- notwithstanding the emerging norm favoring stable exchange rates -- or that it refuse to join the EMS (as Britain did in 1979) or decide to leave (as Britain and Italy did in 1992). In other words, the essential choices in the domain of domestic macroeconomic policy for the open, trade-dependent countries of the European Community in the 1980s depended, ultimately, upon the choices made in the domain of *international* monetary policy -- in particular, the choices made in regard to their currencies' participation and valuation in the EMS.

Policy Choices

The Giscard-Barre Legacy

Most discussions of contemporary French economic policy begin with the coming to power of the Socialists and François Mitterrand in 1981. For several reasons, however, it is useful to begin a summary of the important choices in economic policy several years earlier, during the presidency of Giscard d'Estaing.[13] For one thing, the EMS, which introduced a new external constraint on macroeconomic policy, came into being during the Giscard presidency.[14] For another, it was the macroeconomic policy pursued during the latter part of that presidency, while Raymond Barre was prime minister (from mid-1976 to mid-1981), that set the stage for the policies pursued by Mitterrand and the Socialist-dominated government after they came to power.

When Mitterrand and the Socialists came to power, they inherited an economy mired in a year-long recession. Table 7.3 presents a variety of economic indicators that depict the Giscard-Barre legacy. The data show that the rate of economic growth dropped sharply from between 3 and 4 percent in 1977-1979 to less than 1 percent in 1980-1981. In fact, the economy had slipped into recession in the second half of 1980 and the rate of growth dropped to a negative 0.5 percent, and it remained at that rate during the first half of 1981. The rate of unemployment during the Barre administration increased from less than 5 percent in 1977 to more than 6 percent in 1980 and more than 7 percent -- which translated into 1.7 million unemployed -- by mid-1981. Despite the recession, drop in the rate of growth, and rise in unemployment, however, the rate of inflation had increased over Barre's tenure from about 9 percent in 1977 and 1978 to more than 10 percent in 1979 and more than 13 percent in 1980 and 1981. Some of that increase undoubtedly reflected the impact on domestic prices of the sharp upward surge in oil prices after the Iranian revolution and the start of the Iran-Iraq war. But it also reflected, in part, the high and rising rate of increase in nominal wages; despite Barre's commitment to price stability, the rate of increase in nominal wages -- which had risen by nearly 13 percent in 1977, 1978, and 1979 -- accelerated to nearly 15 percent in 1980 and remained at that level despite the recession of 1980-1981.

In addition to passing on to Mitterrand and the Socialists an economy that was simultaneously mired in recession, low growth, and rising unemployment, on one hand, and high and accelerating inflation, on the other, Giscard and Barre left the new government with a large and rising trade deficit and a rising level of international debt. As Table 7.3 indicates, there was a surplus in the Balance of Trade, a balance in the Current Accounts, and little or no international borrowing in 1978 and 1979.[15] But in 1980 and 1981, the Balance of Trade moved sharply into deficit, the Current Accounts registered a large deficit, and the country was

TABLE 7.3 The Giscard-Barre Legacy: The French Economy, 1977-1982

	Economic Indicators					
	1977	*1978*	*1979*	*1980*	*1981*	*1982*
Economic Growth (% change, G.D.P.)	3.1	3.8	3.3	1.1	0.5	1.8
Unemployment (% workforce)	4.9	5.2	5.9	6.3	7.4	8.1
Inflation (% change, prices)	9.4	9.1	10.8	13.6	13.4	11.8
Wages (% change, hourly wages, manufacturing)	12.9	12.9	12.9	14.9	14.3	15.8
	International Transactions (Billions of Francs)					
	1977	*1978*	*1979*	*1980*	*1981*	*1982*
Exports of Goods and Services	401.9	455.2	535.6	616.1	735.4	822.3
Imports of Goods and Services	407.2	434.2	532.2	664.9	784.6	909.6
Balance of Trade	-5.3	21.0	3.4	-48.8	-49.2	-87.3
Balance on Current Accounts	-13.1	12.5	0.0	-38.3	-45.1	-108.4
Net International Borrowing	14.2	(11.4)	1.5	39.8	46.9	110.2

Source: Organization for Economic Co-operation and Development, *Economic Outlook, 40* (Paris: OECD, December 1986); and earlier volumes. OECD, *National Accounts, vol. 2: 1972-1984* (Paris: OECD, 1986); and OECD, *National Accounts, vol. 1: 1960-1985* (Paris: OECD, 1987.

forced to borrow significant amounts from international creditors. The existence of that large and increasing trade deficit, along with the high and increasing rate of inflation, in the midst of a recession was a sure sign that the franc was overvalued.

It is more than coincidence that the adverse turn in virtually every economic indicator included in Table 7.3 occurs after 1979, for in that year a profound shift occurred in French, and European, exchange-rate policy. Prior to March 1979, the franc floated, having left the "snake" (for the second time) in early 1976.[16] But after the creation of the EMS in March 1979, the franc fluctuated again within a narrow band of +/- 2.25 percent vis-à-vis the other EMS currencies. However, while the franc was closely tied in the EMS to such strong currencies as the mark and the Dutch guilder, France continued to experience a rate of inflation considerably above those more inflation-averse countries. Thus, in 1979, for example, the difference between the rate of inflation in France and Germany, its largest trading partner, was almost 7 percentage points, and in 1980, the difference increased to about 8 percentage points. Despite that cumulative difference of 15 percentage points, however, the franc retained its original exchange rate vis-à-vis the mark, as the Barre government -- committed to a strong franc as weapon against inflation -- refused to devalue. As a result, the franc became increasingly overvalued, and as that happened, the competitiveness of French exports in the markets of other EMS members deteriorated while the competitiveness of goods produced in the other EMS members and sold in France improved.[17] Both developments contributed to the adverse turn in the trade account after 1979.

Table 7.4 presents data on the rate of inflation in France and Germany between 1979 and 1987, as well as data on the timing and magnitude of changes in the central rates of the franc and the mark since the inception of the EMS. The data suggests that the franc may have been overvalued by as much as 15 percent by the time the Socialists came to power in mid-1981. In order for France to have maintained the status quo ante in terms of its competitive position vis-à-vis Germany as of March 1979, it would have had to obtain each year since then a realignment in the exchange rate between the two currencies (either through a devaluation of the franc, a revaluation of the mark, or both) equal to the amount by which its inflation rate exceeded that of Germany. This simply reflects the fact that the relative value of two currencies whose rates are fixed will vary according to the magnitude of the difference in the rates of inflation in the two countries. As a corollary, it reflects the fact that the currency of the country with the higher rate of inflation will become overvalued, relative to that of the country with the lower rate, by an amount equivalent to the cumulative difference in inflation rates less whatever changes occur to increase the value of the currency of the country with the lower inflation rate relative to the value of the currency of the country with the higher rate. However, Table 7.4 indicates that the difference in the French and German inflation rates in 1979 (6.7 percent) was only partially offset by the 2 percent revaluation of the mark, so that the franc was overvalued by roughly 4.7 percent by the end of that year. To that figure, we add the difference in inflation rates of 8.2 percent in 1980 (when no realignment occurred), bringing the overvaluation by the end of 1980 to about 12.9 percent. Adding to that figure a little less than one-half of the 1981 inflation difference of 7.1 suggests a total overvaluation of the franc vis-à-vis the mark of about 16 percent as of mid-1981.

TABLE 7.4   France and Germany, 1979-1987:   Inflation Differential and the Value of the Franc

	Annual Percent Change in Consumer Prices								
	1979	1980	1981	1982	1983	1984	1985	1986	1987
France	10.8	13.6	13.4	11.8	9.6	7.4	5.8	2.5	3.3
Germany	4.1	5.4	6.3	5.3	3.3	2.4	2.2	-0.1	0.2
Difference	6.7	8.2	7.1	6.5	6.3	5.0	3.6	2.6	3.1
Cumulative	6.7	14.9	22.0	28.5	34.8	39.8	43.4	46.0	49.1

Devaluations of the Franc vis-à-vis the Mark

	1979	1980	1981	1982	1983	1984	1985	1986	1987
September 1979	DM 2.0								
October 1981			DM 5.5 Fr -3.0						
June 1982				DM 4.25 Fr -5.75					
March 1983					DM 5.5 Fr -2.5				
April 1986								DM 3.0 Fr -3.0	
January 1987									DM 3.0
Estimated Overvaluation of Franc vs. Mark, End of Year	4.7	12.9	11.5	8.0	6.3	11.3	14.9	11.5	11.6

In addition to contributing to a deterioration of the trade account, the increasing overvaluation of the franc and the Barre government's refusal to contemplate a devaluation introduced a further contractionary impulse into the French economy. As the franc became increasingly overvalued, and as foreign exchange markets perceived that a devaluation was warranted by the continuing inflation differential, the franc weakened and threatened to fall through its floor in its EMS band vis-à-vis the mark. In order to support it, and having opted not to devalue, the Barre government was forced to raise interest rates sharply and reduce the flow of credit into the economy. In addition, it cut the size of the budget deficit sharply in 1979 and again in 1980, giving fiscal policy an overall contractionary impact in those two years. The Barre government presumably would have pursued a tight monetary and fiscal policy in any event, of course, given the high and accelerating rate of inflation, and it had, in fact, been pursuing a tight money policy to support the franc even before the creation of the EMS. But the additional burden of defending a currency that was becoming increasingly overvalued, as devaluation was deferred, resulted in an even tighter macroeconomic policy -- *so* tight, in fact, that before long it pushed the economy into a recession.

Mitterrand, the EMS, and the U-Turn

When François Mitterrand and the Socialist-dominated government took office in 1981, they brought with them a host of programmatic commitments.[18] However, they also inherited from Giscard and Barre responsibility for an economy that had been in recession for a year and in which the number of unemployed had increased dramatically, and in which, despite the recession, the rate of inflation -- already in double-digits -- was still accelerating, the Balance of Trade -- already deeply in deficit -- still deteriorating, the level of international debt -- already unusually high -- still increasing, and the currency -- already overvalued -- still appreciating in real terms.

Enjoying a secure parliamentary majority, the new government had little difficulty in enacting into law a variety of measures in its first years in office that fulfilled many of its programmatic commitments -- for example, increases in the allocations for family allowances, housing, and persons with disabilities, increases in the minimum old age pension and the minimum wage, funds for new jobs in the public sector, a wealth tax, new labor laws, and nationalization of a number of firms, banks, and investment houses.[19] But the economic problems inherited from Giscard and Barre proved far more intractable for the new government. And how they were addressed -- and with what effect -- proved to be far more consequential than the early programmatic victories, both for the government and the Mitterrand presidency itself.

When Mitterrand and the new Socialist government took power, the franc, overvalued by perhaps as much as 15 percent, was under assault in the currency markets. To some extent, of course, that reflected anxiety about the political complexion of the new government -- especially given its likely inclusion of Communists and its commitment to nationalization. However, the speculative pressure also reflected a widespread awareness in the markets that the franc was indeed overvalued and that a devaluation was not only in order but, in fact, long overdue. Many individuals advised Mitterrand to either devalue the franc or withdraw it from the EMS in the first days of his presidency, and many -- including Barre himself as well as the head of the *Trésor* and the Governor of the *Banque de France* -- expected that the new president would have no choice but to emulate his Gaullist predecessors and devalue the currency.[20] But Mitterrand rejected the advice and decided to keep the franc in the EMS at its existing exchange rate.

Mitterrand's decision to maintain the existing exchange rate -- a decision he later acknowledged was a mistake[21] -- may have reflected the pride of the moment or a failure to appreciate the internal logic of the EMS and the consequence of keeping an overvalued currency in it. It may have reflected a concern with the potential political damage that might result from a decision that the government's critics could take as an early indicator of its managerial ineptitude. Or it may simply have reflected the Socialists' visceral antipathy toward financial speculators and their refusal to provide those who had speculated against the franc with a windfall profit.

Whatever the reasons, the decision to maintain the existing exchange rate only postponed the inevitable. And in so doing, it guaranteed that the problem of overvaluation would become increasingly acute, for the longer the franc stayed in the EMS at its existing rate while France had a higher rate of inflation than its trading partners, the more overvalued it would become. That, in turn, would cause the trade deficit to increase even more and subject the franc to increasing speculative pressure (and also, of course, further increase the amount of international borrowing necessary to cover the deficit). Eventually, the exchange rate would have to be adjusted -- and the longer the delay, the larger the magnitude of the adjustment required to eliminate the overvaluation.

After deciding not to deal with the exchange rate, Mitterrand and the Socialist-dominated government turned their attention to the state of the economy -- in particular, the recession and the high and increasing number of unemployed. It was quite reasonable to expect that the government -- especially this one, formed as it was by parties that drew disproportionate support from workers and those most exposed to unemployment -- would attempt to stimulate the economy through fiscal and monetary policy, and the government headed by Pierre Mauroy enacted a number of expansionary measures soon after taking office. Social spending was increased, the social security contributions of employers were reduced, and funds were committed for new jobs in the public sector. In its first supplemental budget in August 1981, the government increased expenditures by 28 billion francs and raised the budget deficit to 57 billion francs, almost double the Barre government's initial projected deficit for the year.[22] Several months later, in its year-end amended budget, the government added another 7 billion francs to spending and the deficit, bringing the latter to a total of 64 billion francs for the year, equivalent to 1.9 percent of G.D.P., which, given the balanced budget in 1980, represented a net fiscal *stimulus* (as measured by the *change* in the magnitude of the deficit) of the same amount. In the domain of monetary policy as well, the Mauroy government pursued a moderately expansionary policy, raising the ceiling imposed by the Ministry of Finance on the expansion of bank credit, lowering the bank base lending rate and the rate on Treasury bills, and raising the targeted growth of the money supply -- all in an effort to increase the flow of credit in the economy.

By the fall of 1981, the franc was again coming under speculative attack in the markets. The Balance of Trade had continued to deteriorate through the summer, as the Barre government's pre-election *relance*,[23] coupled with the new government's moderately reflationary fiscal and monetary policy and the increasing cumulative inflation differential with its trading partners, had increased the French demand for imported goods and reduced the competitiveness of French exports. The franc, by then overvalued by almost 20 percent, came under renewed attack in the currency markets as those who held francs moved into other currencies at an accelerating rate.[24] Foreign exchange reserves plummeted as the *Banque de France* bought up francs in an effort to keep the currency above its EMS floor. By early October, the inevitable moment had arrived, and Mitterrand accepted the recommendation of Jacques Delors, the finance minister, that France negotiate a realignment of exchange rates in the EMS.

The EMS negotiations resulted in a devaluation of the franc of 3 percent and a revaluation of the German mark of 5.5 percent.[25] As the data in Table 7.4 suggest, the October realignment repaired a significant portion -- perhaps almost one-half -- of the loss in competitiveness of French goods vis-à-vis German goods that had occurred since the advent of the EMS. But it did not entirely eliminate the cumulative overvaluation that had occurred since 1979. Since an EMS realignment, by necessity, required the acquiescence of the EMS members, its magnitude depended ultimately on how much of a revaluation the strong-currency countries such as Germany and the Netherlands were willing to accept in order to help France correct its trade and payments problem. And that, in turn, depended on how much the strong-currency countries were willing to spend, in the form of lost exports and increased domestic competition from imports, in order to help the French. As a result, while significant, the October realignment was not large enough to fully neutralize the accumulated inflation differential between the two countries and the franc remained overvalued -- even after the realignment -- by perhaps as much as 11 percent.

Because the October realignment did not eliminate entirely the franc's overvaluation, if the government wished to avoid a renewed attack on the franc in the currency markets, it had no choice -- assuming continued membership in the EMS and no further devaluation -- but to deploy domestic macroeconomic policy, both to defend the currency (e.g., through higher interest rates) and to adjust relative prices (e.g., through a contraction of domestic demand and costs). The shift to a less expansionary macroeconomic policy -- the first step in what would become the U-Turn of the Mitterrand presidency -- began immediately after the October 1981 realignment. To the great consternation of his colleagues in the government, including the prime minister, Delors called for a "pause in the announcement of reforms" and proposed a number of measures that would reduce the fiscal and monetary stimulus then being injected into the economy. He proposed that expenditures be cut by 10 billion francs and that another 15 billion in expenditures be frozen. And in order to reduce the rate of inflation, he proposed a variety of wage and price controls as well as restrictions on the flow of credit.

Delors's proposals were challenged by virtually all of his colleagues in the cabinet -- most notably, Laurent Fabius, the minister of the budget, who claimed that fiscal policy was *his* responsibility -- and it was only Delors's threats to resign, and the perceived need to placate him, that led the president and Prime Minister Pierre Mauroy to accept them. But Fabius had his revenge in the budget for 1982 that he submitted a few weeks later. By then, the economy was in recovery and was growing at a rate of more than 3 percent, and the government projected a comparable growth rate for 1982. Despite that, the 1982 budget called for dramatic increases in spending and the deficit. Expenditures would increase by 28 percent and the deficit -- after a 19 percent increase in revenues -- would increase by more than 30 billion francs, to *95 billion*, equivalent to 2.6 percent of G.D.P. Given the 1981 deficit of 1.9 percent of G.D.P., that would introduce a fiscal stimulus -- during a time of recovery and relatively high growth -- equivalent to 0.7 percent of G.D.P.

The fiscal stimulus contained in the 1982 budget created demand that continued to manifest itself in a surge of imports, and the balance of trade continued to deteriorate through the winter of 1981-1982 and the spring of 1982. Both the surge of imports and growth of the deficit were accentuated by the continuation -- despite the price and wage controls -- of double-digit inflation that added to the overvaluation of the franc. The lower rate of inflation in Germany contributed to a further increase in the cumulative inflation differential between the two countries, which, in turn, caused the franc to become increasingly overvalued -- to such an extent, in fact, that by mid-1982 the favorable effect of the 1981 realignment had been almost entirely eliminated. Not surprisingly, the franc again came under attack in the currency markets, foreign exchange reserves flowed out in defense of the currency, and, despite massive interventions by the *Banque* in the markets, the franc fell to its floor in the EMS. Once again, devaluation was imminent.

As Delors and Mauroy prepared for a second realignment of exchange rates in the spring of 1982, it was apparent that, as in 1981, devaluation would bring with it, in its wake, a turn to a less expansionary, more contractionary fiscal and monetary policy. Thus, the detailed plan they prepared for Mitterrand included price and wage controls, cuts in expenditures and the budget deficit, higher interest rates, and a contraction of the money supply. After some delay (to let his Versailles G-7 summit take place without the embarrassment of another devaluation), Mitterrand agreed to the plan and authorized Delors to initiate negotiations in the EMS and in mid-June, immediately after the summit, the EMS members agreed to a 5.75 percent devaluation of the franc and a 4.25 percent revaluation of the mark and guilder.[26] Although larger than the first one, the June 1982 realignment was not large enough to entirely eliminate the cumulative inflation difference (less the previous realignments) since 1979. As a result, the franc remained overvalued and pressure remained on domestic macroeconomic policy to defend the currency and reduce inflation and imports by contracting demand.

In return for the German agreement to revalue the mark a second time in less than a year, Delors had committed France to remaining in the EMS and to instituting the policy of austerity that he and his aides had drafted with Mauroy and his aides. That the two domains of policy were linked, and that a negotiated realignment of EMS exchange rates carried with it the obligation to shift to a more contractionary macroeconomic policy, was evident in the statement issued by the Monetary Committee after the negotiation: it noted that it had "taken into consideration the important program that the French government planned to put into effect. The ministers noted their appreciation of this program."[27] Interestingly -- and symbolic of the constraint on domestic policy posed by the EMS -- the French cabinet had not yet discussed and approved the program! That occurred the next day, at a special meeting, which formally adopted the various provisions in the Delors-Mauroy program that came to be known as *rigueur*.

The commitment to *rigueur* in June 1982 represented, many observers believe, the *tournant décisif*, or *tournant majeur*, or *grand tournant* of the Mitterrand presidency.[28] During the remainder of that year, fiscal policy lost much of its expansionary thrust. Thus, while the supplementary budget introduced later in June increased spending by 12 billion francs, revenues were increased by a similar amount and the overall deficit and magnitude of fiscal stimulus remained unchanged. A second amended budget in December raised expenditures, and the deficit, by four billion francs. But that was the only unfunded spending increment in the year -- in marked contrast to the 35 billion of unfunded spending in the previous year. In its draft budget for 1983, expenditures were increased by 12 percent (compared with 28 percent in the previous budget), an amount that barely exceeded the increase in nominal G.D.P. At the same time, however, revenues were increased by 9 percent, so while the deficit was increased by some 19 billion francs, from 99 billion to 118 billion, the fiscal stimulus was limited to only 0.4 percent of G.D.P. And two months after passage of the Finance Act, an amount comparable to the projected increase in the deficit was frozen and placed in reserve.

Despite having been devalued twice in less than nine months, the franc remained overvalued vis-à-vis the stronger currencies of the EMS. The inflation difference between France and Germany did not diminish, as reductions in the German rate of inflation matched the decrease in the French rate, which, by then, was about 10 percent. As a result, the trade deficit continued to deteriorate in the second half of 1982 and approached 90 billion francs for the year. The franc remained under attack in currency markets and hovered near its floor in the EMS, and foreign exchange reserves flowed out of the country as the *Banque* sought to maintain the franc within its EMS band. Although Mitterrand deferred a decision about the exchange rate until after the municipal elections scheduled for

March 1983, devaluation -- and a further tightening of macroeconomic policy --
was once again on the agenda.

In March 1983, after a protracted and stormy debate within the government
-- during which, at one point, Mitterrand decided to take the franc out of the
EMS, only to reverse himself a few days later[29] -- France negotiated a third devaluation of the franc within the EMS. The 1983 realignment resulted in a devaluation of the franc by 2.5 percent and a revaluation of the mark by 5.5 percent.[30] Taken on top of the 8.5 percent realignment vis-à-vis the mark in 1981
and the 10 percent realignment in 1982, the 8 percent realignment in 1983 effected a substantial reduction in the overvaluation of the franc. Indeed, as Table
7.4 suggests, the overvaluation was reduced to such an extent that, by the end of
the year, it was perhaps no more than 6 percent -- less than half of what it was
when Mitterrand and the Socialist government took office in 1981.

As was the case in 1982, the 1983 devaluation carried with it the need to use
domestic macroeconomic policy -- both to defend a currency that still remained
overvalued and that would become increasingly so as long as Germany kept pace
with the reductions in French inflation, and to continue the effort to reduce relative prices. As in 1982, German agreement to revalue the mark carried a price;
Delors had to agree that the government would implement an increasingly
contractionary fiscal and monetary policy. Thus, at the meeting that negotiated
the realignment, Germany demanded, and Delors committed the government to,
"supplementary guarantees" of fiscal restraint -- most notably, an increase in the
social insurance contribution paid by wage earners, a compulsory loan on taxpay-
ers, and a reduction in expenditures by 20 billion francs -- in exchange for revaluation of the mark.[31] At its next meeting, the French cabinet accepted the German
conditions (albeit with some resistance and some minor modifications),[32] and in
so doing moved from *rigueur* to full-fledged austerity.

The fiscal measures adopted after the 1983 realignment introduced a marked
contractionary effect in the economy. Some 27 billion francs of additional rev-
enue were generated through the income surtax and three-year compulsory loan
of 10 percent of the tax of those with high incomes. And some 24 billion francs
of expenditures were cut -- some from the already-frozen reserves, some from the
funds allocated to public enterprises, and the rest through a variety of other cuts.
The 1984 budget accentuated this contractionary impulse by raising expenditures
only 6 percent -- considerably less than the projected increase in nominal G.D.P.
-- while raising revenues 6.3 percent. As a result, although the deficit would
increase by 4 billion francs in 1984 (compared to 38 billion in 1982 and 19 billion in 1983), to a total of 125 billion francs, the ratio of the deficit to the G.D.P.
would decrease slightly, to just under 3 percent, causing fiscal policy to have, for
the first time since 1980, a net *contractionary* effect.

The New-Found Aversion to Devaluation

The preceding discussion has described the evolution of economic policy in the early years of the Mitterrand presidency, from one that was stimulative and reflationary to one that was increasingly contractionary and that culminated in *rigueur* and then outright austerity. The discussion suggests that the shift in domestic policy was driven by the government's exchange rate policy; by the logic of the EMS, the extent to which the government was required to pursue a contractionary course in its domestic economic policy was a function of the choices made with regard to the exchange rate -- in particular, in view of the overvaluation of the franc, the *timing* and *magnitude* of devaluation. The *earlier* the devaluation (or devaluations), and the *larger* they were, the *smaller* the macroeconomic contraction needed to defend the franc and adjust relative prices. Conversely, the *later* the devaluations, and the *smaller* they were, the *larger* the necessary macroeconomic contraction. To the extent that the Socialist-dominated government delayed any correction in the overvaluation of the franc that it inherited from Giscard and Barre, and then negotiated a series of *modest* devaluations -- modest precisely because they *were* negotiated -- it was forced to implement a macroeconomic policy that was more contractionary than might otherwise have been necessary, with obvious consequences both for the rate of economic growth and the level of unemployment.

Constituting as they do a major turning point -- most would say *the* major turning point -- in the Mitterrand presidency, the exchange rate and macroeconomic decisions of the 1981-1983 period have been subjected to considerable analysis and a good deal of second-guessing. One can certainly question whether the Socialist government moved quickly enough to redress the overvaluation of the franc, whether it responded with sufficiently large devaluations in those early years, and whether it might have effected larger devaluations by withdrawing the franc, at least temporarily, from the EMS. Nevertheless, however questionable the timing and magnitude of those early devaluations, the deterioration in the rate of growth and unemployment that characterized the later years of the Mitterrand presidency cannot be attributed entirely to them. Indeed, the data in Table 7.4 suggest they should probably be attributed, instead, to exchange rate policy *after* 1983; after the 1983 realignment, the several Socialist-controlled governments, beginning with the last Mauroy government and the one headed by Laurent Fabius in 1984-1986,[33] did not once devalue the franc -- despite the fact that the rate of inflation in France exceeded that of Germany in every year until 1991.

As noted above, the data in Table 7.4 indicate that the three realignments of the franc vis-à-vis the mark in 1981-1983, taken together, reduced the overvaluation of the franc appreciably -- by about 60 percent -- from the 15 percent level inherited from Giscard and Barre to roughly 6 percent by the end of 1983. The data also indicate, however, that because the Mauroy-Delors strategy of periodic, negotiated devaluation was not continued after 1983, the extent of overvaluation increased dramatically after that date -- so much so that by 1986 the franc was as overvalued as it had been when the Socialists first came to power! This turnabout occurred in 1984 and 1985 because the continuing difference in French and German rates of inflation (5 percent in 1984 and 3.6 percent in 1985, despite the marked deceleration in the rate of increase in French prices) was not offset by any revaluation of the mark and/or devaluation of the franc. As a result, by the end of 1984, the franc was overvalued by about 11 percent, and by the end of 1985, that figure had increased to roughly 15 percent -- about what it had been in mid-1981.[34]

With the last Mauroy and the Fabius governments eschewing any realignment of the exchange rate between an increasingly overvalued franc and the mark, domestic macroeconomic policy continued to be constrained by the franc's participation in the EMS. Despite the low rate of growth and the high and rising level of unemployment, domestic policy was sharply contractionary in 1984, neutral, at best, in 1985, and contractionary again in 1986. Thus, real interest rates (that is, nominal rates net of inflation) rose by more than a point in 1984, remained at that level in 1985, and then moved up another point in 1986. Meanwhile, the size of the budget deficit relative to G.D.P. decreased in 1984, giving fiscal policy an overall *contractionary* effect, and after remaining unchanged in 1985, decreased again in 1986, introducing an additional contractionary impulse. Not surprisingly, the rate of growth remained low -- about 1.3 percent in 1984 and 1.9 percent in 1985, after 1983's 0.7 percent -- and the rate of unemployment continued its upward drift, to 9.7 percent in 1984, 10.3 percent in 1985, and 10.6 percent in 1986.

Why did the Socialist governments eschew any devaluation of the franc after the 1983 realignment -- and in so doing revert to the strong-franc policy of the Barre government? For one thing, if it is the case that governments tend not to engage in preemptive devaluations to correct an overvaluation of their currency but, rather, devalue only when they have to -- after the currency has come under attack in the markets (and sometimes, of course, not even then) -- the Socialist governments may have kept the franc at its existing exchange rate in 1984 and 1985 simply because it did not come under pressure sufficient to force a devaluation. That it did not was no doubt at least partly attributable to the larger international environment -- in particular, the dramatic rise of the U.S. dollar in those years, in the wake of the Federal Reserve's toleration of historically high interest rates, relative to the mark and the currencies (including the franc) linked to the mark. But the absence of pressure no doubt derived, also, from France's lower inflation rate and its downward trajectory (see Table 7.4), coupled with the credibility of the government's commitment to stabilizing prices and remaining in the EMS even at the cost of domestic contraction.

Other, more political factors may have contributed as well to the Socialist governments' new-found aversion to devaluation. For one thing, both Fabius and Bérégovoy, the finance minister in 1984-1986 (and 1988-1992), had been among the leading advocates of a withdrawal of the franc from the EMS in the 1981-1983 debates about exchange rate policy. As such, they were among the fiercest critics of the Mauroy-Delors policy of periodic, negotiated devaluations. Both may have had little interest in pursuing a negotiated devaluation, given the implicit endorsement which would represent of the earlier policy -- especially, of course, since the franc was not in immediate danger of falling through its floor.

If Fabius and Bérégovoy were not interested in continuing the Mauroy-Delors policy (unless perhaps absolutely forced to do so by the currency markets), Mitterrand, too, was not inclined to negotiate yet one more devaluation. By the end of the March 1983 currency crisis, the president was fed up with the recurring pattern in each crisis -- protracted and time-consuming debate and dissension within the government, followed by a negotiation in which France was forced to accept, as the price for a modest German revaluation and modest devaluation of the franc, further contraction of the economy.[35] Moreover, he continued to believe -- as he had in 1983, when he delayed a decision about exchange rate policy until after the municipal elections -- that the Socialists would suffer electoral retribution for a devaluation. With important legislative elections looming in early 1986, and with the government in danger of losing its majority, the president may have been quite happy to avoid yet another devaluation crisis.

The Balladur Correction

In the 1986 election, the Socialist Party and its allies did in fact lose their majority in the *Assemblée* and a *co-habitation* government headed by Jacques Chirac, the Mayor of Paris and long-time leader of the neo-Gaullist *Rassemblement pour la République*, was formed by the R.P.R. and the Giscardian *Union pour la démocratie française*. The new government appeared to recognize -- in a way that the one headed by Fabius had not -- the necessity of addressing the problem of an overvalued franc in the EMS and the constraint which imposed on domestic policy. Thus, although it was in office only a little more than two years, the Chirac government effected *two* realignments in the franc-mark exchange rate. The first occurred within a month of taking office, when Edouard Balladur, the minister of economics, finance, and privatization, and a close ally of Chirac, negotiated a modest realignment in the franc-mark rate. That realignment, consisting as it did of a 3 percent revaluation of the mark and a 3 percent devaluation of the franc, eliminated roughly two-thirds of the increase in overvaluation that occurred in 1984 and 1985 because of the still-higher rate of French inflation and absence of any EMS realignment.

Whether or not Balladur and Chirac understood the inherent logic of the EMS better than Bérégovoy and Fabius, they *acted* as if they did. Thus, less than a year after the first devaluation, they effected a second realignment in the franc-mark rate. In January 1987, the franc -- still overvalued and increasingly under pressure in the currency markets as the U.S. dollar dropped from its 1985 high and the German mark moved up -- weakened against the mark and moved toward its floor in the EMS. Balladur deliberately let the franc fall through its floor in order to force the Bundesbank to intervene in the markets in support of the franc and, ultimately, to force the German government to revalue the mark. Reflecting a perception that the mark was undervalued and that Germany, as a result, enjoyed an unfair advantage in intra-EC trade, as well a sense that the weaker-currency countries were increasingly required to bear a disproportionate share of the costs of adjustment, the Balladur gambit resulted in the first unilateral revaluation of the mark since 1979.[36]

Consisting as it did of another 3 percent revaluation, the 1987 realignment did not entirely eliminate the overvaluation of the franc. As a result, fiscal and monetary policy remained contractionary, with real interest rates increasing slightly in 1987 and fiscal policy having its largest contractionary effect since 1980. Nevertheless, when taken together, the 1986 and 1987 realignments *did* offset the cumulative difference in French and German inflation rates after 1984 and, in so doing, effected a considerable reduction in the extent of overvaluation of the franc. That, in turn, contributed to an increase in the rate of growth, a diminution in the level of unemployment, and a slight reduction in the trade deficit in 1988.

The Socialists Return: The Advent of the Franc Fort

Although the two Balladur realignments contributed to a somewhat higher rate of growth and a reduced trade deficit and level of unemployment, their effects were slight in magnitude and late in coming, and, for both reasons, they provided Chirac and the governing parties little assistance in the 1988 elections. As a result, Mitterrand easily defeated the leader of the R.P.R. in the presidential election and the Socialist Party, helped by the president's coattails, was able to equal its 1981 vote in the subsequent legislative elections. Although it failed to win a majority of the seats in the *Assemblée*, as it had in 1981, the party was nevertheless able to form a series of minority governments that held power over the next five years.[37]

While differing in several respects, the Socialist governments that held office between 1988 and 1993 shared an aversion to devaluation. Rather than continuing the policy of periodic, limited devaluation initiated by Delors and later adopted by Balladur, those governments reverted to the policy followed in 1984-1985 by Fabius and Bérégovoy (who returned as finance minister and remained in the post until 1992, when he succeeded Cresson as prime minister) -- and Barre before them -- of maintaining the existing franc-mark exchange rate. They did so despite the fact that, as of mid-1988, the franc was overvalued vis-à-vis the mark by perhaps 12 percent,[38] and the additional fact that France continued to have a higher rate of inflation than Germany until 1991. Even when the franc was subjected to unprecedented speculative pressure in the currency markets, as it was during the 1992-1993 EMS crisis, the government adhered to that policy.[39]

As was the case between March 1983 and March 1986, the Socialists' aversion to devaluation and commitment to a franc fort reflected, in part, a diminished need to devalue, as speculative pressure on the franc abated after the realignments of 1986 and 1987. With the stabilization of the rate of inflation in France in the range of 3 percent, and the acceleration of the rate of inflation in Germany after 1988, the difference in the rates in the two countries not only continued to decrease but became negligible. Thus, the French rate, which exceeded the German rate by 1.4 percent in 1988, exceeded it by only 0.8 percent in 1989 and 0.7 percent in 1990. And after 1990, the difference actually favored *France*, as the continued acceleration of the German rate caused it to surpass the French rate -- by 0.3 percent in 1991, 1.6 percent in 1992, and 2.0 percent in 1993.[40]

The Socialist governments' aversion to devaluation and commitment to a *franc fort* was not simply the result of a diminution of speculative pressure against the franc in the late 1980s. As Blanchard and Muet note, it reflected, also, a conscious choice about policy -- specifically, about how to improve the country's competitiveness vis-à-vis its trading partners.[41] The governments' aversion to devaluation reflected a belief -- one that became especially widespread as the EMS took on the character of a quasi-fixed exchange rate regime in the mid-to-late 1980s -- that devaluation provides only a short-term and transitory correction of the erosion in competitiveness that has already occurred. Because devaluation cannot effect the changes in wages and other costs that are necessary if relative prices are to be altered in the future, it was thought to be incapable of restoring a country's external competitiveness. Restoring competitiveness requires, instead, a reduction in relative costs and prices, which could only occur through a process of "competitive disinflation." Therefore, improving the competitive position of the French economy in the long term -- an improvement that would be reflected in the attainment of a balance of trade, a stable exchange rate, and a reasonable rate of growth and employment -- required that its prices, relative to those of the competition, be driven down -- something that could only be done by pursuing, attaining, and maintaining a lower rate of inflation than its trading partners. That, in turn, required the government to adhere to a contractionary macroeconomic policy.

If the strategy of restoring external competitiveness through competitive disinflation, rather than competitive devaluation, required the government to pursue a contractionary macroeconomic policy, the duration and magnitude of macroeconomic contraction depended on both the rates of inflation in other countries and the degree of flexibility in costs within France. Obviously, any gains in competitiveness achieved through a reduction in the rate of inflation in France would be neutralized by a comparable reduction in the rate of inflation in its trading partners. Likewise, any gains in competitiveness achieved through macroeconomic contraction would be diminished to the extent that costs proved to be relatively unresponsiveness to contractionary policy. In either circumstance, a restoration of competitiveness would require a longer and/or more severe macroeconomic contraction.

Unfortunately, the Socialist governments encountered *both* obstacles as they pursued their policy of competitive disinflation. Most of France's trading partners experienced reductions in their rates of inflation in the 1980s, thereby reducing the gain in competitiveness earned by France through its own policy of disinflation. And costs within France -- most notably, as Blanchard and Muet note,[42] the costs of labor, both in terms of wages and social contributions -- proved to be less responsive and more rigid in the face of contraction and rising unemployment than many had anticipated. For both reasons, therefore, the several Socialist governments were required to adhere to their contractionary economic policy, and to accept low rates of growth and high levels of unemployment, for a longer period than might have otherwise been necessary -- indeed, for their entire term in office. Thus, nominal and real interest rates were pushed sharply upward in 1989 and again in 1990 and remained at those high levels for the duration of their tenure. Fiscal policy remained contractionary in 1988 and 1989 and was only mildly expansionary in 1990 and 1991. As a result, the rate of growth dropped in 1990 and again in 1991, and the rate of unemployment rose toward the 10 percent level in 1991 and again in 1992.

If the simultaneous deceleration of rates of inflation in France's trading partners and the rigidities in wages and other domestic costs diminished the gains produced by the strategy of competitive disinflation, and deepened and lengthened the macroeconomic contraction required to reduce relative prices, that contraction was further deepened by the Socialist government's adherence to the existing franc-mark exchange rate throughout the 1992-1993 EMS currency crisis. On several occasions -- in late September 1992, again in December 1992 and January 1993, and finally in July 1993 -- the franc (like most of the currencies in the Exchange Rate Mechanism of the EMS) came under sustained assault in the currency markets and threatened to fall through its floor against the mark -- despite the fact that France had, by then, a lower rate of inflation than Germany and a surplus in its Balance of Trade. Concerted and coordinated defenses mounted by the French and German governments and central banks kept the franc above its floor against the mark on each occasion.[43] But, as part and parcel of each wave of speculative pressure, the French government was forced to raise its short-term rates and to maintain them at unusually high nominal and real levels throughout late 1992 and early 1993. The government -- by then headed by Pierre Bérégovoy -- attempted to offset the increasingly contractionary effect of monetary policy by providing the first significant fiscal stimulus since 1981; nevertheless, the overall effect of macroeconomic policy was to further diminish the rate of growth and to drive the rate of unemployment above 10 percent. Not surprisingly, in the wake of those developments, the Socialist Party suffered the worst electoral defeat of its history!

Lessening the EMS Constraint: The Balladur Recovery

In the election for the *Assemblée Nationale* in March 1993, the *Parti Socialiste* lost more than fifty percent of its vote compared to 1988. Although they did not substantially increase their overall share of the vote, the two conservative parties won more than 80 percent of the seats in the *Assemblée*, and, once more, a *co-habitation* government took office. Convinced that Jacques Chirac's occupancy of the *Matignon* in 1986-1988 had damaged his chances in the 1988 presidential election, and wishing to avoid a similar fate in 1995, Chirac and Edouard Balladur agreed that the latter would become prime minister.[44] Balladur appointed Edmond Alphandéry as minister of the economy. But he retained for himself responsibility for monetary policy in the new government.

On one hand, the Balladur government brought with it to office a strong public commitment to the *franc fort* and the EMS, notwithstanding the opposition of many within the R.P.R. to both. Balladur, one of the few R.P.R. members to vote in favor of the Maastricht Treaty in the *Assemblée* in 1992,[45] had voiced that commitment on many occasions. And Alphandéry was a protegé of Raymond Barre, who had presided over the creation of the EMS and had pursued a strong currency policy in 1979-1981. On the other hand, as the 1987 currency crisis had demonstrated, Balladur also brought with him -- partly, no doubt, because of the considerable opposition within the R.P.R. to the EMS, the *franc fort*, and Maastricht -- a greater propensity to challenge German policy and leadership within the EMS than had been exhibited by his Socialist predecessors. And, indeed, that propensity reappeared almost immediately after the new government took office, and in a manner that bore a striking resemblance to the events of 1987. Specifically, Balladur challenged the presumption that the German Bundesbank sets the floor for interest rates in the EMS and pursued an aggressively expansionary monetary policy, marked by unilateral reductions of interest rates in order to stimulate an economic recovery. Ultimately, he challenged Germany to either leave the EMS or agree to a lessening of the constraint imposed on other economies by German monetary authorities working through the EMS. The result was, of course, the decision to widen the bands of the EMS in August 1993.

When the Balladur government came to power, the expected rate of economic growth for the year was close to zero and the rate of unemployment was above 10 percent. The intervention rate was 9 percent and three-month money market rates were around 12 percent -- meaning, given an inflation rate of roughly 2 percent, that borrowers faced very high real interest rates. At the same time, the Bérégovoy government had so loosened fiscal policy by then that the overall government deficit for the year was expected to be roughly 400 billion francs, almost 6 percent of G.D.P., leaving little leeway for further fiscal expansion to counter the recession.

During its first month and one-half in office, the Balladur government followed a policy of reducing interest rates in small increments, and attempting at the same time to reduce the large budget deficit. By mid-May 1993, although the Bundesbank had resisted making any further cuts in interest rates after its reduction of the discount rate in late April,[46] French rates had been reduced six times in six weeks. The intervention rate had dropped to 7.75 percent. And money market rates had also dropped -- by enough to eliminate the differential of roughly 5 percentage points that had existed between French and German rates prior to the election. In late May, as government agencies published increasingly pessimistic projections of growth and unemployment -- negative growth for the year and year-end unemployment over 12 percent -- and as various members of the coalition government challenged his contractionary budgetary stance, Balladur proposed a series of measures to promote public works and infrastructure and jobs, to be funded with a 40 billion franc loan.[47] And the government reduced interest rates yet again.

Despite the Bundesbank's continued resistance to further reductions of interest rates, the French government reduced its interest rates again in mid-June and, in so doing, eliminated the differential that had existed between the French intervention rate and its German equivalent, the discount rate. A week later, the government reduced the intervention rate again, to 7 percent, one-quarter of a point *below* the German discount rate -- in effect challenging the presumption that Germany sets the floor for rates in the EMS. Several days later, in announcing a meeting of the Franco-German Economic and Finance Council, Alphandéry said Europe was suffering from "overly restrictive monetary policies, notably the unduly restrictive German policy" and suggested that "the Germans must speed up their rate cuts." Needless to say, the Germans were offended and cancelled the meeting.[48]

The currency markets began to sense trouble in the Franco-German axis of the EMS. And they began to fear that the French government would let its domestic objectives override its commitment to maintaining the value of the franc. The government appeared to be so preoccupied with the deteriorating economy and rising rate of unemployment (and, of course, the 1995 presidential election) that it would continue to reduce interest rates, even if Germany did not, and would not raise them, even if the franc came under speculative attack. Not surprisingly, as those perceptions developed, the franc began to come under pressure in the markets. In early July, the Bundesbank did finally cut its rates. But the French government matched those cuts immediately and the franc continued to move toward its floor in the EMS. For the third time in the past year, the German and French central banks began joint intra-marginal interventions in defense of the franc.[49]

By mid-July, it was increasingly apparent that the German Bundesbank would not implement another reduction in its rates before its summer recess. At the same time, it was apparent that, given the negative growth rate being projected for the year,[50] the anticipated year-end unemployment rate in excess of 12 percent, and the pending presidential elections, the French government would continue reducing *its* rates. It was also apparent, however, that if this divergence in monetary policy caused the franc to drop to its floor against the mark, the French government would *not* devalue; Balladur was, he had said, "indestructably attached to the stability of the franc within the EMS."[51] While many believed that France ultimately would have to devalue or allow the currency to float, just as the British had the previous autumn, the French government's position was in fact not unlike its position in the 1987 crisis: Market pressure would continue to drive the franc downward, provoking massive interventions in the currency markets by the central banks. Sooner or later, those interventions would reach a limit as the French bank exhausted its reserves and borrowing capacity. At that point, the Bundesbank would either have to continue intervening unilaterally or cease its support -- which, of course, would constitute a de facto withdrawal of the mark from the EMS. At that point, either the EMS would go out of business (which the French would not allow, since that would inevitably be viewed as a defeat for the *franc fort* and a certain prelude to a devaluation), or a scheme would be concocted that would simultaneously allow France to continue reducing its rates without devaluing and Germany to continue its membership in the ERM without having to conduct the massive interventions necessary to support weak currencies. Concocting such a scheme was, of course, precisely what the finance ministers did in August 1993, when they agreed to a French proposal to widen the bands of the EMS from +/- 2.25 to +/- 15 percent.[52]

The decision to widen the bands of the EMS significantly lessened the exchange rate constraint on French macroeconomic policy that had existed since 1979. For the Balladur government, the decision meant it could continue its policy of reducing interest rates in small increments, in order to stimulate a recovery, without provoking speculative pressures that would confront it with a choice between shifting to a more contractionary policy or devaluing the currency.[53] More generally, widening the range of fluctuation for the exchange rate meant that the range of choices in the domain of macroeconomic policy available to the French government -- and, indeed, to every government that participated in the EMS -- was widened as well. Governments could, of course, opt for continuing contractionary fiscal and monetary policies. But, to a greater extent than was the case in the old mark-dominated, narrow-band EMS, they could opt, instead, for more *expansionary* economic policies.

The French government's willingness to challenge German leadership in monetary policy in the spring and summer of 1993 and, ultimately, to provoke a crisis that resulted in a lessening of the EMS constraint on domestic policy, was not the only source of the recovery that began later that year. Responding largely to the recession that had been created by its predecessors' contractionary policies, the Bérégovoy government had dramatically increased the stimulative effect of fiscal policy in 1992 and 1993, and that stimulus alone, coupled with a gradual easing of monetary policy as German rates came down, undoubtedly would have fuelled a recovery of some magnitude. Nevertheless, the government's commitment to an aggressively expansionary monetary policy, and its willingness to adhere to that commitment even in the face of unprecedented speculative pressures, German opposition, and the possible demise of the EMS, *did* play a significant role in generating, accelerating, and deepening the recovery.

Consequences

Monetary and Fiscal Policy

The cumulative effect on monetary and fiscal policy of the choices made by French governments in the face of the EMS constraint is apparent in time-series data on interest rates and budget deficits. Table 7.5 presents data on both for the period since 1979. The data suggest that real short-term interest rates -- that is, nominal rates minus the rate of inflation -- were positive over the period since 1980. And more important, they increased substantially over that period to unusually high levels, especially during Mitterrand's second term and, within that *septennat*, especially during 1989-1992. That, of course, was precisely the period when the *franc fort* became enshrined as policy dogma. The Balladur government's sustained drive to lower nominal rates in 1993 and 1994 *did* bring real rates back to the range of a decade earlier. Despite that, however, they remained above the levels that existed during the Barre administration and the first years of the Mitterrand presidency.

Table 7.5 also presents data pertaining to the magnitude of the overall public sector budget deficit, relative to G.D.P., and the year-to-year change in that magnitude. The latter provides a measure of the net stimulative (or contractionary, if the relative size of the deficit decreases) effect of fiscal policy. The data indicate, for example, that after having been contractionary in 1979 and 1980, fiscal policy was expansionary in 1981 (with an effect equivalent to 1.9 percent of G.D.P., meaning the deficit increased by that amount) and 1982 (0.9). But after 1982, fiscal policy was generally contractionary or, at most, only mildly expansionary, for the next decade. In particular, during the period between 1983 and 1990, fiscal policy was stimulative, in the aggregate, in only *one* year -- and then only by the slightest amount. Only in 1992 and 1993, when the deficit increased to almost 6 percent, largely in response to the cyclical downturn, did fiscal policy become as stimulative as it had been in the first years of the Mitterrand presidency.

TABLE 7.5 Interest Rates and Fiscal Policy in France, 1979-1994

	Nominal Short-Term Interest Rates (average 3-month interbank rate)	*"Real" Short-Term Interest Rates (nominal 3-month rate-inflation)*	*Budget Deficit as % of G.D.P.*	*Net Fiscal Stimulus of Budget*
1979	9.8	-1.0	0.8	-1.3
1980	12.2	-1.4	0.0	-0.8
1981	15.3	1.9	1.9	1.9
1982	14.6	2.8	2.8	0.9
1983	12.5	2.9	3.2	0.4
1984	11.7	4.3	2.8	-0.4
1985	9.9	4.1	2.9	0.1
1986	7.7	5.0	2.7	-0.2
1987	8.3	5.2	1.9	-0.8
1988	7.9	5.2	1.7	-0.2
1989	9.4	5.8	1.3	-0.4
1990	10.3	6.9	1.6	0.3
1991	9.6	6.4	2.2	0.6
1992	10.3	7.9	3.9	1.7
1993	8.6	6.5	5.8	1.9
1994 (est.)	5.3	3.8	5.9	0.1

Source: Organization for Economic Co-operation and Development, *Economic Outlook 55, June 1994* (Paris: OECD, 1994), pp. A18, A31, and A37; and earlier volumes.

Inflation, Unemployment, Growth, Trade

The monetary and fiscal policies pursued by the various French governments had a variety of consequences, in terms of economic performance. Some of those are summarized in Table 7.6. Those data demonstrate, for example, that the secular upward trend in real interest rates, when coupled with the largely neutral, or contractionary, fiscal policy pursued between 1983 and 1992, resulted in a dramatic diminution over time in the rate of inflation. As Figure 7.1 demonstrated, especially during 1982-1986, but also again in the 1990s, the rate of inflation decelerated to exceptionally low levels. To some degree, of course, the earlier deceleration was a result of the price and wage controls instituted during the period of *rigueur*; nevertheless, that was only part of the explanation, and even after their removal the rate of inflation remained well below earlier levels (and, indeed, even below the levels in post-unification Germany).

The substantial deceleration in the rate of change in prices occurred in large part through the dampening of demand effected by monetary and fiscal policy.

TABLE 7.6 Inflation, Unemployment, Economic Growth, and Trade in France, 1979-1994

	Inflation (% Change, Consumer Prices)	Unemployment (% of Labor Force)	Growth (% Change, "Real" G.D.P.)	Balance of Trade ($ Billion)
1979	10.8	5.9	3.2	-2.1
1980	13.6	6.3	1.6	-13.0
1981	13.4	7.4	1.2	-10.1
1982	11.8	8.1	2.5	-15.5
1983	9.6	8.3	0.7	-8.2
1984	7.4	9.7	1.3	-4.1
1985	5.8	10.3	1.9	-5.4
1986	2.7	10.4	2.5	-2.8
1987	3.1	10.5	2.3	-9.2
1988	2.7	10.0	4.5	-8.5
1989	3.6	9.4	4.3	-10.1
1990	3.4	8.9	2.5	-12.9
1991	3.2	9.5	0.8	-8.8
1992	2.4	10.4	1.2	2.9
1993	2.1	11.7	-0.9	9.3
1994 est.	1.5	12.3	1.8	16.1

Source: Organization for Economic Co-operation and Development, *OECD Economic Outlook, 55, June 1994* (Paris: OECD, 1994), pp. A4, A18, A23, and A48.

As a result, the substantial decrease in the rate of inflation was accompanied by a diminution of the rate of growth to low levels for substantial periods -- most notably, in 1983-1986 and in the period after 1990. Those periods of sustained low growth resulted, in turn and after a lag, in increased levels of unemployment, especially in 1984-1985 and 1991-1993. The cumulative effect was the pattern illustrated in Figure 7.1: The rate of inflation decelerated sharply -- indeed, unusually sharply, relative to the experience in other neighboring countries. And the rate of unemployment increased dramatically -- like the inflation rate, by an unusually large amount, relative to the experience of France's European neighbors.

The data in Table 7.6 pertaining to trade present an intriguing wave-like pattern. After the dramatic deterioration that began in the last years of the Barre administration and continued in the first eighteen months of the Mitterrand presidency, the Balance of Trade improved substantially by the mid-1980s. But then it began to deteriorate again, only to improve once more -- to such an extent, indeed, that it registered a surplus after 1991. As crude as the data are, there is some suggestion that the strategy pursued by Mauroy and Delors (and later

TABLE 7.7 French Balance of Trade, 1979-92 ($ Billions)

	French Balance of Trade with:									
	Germany	*Italy*	*Bel-L*	*U.K.*	*Neth*	*Spain*	*All EC*	*Japan*	*U.S.*	*World*
1979	-2.3	0.4	-0.1	1.5	-1.3	-0.5	-1.4	-3.3	-1.2	-6.3
1980	-4.0	1.2	-0.9	0.5	-1.9	-0.7	-5.0	-5.8	-1.7	-18.9
1981	-4.1	0.8	-0.6	0.6	-2.5	-0.3	-5.4	-4.3	-1.7	-14.6
1982	-5.8	-0.6	-0.9	-0.3	-2.1	-0.6	-10.0	-3.9	-1.9	-19.0
1983	-3.7	-0.7	-0.7	-0.5	-2.0	-0.9	-8.4	-2.4	-1.6	-11.0
1984	-3.2	0.0	-0.5	-0.9	-1.9	-0.4	-7.0	-0.5	-1.7	-6.8
1985	-3.3	-0.2	-0.9	-0.8	-1.8	-0.8	-7.7	0.2	-1.8	-6.6
1986	-5.7	-0.9	-1.3	2.1	-1.5	-0.3	-7.8	-0.9	-3.1	-4.5
1987	-7.4	-1.2	-1.5	1.4	-1.6	0.8	-9.6	-0.9	-3.8	-10.1
1988	-8.4	-0.8	-1.6	2.9	-0.3	1.3	-7.0	-1.8	-4.6	-11.7
1989	-9.3	-1.0	-2.2	2.9	-0.1	1.6	-8.4	-3.3	-4.5	-13.6
1990	-7.7	-3.1	-0.9	2.6	0.0	2.5	-7.3	-6.3	-5.2	-17.7
1991	-1.2	-1.9	-0.2	1.7	-1.3	2.8	0.0	-8.5	-5.1	-14.2
1992	-3.9	-0.1	0.7	3.0	-0.8	3.9	3.2	-5.0	-5.6	-3.3
Total	-70.0	-8.1	-11.6	16.7	-19.1	8.4	-81.8	-46.7	-43.5	-158.3

Source: International Monetary Fund, *Direction of Trade Statistics Yearbook, 1993*
(Washington: I.M.F., 1993), pp. 177-179; and earlier volumes.

Balladur) of periodic, limited realignments of the exchange rate contributed to a
marked diminution in the trade deficit. Thus, the deficit decreased markedly in
the four years after 1982. (It also decreased after 1991, although this latter decrease was undoubtedly a product -- at least in part -- of the severe cyclical contraction in demand for imports.) In contrast, the strategy of maintaining a strong
currency and stable exchange rate, such as existed during the Barre and Rocard
governments, appears to have contributed to a dramatic deterioration in the trade
account.

As intriguing as the changes in the Balance of Trade described in Table 7.6
are, the inferences that can be drawn from them are rather ambiguous, in part
because they aggregate all French trade with the world as a whole. Because the
trade account provides the litmus test for the various strategies designed to restore competitiveness, it is useful to disaggregate the data and consider French
trade with specific countries. Table 7.7 presents data on the bilateral Balance of
Trade between France and its six most important trading partners in the European Union, and the Union as a whole, as well as Japan, the United States, and
the world as a whole. The data indicate that over the period between 1979 and

1992 France experienced a cumulative trade deficit of roughly $158 billion. [54] The largest portion of that cumulative deficit -- some $82 billion -- was incurred in its trade with other member states of the European Community, and the largest portion of *that* deficit, by far, was incurred in its trade with Germany ($70 billion). Taken together, the cumulative deficit on intra-EC trade, along with the large cumulative deficits with Japan (some $47 billion) and the United States (some $44 billion), accounted for the *entire* cumulative deficit since 1979. [55]

The data in Table 7.7 pertaining to French trade with other EC member states are especially interesting for what they imply about the impact of French economic and exchange-rate policy. They suggest that the Mauroy-Delors negotiated devaluations had a measurable, but nevertheless relatively modest, effect on the trade deficit in the early 1980s and that the commitment to the *franc fort* in the late 1980s contributed to a marked deterioration in the trade deficit, notwithstanding the success in stabilizing prices. These effects are most clearly illustrated by the changes in the magnitude of the recurring deficit with Germany. Thus, we note that this deficit -- and the deficit with the EC as a whole -- decreased by a total of two to three billion dollars in 1983 and 1984 in the wake of the three devaluations of 1981-1983. But after the mid-1980s, the deficit in trade with Germany grew substantially, to such an extent that by 1988 and 1989 it was twice as large as the deficit that had plagued the Mauroy government in the first years of the Mitterrand presidency. And whereas the deficit with Germany had constituted only a portion -- albeit a considerable one -- of its overall deficit with the EC member states in the early 1980s, it accounted for the *entire* EC deficit in the late 1980s.

The data in Table 7.7 suggest, in short, that the franc remained substantially overvalued against the mark throughout the 1980s and became *increasingly* overvalued as time went by -- notwithstanding the decade-long commitment to austerity and the success in stabilizing prices. They also suggest that the diminution in France's trade deficit with Germany, and the EC as a whole, in 1991 and 1992 was, to a very large extent, the result of an altogether unique, and probably transitory, development -- German unification -- rather than the result of a restoration of competitiveness through disinflation. Moreover, they suggest that the improvement in the Balance of Trade with the EC after 1990 derived not only from the effects of German unification but, also, from compositional changes in the structure and locus of trade -- changes that may have resulted, in part, from temporary overvaluations of other currencies in the EMS. Thus, in 1991 and 1992, France enjoyed a marked improvement in its balance of trade with Italy, Britain, and Spain -- the three countries whose currencies were most overvalued at the time in the EMS. [56] Given the likely temporary effect of German unification on French-German trade, the improved competitive position of Britain, Italy, and Spain vis-à-vis France after the withdrawal of the pound sterling and lira from the EMS and their subsequent depreciation and the three devaluations of the peseta in 1992-1993, and the likely resurgence of French imports as demand increases with the economic recovery, it is by no means obvious -- despite the enormous price paid over the last decade in low growth and high unemployment in return for disinflation -- that France has so improved its competitive position as to avoid a return to the large deficits with Germany, Europe, and the world that characterized its trade throughout most of the EMS era.

Political Consequences

In addition to their direct effect on the economy, the choices made by governments in the linked domains of international financial and domestic macroeconomic policy had more distal -- but nevertheless important -- *political* consequences as well. This is best illustrated by the electoral fate of the Socialist Party -- especially in the last years of Mitterrand's second *septennat* as former supporters defected in large numbers to neighboring movements (or simply did not vote). On the first ballot of the legislative elections of March 1993, for example, the party obtained less than 18 percent of the vote, less than one-half its vote in the 1988 election and its smallest vote in its two decades of existence. (In contrast, three ecology-oriented parties -- two of which were running for the first time -- won more than 10 percent of the vote.)[57] Even a year in the opposition was insufficient to restore the party's electoral fortunes; in the 1994 elections for the European Parliament, its vote continued to drop, to 14.5 percent, only 2 percentage points ahead of Bernard Tapie's new *Energie Radicale*.[58]

Many factors other than economics -- scandals, length of time in office, and so forth -- contributed to the erosion in support for the Socialist Party in the last years of the Mitterrand presidency. And, of course, some of the Socialist defectors may return in future elections -- for example, in a presidential election with a party candidate in the second round. Nevertheless, insofar as the economic policies of the Socialist-dominated governments resulted in a decade-long commitment to an overvalued currency, austerity, low growth, and high and rising unemployment, and insofar as voters were more inclined to punish governing parties for austerity, low growth, and high and rising unemployment than to reward them for low rates of inflation and a strong currency, it is reasonable to assume that they contributed to the party's near-demise as an electoral force and that at least some of the defectors who left the party because of those policies will not return.

The political consequences of the economic policies pursued by French governments in the 1980s and early 1990s may have extended beyond political parties. In addition to contributing to the erosion of support for the Socialist Party, the austerity, low growth, and high unemployment that were by-products of the commitment to the *franc fort* and the EMS may have contributed to a sharp erosion in support in the French public for the European Community and Union -- an erosion that was evident in the run-up to, and near defeat of, the Maastricht

Treaty in, the referendum of September 1992, the surge of support in 1994 for de Villiers' anti-Maastricht movement, and Eurobarometer survey data. Indeed, the latter indicate that over the past five years, France not only experienced an erosion in support for the Union but experienced a *larger* erosion in support than *any* other member state! Thus, whereas in 1989 many more French citizens (60 percent of those surveyed) believed France benefitted on the whole from membership in the EU than believed it did not (20 percent), by 1994, more French citizens (40 percent) thought the country did *not* benefit from membership than thought it *did* (38 percent). No other country experienced as sharp a reversal over that period in the public's assessment of the net advantage of EU membership, and only Spain and Britain among the other member states resembled France in having more citizens who believed the country did not benefit from the EU than believed that it did.[59] Obviously, as with the Socialist vote, many factors contributed to the erosion of support for the EU. Nevertheless, it is plausible that the state of the economy -- and perhaps even the growing recognition that the country's economic problems were linked to its exchange rate policy (a view that was articulated forcefully by Philippe de Villiers and the leading Gaullist critic of Maastricht and the EMS, Philippe Séguin) -- contributed to that erosion.

If the economic policies adopted by the Socialist-dominated governments contributed to the erosion of electoral support for the Socialist Party and for the European Union itself in the late 1980s and early 1990s, the brief experience of the Balladur government stands in sharp contrast -- although nevertheless demonstrating that economic policy choices have political consequences. This is best illustrated by the dramatic change in personal support for Balladur that occurred in 1994. After the July 1993 crisis in the EMS, the Balladur government continued to pursue its aggressively expansionary monetary policy by driving down interest rates in a series of small steps. By the turn of the year, the economy had begun to revive. The rate of economic growth, which had declined throughout 1993, turned positive in the first quarter of 1994, increasing by 1 percent on an annual basis, and accelerated to 1.8 percent in the second quarter. The unemployment rate stabilized and, in June 1994, turned down for the first time in four years.[60] As the recovery gathered momentum in the spring of 1994, Balladur's personal popularity, which had decreased steadily throughout the winter, turned around and began increasing dramatically -- indeed, to such an extent that by mid-1994 he was the most popular choice for president in the impending election![61]

Conclusion

From 1982-1994, France has experienced a sharp and dramatic deceleration in the rate of inflation, protracted periods of low growth, and a marked increase in unemployment to one of the highest levels in Europe. Even as the country recovers from the deepest recession since 1945, the growth rate remains low, the unemployment rate remains well into double digits, and a substantial portion of the unemployed remains beyond the reach of the cyclical upturn. More so in the mid-1990s than in the 1970s -- and despite the Socialist Party's control of government for much of the period since 1980 -- France is a country that, compared with others, appears to be averse to inflation and willing to accept high levels of unemployment in the name of price stability.

This chapter has sought to understand why that mutation in collective macroeconomic preferences occurred. That France came to be marked, during the 1980s and early 1990s, by unusually low rates of inflation and unusually high levels of unemployment was, of course, the result of the commitment of most governments over that period to a contractionary macroeconomic policy marked by high and rising real interest rates and, at best, fiscal balance. Macroeconomic contraction was, in turn, a response to the constraints posed by the international context within which the French economy was, and is, embedded -- in particular, its high and rising dependence on trade with its partners in the European Community and Union and its continuing participation in the European Monetary System. Dependent on trade and thus sensitive to relative prices, suffering from a relatively high and accelerating rate of inflation as the EMS came into existence in 1979, and suffering, also, from an endemic trade deficit, France faced a recurring choice about how to adjust its prices relative to those of its major trading partners. It could reduce relative prices, and the perpetual overvaluation of the franc within the EMS and trade deficit within the EC, by domestic macroeconomic policy -- that is, by monetary and fiscal contraction. Or it could reduce them by devaluing the franc or withdrawing it from the EMS. To the extent that it pursued a policy of frequent and/or large devaluations of the franc, it could alter relative prices without incurring the costs associated with macroeconomic contraction -- although by allowing it to avoid changing its domestic cost structure, devaluation increased the likelihood that it would have to devalue again in the future. However, to the extent it avoided devaluation, or instituted modest devaluations that did not fully neutralize the accumulated overvaluation of the currency, the government shifted the burden for adjusting relative prices entirely to domestic macroeconomic policy, thereby deepening the magnitude of the necessary contraction.

Our discussion of the policy choices made by French governments in the era of the EMS suggests an oscillation between complete aversion to devaluation accompanied by sharp macroeconomic contraction, on one hand, and periodic, modest devaluations negotiated within the EMS accompanied by somewhat less severe domestic contraction, on the other. Interestingly, the choice between these two alternatives did not correspond perfectly with the ideological center of gravity of successive governments. In particular, it was not always the case that governments formed by the Left pursued the strategy of periodic, negotiated devaluation, in order to mitigate the costs of domestic contraction, and governments formed by the non-Left pursued the strategy of non-devaluation accompanied by more severe domestic contraction. Thus, although the Barre government *did* refuse to devalue, allowed the franc to become overvalued, and drove the economy into a recession, and although the Mauroy government *did* devalue the currency three times within eighteen months, the Socialist governments headed by Fabius and Rocard, Cresson, and Bérégovoy were no less averse to devaluation than Barre's. Conversely, over the last decade, only the *co-habitation* governments headed by Chirac and Balladur sought to reduce the EMS constraint on macroeconomic policy -- either by implementing periodic realignments of the franc-mark exchange rate, as in 1986-1987, or by forcing an alteration of EMS rules, as in 1993.

Balladur's challenge to German leadership in monetary policy in 1993, cul-minating in the decision to widen the bands of the EMS, dramatically lessened the extent to which participation in the EMS constrained domestic economic policy. Nevertheless, we should note, in closing, that the constraint has not alto-gether disappeared. The government continues to adhere to its commitment to the *franc fort* and, although lowering rates, has kept them high enough to support the currency inside its old narrow band in the EMS. Meanwhile, the rate of economic growth remains low and the level of unemployment remains high, even as the economy recovers, and there is no reason to think that the rate of growth will increase dramatically, and the level of unemployment will drop dramatically, in the foreseeable future. However, although the government continues to expe-rience low growth and high unemployment, it will confront an additional EU-generated contractionary impulse in the form of the "convergence criteria" that must be satisfied if France is to move with other EU members to the third and final stage of Economic and Monetary Union in the late 1990s -- criteria that, among other things, stipulate a sharp reduction from present levels in the size of the budget deficit, a low rate of inflation, and continued membership within the EMS. Meanwhile, as it attempts to meet those inherently contractionary criteria in an era of low growth and high unemployment, the conservative government must confront, at the same time, its own deep, internal divisions over Maastricht, EMU, and the European Union and simultaneously implement the Maastricht Treaty, charting the way to stage three of EMU, and negotiating institutional reform of the EU in the Intergovernmental Conference scheduled for 1996. Not-withstanding the lessening of the EMS constraint in 1993, then, the European issue -- in particular, the extent to which and ways in which its membership in the EU constrains domestic policy -- will remain at the fore and dominate politi-cal debate in France in the years ahead. How that issue is resolved -- indeed, *whether* it is resolved -- will, more than anything else, define the country's role in the new Europe.

Notes

A preliminary version of portions of this chapter was presented at the Colloquium on the New France in the New Europe at Georgetown University in October, 1993. For their helpful comments and suggestions, I wish to thank Marc-Antoine Autheman, Greg Flynn, Peter Hall, Jacques Le Cacheux, George Ross, and Martin Schain.

1. Stanley Hoffmann, "France: Keeping the Demons at Bay," *New York Review of Books*, 3 March 1994, p. 10.
2. Among the members of the Union, the French rate was exceeded only by those of Belgium (about 13 percent), Ireland (18 percent), and Spain (24 percent). (Finland and Sweden, entrants in 1995, also had unusually high rates of unemployment.) See *OECD Econmonic Outlook, 55* (Paris: OECD, June 1994), and *OECD Observer No. 188* (Paris: OECD, July 1994), pp. 39-40.
3. In May 1994, the rate of unemployment peaked at 12.7 percent. The next month it dropped, for the first time in four years, to 12.6 percent, and it remained at that level in July 1994. See John Ridding, "Another rise in French unemployed," *Financial Times*, 1 July 1994, p. 2; Ridding, "Largest fall for years in French jobless," *Financial Times*, 2 August 1994, p. 2; and *Financial Times*, 1 September 1994, p. 3. That a substantial portion of the unemployment is structural in nature is suggested by the high rate of long-term unemployment; of the 3.3 million unemployed in mid-1994, more than 1 million had been unemployed for more than a year. See Ridding, "Largest fall."
4. See John Ridding, "France adjusts slowly to recovery," *Financial Times*, 16 August 1994, p. 2; and "France: Survey," *Financial Times*, 12 July 1994, p. II.
5. See Alice Rawsthorn, "French trade surplus continues," *Financial Times*, 22 July 1994, p. 2. The 1993 figure also appears in "France: Financial Times Survey," p. IV.
6. The most substantial changes occurred in the protracted crisis in the European Monetary System in 1992 and 1993, in the course of which the British pound and the Italian lira were withdrawn from the Exchange-Rate Mechanism and allowed to float, the Spanish peseta was devalued three times, the Portugese escudo twice and the Irish punt once. See David R. Cameron, "British Exit, German Voice, French Loyalty: Cooperation, Domination and Defection in the 1992-93 ERM Crisis," unpublished manuscript, 1994.
7. The data for Figure 7.1 are reported in Organization for Economic Co-operation and Development, *OECD Economic Outlook, 55*, June 1994, (Paris: OECD, 1994), pp. A4 and A18. The data for unemployment are standardized to make the rates cross-nationally comparable.
8. See Etienne S. Kirschen et al., *Economic Policy in Our Times, Vol. 1* (Amsterdam: Northholland, 1964), p. 257.
9. For descriptions and analyses of the economic policies of the Socialist governments, see, among many, Philippe Bauchard, *La Guerre des deux roses: Du Rêve à la réalité 1981-1985* (Paris: Grasset, 1986); David R. Cameron, "Exchange Rate Politics in France, 1981-1983: The Regime-Defining Choices of the Mitterrand Presidency," in Anthony Daley, ed., *The Mitterrand Era* (New York and London: New York University and Macmillan, forthcoming); Pierre Favier and Michel Martin-Roland, *La Décennie Mitterrand: 1. Les ruptures (1981-1984)* (Paris: Seuil, 1990); Alain Fonteneau and Pierre-

Alain Muet, *La Gauche face à la crise* (Paris: Foundation Nationale des Sciences Politiques, 1985); Peter A. Hall, "The Evolution of Economic Policy under Mitterrand," in George Ross, Stanley Hoffmann, and Sylvia Malzacher, eds., *The Mitterrand Experiment* (New York: Oxford, 1987); and Jeffrey Sachs and Charles Wyplosz, "The Economic Consequences of President Mitterrand," *Economic Policy, 2* (April 1986), pp. 262-322.

10. The EMS retained several features of the "snake," such as its bilateral parity grid of currencies and its fluctuation range of +/-2.25 percent, while instituting a mechanism for joint interventions in currency markets and for negotiating realignments among exchange rates, both of which were lacking in the "snake." For the definitive account of the creation of the EMS, see Peter Ludlow, *The Making of the European Monetary System: A Case Study of the Politics of the European Community* (London: Butterworth, 1982).

11. September 1992, of course, marks the advent of the year-long crisis in the Exchange-Rate Mechanism of the EMS, which, in a matter of months, undid the stabilizing effects of the first thirteen years. See Cameron, "British Exit, German Voice, French Loyalty."

12. See David R. Cameron, "The 1992 Initiative: Causes and Consequences," in Alberta M. Sbragia, ed., *Euro-politics: Institutions and Policymaking in the 'New' European Community* (Washington, D.C.: The Brookings Institution, 1992), Tables 2-7, p. 46.

13. One study that begins the story where it should begin, in the Barre administration, is Sachs and Wyplosz, "The Economic Consequences of President Mitterrand," pp. 268-269. For an extensive treatment of the policy of the Barre government, see Fonteneau and Muet, *La Gauche face à la crise*.

14. On Giscard's role in the creation of the EMS, see, in addition to Ludlow, *The Making of the European Monetary System*, Valéry Giscard d'Estaing, *Le Pouvoir et la vie* (Paris: Compagnie 12, 1988).

15. France normally experienced a net outflow of one to two billion francs in its capital accounts; therefore, its international borrowing (or lending) was roughly one or two billion more (or less) than its Current Accounts deficit (or surplus) -- which, in turn, reflected, to a very large degree, its deficit (or surplus) in its Balance of Trade.

16. Since the "snake" lacked both the institutional mechanisms and norms that would promote joint interventions in currency markets and/or realignments of exchange rates, when currencies weakened and fell through their floors against strong currencies, they simply dropped out of the "snake."

17. Only one rather small change in exchange rates was instituted between March 1979, when the EMS was created, and May 1981. That involved a 2 percent revaluation of the German mark in September 1979.

18. The commitments were embodied in the *Cent Dix Propositions* that constituted Mitterrand's campaign platform. They were based on the positions developed by the Partie Socialiste after its 1979 congress at Metz and published in *Projet socialiste pour la France des années 80* (Paris: Club Socialiste du Livre, 1980).

19. For summaries of the plethora of legislation in the first Mitterrand septennat, see, among many, John S. Ambler, ed., *The French Socialist Experiment* (Philadelphia: Institute for the Study of Human Issues, 1985); Philip G. Cerny and Martin Schain, eds., *Socialism, the State and Public Policy in France* (New York: Methuen, 1985); Fonteneau and Muet, *La Gauche face à la crise*; and Ross, Hoffmann, and Malzacher, eds., *The Mitterrand Experiment*. See, also, David R. Cameron, "The Colors of a Rose: On the

Ambiguous Record of French Socialism," *Center for European Studies Working Paper Series* (Cambridge: Harvard University Press, 1988).

20. In December 1958, de Gaulle had devalued the franc by 17.5 percent. In August 1969, Pompidou devalued the currency by 11 percent. On the internal debate within the government, see Cameron, "Exchange Rate Politics."

21. See his comments in interviews, reported in Serge July, *Les Années Mitterrand: Histoire baroque d'une normalisation inachevée* (Paris: Grasset, 1986), p. 110; and Stéphane Denis, *La Leçon d'automne: Jeux et enjeux de François Mitterrand* (Paris: Albin Michel, 1983), p. 15.

22. Under the pressure of the recession and the 1981 elections, the Barre government had increased expenditures and raised the deficit for the year to about 52 billion francs by the time the Socialists took office. As a result, the increase in the deficit attributable to the latter was much less -- roughly 5 billion francs. See Fonteneau and Muet, *La Gauche face à la crise*, p. 93.

23. In the months before the 1981 elections, the Barre government reduced the employees' contribution for sickness insurance by 1 percent, provided farmers with a multi-billion franc income supplement, increased the minimum pension and aid to the elderly and persons with disabilities, and increased the investment tax credit for companies. See Fonteneau and Muet, *La Gauche face à la crise*, p. 93.

24. The estimate of a 20 percent overvaluation in late 1981 is based on the data in Table 7.4 -- specifically, the estimated overvaluation as of the end of 1980 of 12.9 percent plus the inflation difference of 7.1 percent in 1981.

25. Also, the Dutch guilder was revalued by 5.5 percent and the Italian lira was devalued by 3 percent.

26. In addition, the Italian lira was devalued by 2.75 percent.

27. Quoted in Cameron, "Exchange Rate Politics."

28. Favier and Martin-Roland, *La Décennie Mitterrand*, pp. 401 and 424, use the first two terms; Marie-Paule Virard, *Comment Mitterrand a découvert l'économie* (Paris: Albin Michel, 1993), p. 51, uses the third.

29. On the "dix jours qui s'ébranlerent Mitterrand," see Bauchard, *La Guerre des deux roses*; Favier and Martin-Roland, *La Décennie Mitterrand*; and July, *Les Années Mitterrand*. See, also, the discussion in Cameron, "Exchange Rate Politics."

30. In addition, the Dutch guilder was revalued by 3.5 percent, the Danish krone by 2.5 percent, and the Belgian franc by 1.5 percent. The Italian lira was devalued by 2.5 percent and the Irish punt by 3.5 percent.

31. See Bauchard, *La Guerre des deux roses*, pp. 145-147.

32. Pierre Bérégovoy, then the minister of social affairs (and later the minister of finance in 1984-1986 and 1988-1992, and prime minister in 1992-1993), described the German conditions as an "unacceptable diktat." He demanded that the proposed increase in employees' social insurance contributions be changed to a 1 percent surtax on household incomes. See July, *Les Années Mitterrand*, p. 97.

33. Fabius replaced Mauroy as prime minister in mid-1984. Bérégovoy was named minister of finance in the Fabius government in place of Delors, who was appointed president of the European Commision.

34. The French and German rates of inflation are reported in Organization for Economic Cooperation and Development, *OECD Economic Outlook, 55, June 1994* (Paris: OECD, 1994), p. A4.

35. This was perhaps best exemplified by Mitterrand's comment after Fabius and others convinced him he could not take the franc out of the EMS: "We do not control our policy. In remaining in the EMS, we are in fact condemned to the policy of the dog that kills itself swimming against the current. Only for the profit of Germany." Quoted in July, *Les Années Mitterrand*, p. 96.

36. We might note the important role played by the 1987 Franco-German currency dispute, and Balladur, in the development of the initiative that eventually culminated in the Treaty on European Union signed at Maastricht in 1992. Several months after the January dispute, Balladur issued a series of proposals for improving the EMS that resulted in the Basle-Nyborg agreements of September 1987 pertaining to intra-margin interventions. Later, in December 1987 and January 1988, he issued a larger set of proposals to improve the EMS that, in effect, put the issue of Economic and Monetary Union back on the agenda of the EC. See David R. Cameron, "Transnational Relations and the Development of European Economic and Monetary Union," in Thomas Risse-Kappen, ed., *Bringing Transnational Relations Back In: Non-State Actors, Domestic Structures, and International Institutions* (Cambridge: Cambridge University Press, Forthcoming).

37. The P.S. won 36.6 percent of the vote on the first ballot of the June 1988 election for the *Assemblée*, compared with 31.3 percent in 1986. Michel Rocard served as prime minister from 1988 to mid-1991, when he was replaced by Edith Cresson, who, in turn, was replaced by Bérégovoy in April 1992.

38. From Table 7.4, the franc was overvalued by 11.6 percent vis-à-vis the mark by the end of 1987. In 1988, the rates of inflation in France and Germany were, respectively, 2.7 percent and 1.4 percent. Adding one-half of that difference to 11.6 brings the figure to roughly 12 percent as of mid-1988.

39. See Cameron, "British Exit, German Voice, French Loyalty."

40. In 1988, the rates of inflation in France and Germany were 2.7 percent and 1.4 percent. In 1989, they were 3.6 percent and 2.8 percent, and in 1990, they were 3.4 percent and 2.7 percent. In 1991, for the first time, the French rate was lower than the German, 3.2 percent versus 3.5 percent. In 1992, they were 2.4 percent and 4.0 percent, and in 1993, they were 2.1 percent and 4.1 percent.

41. See Olivier Jean Blanchard and Pierre Alain Muet, "Competition Through Disinflation: An Assessment of the French Macroeconomic Strategy," *Economic Policy*, 16 (April 1993), pp. 12-56.

42. Blanchard and Muet, "Competition Through Disinflation." See, also, Sachs and Wyplosz, "The Economic Consequences of President Mitterrand."

43. On the defense mounted in late September 1992 that set the pattern for the later ones, see William Dawkins, "French weaponry secured win in battle for franc," *Financial Times*, 3 November 1992, p. 2; Dawkins and David Buchan, "How the French fought to save the franc," *Financial Times*, 20 November 1992, p. 15; and Cameron, "British Exit, German Voice, French Loyalty." Eventually, in early August, 1993, the Community widened the fluctuation bands of the EMS from +/-2.25 percent to +/-15 percent.

44. It was understood at the time that Chirac would be the Gaullist candidate in the 1995 election. Balladur, the architect of *co-habitation* in both its 1986 and 1993 forms, readily acknowledged this on several occasions after 1990. See Edouard Balladur, *Dictionnaire de la Réforme* (Paris: Fayard, 1992). See, also, Claire Chazal, *Balladur* (Paris: Flammarion, 1993).

45. On 13 May 1992, the *Assemblée* voted to approve the constitutional revisions necessary for the Treaty on European Union by 398 to 77, with 99 abstentions. Eighty-eight members of the R.P.R. (including Chirac) abstained and thirty-one voted against. Only seven R.P.R. members (one of whom was Balladur) voted in favor. Among the leaders of the opposition within the R.P.R. was Philippe Séguin, who spoke for the opposition in a televised debate with Mitterrand before the 20 September 1992 referendum and who became president of the *Assemblée* after the 1993 election. For his views, see Philippe Séguin, *Discours pour la France* (Paris: Grasset, 1992) and Philippe Séguin, *Ce que j'ai dit* (Paris: Grasset, 1993).

46. See Christopher Parkes and James Blitz, "Bundesbank resistance grows to further cuts in interest rates," *Financial Times*, 29-30 May 1993, p. 2.

47. See David Buchan and Alice Rawsthorn, "Balladur to borrow $7 billion to boost economic revival," *Financial Times*, 25 May 1993, p. 2; Buchan, "Balladur moves to create more jobs," *Financial Times*, 26 May 1993, pp. 1, 16; Buchan, "Balladur's jobs package averts rift," *Financial Times*, 27 May 1993, p. 2; and Buchan, "Springtime in Paris," *Financial Times*, 29-30 May 1993, p. 9.

48. See Christopher Parkes, Alice Rawsthorn, Peter John, "Waigel cancels French talks after attack," *Financial Times*, 25 June 1993, pp. 1, 38; and Parkes, "Waigel rejects advice on interest rates from Paris," *Financial Times*, 26-27 June 1993, p. 24. Theo Waigel was the German finance minister.

49. See Alice Rawsthorn and James Blitz, "Franc falls close to ERM floor," *Financial Times*, 10-11 July 1993, p. 1.

50. See David Buchan, "French output forecast worsens," *Financial Times*, 8 July 1993, p. 4.

51. See *Financial Times*, 13 July 1993, p. 1; and *Financial Times*, 14 July 1993, p. 2.

52. On the pressure on the franc in July 1993 and the negotiations that resulted in a widening of the fluctuation bands of the EMS, see Peter Norman, "Lines of defence keep falling," *Financial Times*, 24-25 July 1993, p. 8; Peter Marsh, James Blitz, Lionel Barber, John Ridding, "Future of ERM in balance," *Financial Times*, 31 July-1 August 1993, pp. 1, 13; Marsh and Barber, "EC holds crisis talks in struggle to save ERM," *Financial Times*, 2 August 1993, p. 1; Barber, "Politicians usurp the technocrats," *Financial Times*, 2 August 1993, p. 4; Barber, "ERM bands produce sort of harmony," *Financial Times*, 3 August 1993, p. 2; and the account in Cameron, "British Exit, German Voice, French Loyalty."

53. Lessening the EMS constraint did not mean, however, that the French government would let the franc depreciate significantly. Indeed, within a few months of the decision to widen the EMS bands, the franc was trading above its old narrow-band floor against the mark, and it has remained above that floor ever since. See Samuel Brittan, "Single currency rises again," *Financial Times*, 12 May 1994, p. 16.

54. The I.M.F. data reported in Table 7.7 are based on a slightly more inclusive definition of exports and imports than the O.E.C.D. data reported in Table 7.6. For that reason, the figure for the overall Balance of Trade reported in Table 7.7 is more accurate than the figure reported in Table 7.6.

55. On the negligible contribution of trade with developing countries to the French deficit, see Suzanne Berger's chapter. We might note that French trade with all countries *except* the member states of the EU, Japan, and the United States earned, in the aggregate, a surplus every year after 1982 except 1991 (when the deficit was $600 million). In 1992,

the most recent year for which data are available, for example, its aggregate surplus with all countries except the United States, Japan and those of the EU was $4.1 billion. Only in 1980-1982 did France incur substantial deficits with the rest of the world (-$6.4 billion in 1980, -$3.2 billion in 1981 and 1982) -- undoubtedly the result of the second OPEC price shock.

56. See Cameron, "British Exit, German Voice, French Loyalty."

57. Allied in the *Union pour la France* and fielding single candidates in most districts, the R.P.R. and U.D.F. won about 40 percent of the vote in the election. See *Le Monde*, 24 March 1993, p. 9.

58. We should note that Tapie was a former minister in a Socialist government, and he received some presidential encouragement in the 1994 election -- perhaps in order to force Michel Rocard's departure as head of the P.S. (which in fact happened shortly after the election). The R.P.R. and U.D.F. received 25.5 per cent of the vote in the 1994 election; they, too, suffered large defections to a new movement -- in their case to Philippe de Villiers' anti-Maastricht, anti-EU *l'Autre Europe,* which won 12.5 per cent.

59. Only two countries, Belgium and Italy, experienced erosions in support that approached the magnitude found in France, and in both, substantially more people felt the country benefitted from membership than believed it did not. In the EC as a whole in 1989, 55 per cent thought their country benefitted from membership and 28 per cent thought it did not. In 1994, the figures were 46 per cent and 34 per cent, respectively. See David Marsh, "Partners dance to different tunes," *Financial Times,* 18-19 June 1994, p. 8.

60. On the quarterly growth rates in 1994, see *Financial Times,* 8 September 1994, p. 2. In 1993, the annual rates of change in the G.D.P., quarter by quarter, were -2.0, -1.5, -1.2 and -0.9 per cent. On the recovery, see David Buchan, "French growth forecast improves," *Financial Times,* 20 May 1994, p. 2; John Ridding, "Up off the floor," *Financial Times,* 12 July 1994, II; and Alice Rawsthorn, "French recovery accelerating," *Financial Times,* 23-24 July 1994, p. 2. On the rate of unemployment, see Alice Rawsthorn, "French jobless rate stabilizes," *Financial Times,* 30 April-1 May 1994, p. 3; and John Ridding, "Largest fall for years in French jobless."

61. See, for example, "Who's for president?" *The Economist,* 21 May 1994, pp. 55-56; David Buchan, "France and Balladur -- on recovery road," *Financial Times,* 25 May 1994, p. 3; and *The Economist,* 3 September 1994, pp. 50-52. The latter provides survey evidence of the sharp and sustained upturn in Balladur's popularity after April 1994.

PART THREE

Social Change and
Political Institutions

8

Change and Stability in
French Elites

Ezra Suleiman

Despite the political, economic, and social transformations of postwar France, two things have remained unchanged: the manner in which France recruits its leaders and the hold this elite has had on key positions in society. At the same time, although France has preserved its elitist institutions throughout all the tumultuous changes of the last half-century, elitist institutions have been modified in important ways, and the elites themselves have experienced enormous changes. The structural continuities are significant, but the changes in the ways these elite structures operate in French society have produced a fundamental shift in the way France is governed.

Traditionally, the power and autonomy of France's administrative bureaucracy have been a distinguishing characteristic of French political life. Today, France's administrative elites retain their power; in many ways their position in society is less challenged than it has ever been. But the elite has not retained its autonomy. Indeed, in critical ways, the elite has become indistinguishable from the political class in France. The barriers between serving the state, serving one's personal interests, and serving political interests have been blurred to the point of becoming, for all practical purposes, nonexistent.

Thus, France continues to possess elites who utilize an educational system in order to perpetuate themselves. For the most part, the elites also remain a manifestation of a class system that has been unshakable. But despite the preservation of basic elite structures, changes within the elitist institutions and in French society have produced changes within the elites themselves. Three factors are of particular importance: the Left's contribution to the legitimacy of the elitist structures; the impact of changes in the society on the elites; and, finally, the impact of changes in political structures on the elites. The combination has produced a profound change in elite ethics.

A Renewed Legitimacy

France has a system of nurturing elites that has had its admirers (mostly foreign) and its critics (mostly internal). The debate concerning elitist structures takes place periodically, particularly during times of crisis. In the aftermath of the French defeat by the Prussians in 1870, a national debate centered on the adequacy not just of the military structures but of the institutions responsible for training the nation's leaders. Following the liberation of France in 1944, critics once again questioned the judgment, values and competence of the elites. Men like Renan, in his *La Réforme intellectuelle et morale*, and Marc Bloch, in *L'Etrange defaite*, held the elites responsible for France's unpreparedness and ultimate collapse. More recently, the Left, in opposition during the 1960s and 1970s, denounced the undemocratic, elitist, and politicized nature of France's governing princes.

The extraordinary transformations of France in the postwar era allowed the elites to ward off criticism and to improve their image. They were lauded for their competence, and many outside observers wished to emulate the institutions that allowed France to harvest each year such a remarkable crop of qualified leaders. Starting in the 1960s, however, the elite training mechanisms came under mounting criticism for their social bias. In most of these attacks, the competence of France's leaders was not the primary issue. Critics bemoaned the lack of equality and democracy in the French institutions. It did not matter whether the schools produced competent and well-trained engineers, industrialists, and public servants. What mattered was that these schools perpetuated social inequalities, privileging those who already possessed the largest stock of "cultural capital." The elites simply reproduced themselves.[1]

The anti-elitist criticisms of Pierre Bourdieu and others coincided with the restructuring of the Left during the 1960s and 1970s. The Left was careful not to draw up detailed plans for reforming the mechanisms through which the elites perpetuated themselves. It nonetheless gave signals, and thereby hope to many, that it would try to institute a more democratic elite-forming structure as part of its project to *"changer la société."*

After over a dozen years of Socialist rule, however, the institutions that train and nurture France's governing elites are alive and well. In fact, at no time since the early postwar era have they been the object of such insignificant criticism. The Left has ceased its vitriolic attacks on these institutions, and has granted them a legitimacy they rarely possessed in the past. The Left itself has come to depend on the products of these institutions; it respects their traditions and objectives; and is as much in awe of what they represent as the Right was in its most defensive days. More importantly, however, the Left has learned to use, and allowed itself to be used by, these elites, more often than not to the detriment of the moral and ethical values with which the Left was long associated.

The result of the experience under the Left is thus quite the opposite of initial expectations. Indeed, after the May 1981 elections, the prospects of a Socialist government sent tremors through the administration. It was generally assumed that a Socialist government could not accept to work in, and with, an administrative structure that had long served the Right.[2] There were also signs during the early phases of the Left in power that changes would be forthcoming. Louis Mermaz, one of President Mitterrand's closest allies and a former president of the National Assembly, as well as minister of agriculture in the last Socialist government, expressed a widespread view when he noted in a 1982 interview with *Le Monde*: "It is necessary to make changes at certain levels of the state administration, whether for political or economic reasons. There is no longer any doubt that an administration mobilized for the construction of a socialist society cannot have the same behavior as an administration which had the responsibility of managing a strictly capitalist France."[3] Two Socialist projects for administrative renewal received the greatest attention: changing the personnel at the highest levels of the civil service, and reforming the procedure for recruitment into the state bureaucracy.

There were changes in personnel, but the purge anticipated and called for by a number of Socialists did not take place. In 1981, out of 139 directors of the central administration, fifty-nine (42 percent) were kept in their posts, sixteen (6 percent) were transferred to other directorial posts, sixty-four (46 percent) were changed, and ten new posts were created. Thus, over half of the directors of the central administration were changed in the first year of Socialist government. However, as Yves Agnés noted, "it is utterly wrong to maintain, with respect to changes in the state apparatus, that there was a systematic witch hunt. But it is plausible to maintain that a certain number of people who belonged to the *'phalanges de Giscard'* were cast aside."[4] Despite the important number of changes of personnel in both the administration proper and the semi-public and nationalized sectors, the personnel changes in the 1981-1982 period were ultimately of the same order of magnitude as when Giscard d'Estaing became president.[5]

In the area of recruitment much was also expected to change, particularly in view of the fact that Mitterrand himself was known to be hostile to the elitist nature of ENA and to the *grands corps* structure. It soon became clear, however, that the Socialists had no intention of abolishing ENA, despite the naming of a Communist as Minister of the Civil Service in 1981. There nonetheless remained the expectation that some structural reforms would be introduced. But the reform as presented to parliament on 5 October 1982 aimed only to widen the recruitment of higher civil servants. At the time of preparing the reform, the minister,

Anicet Le Pors, had said that the main goal would be to ensure that "the higher civil service reflects the social reality of the nation."[6]

The principal innovation of the reform was the introduction of a "third avenue" of entry into ENA. Since 1945 there had been two paths into ENA: the *concours d'etudiants* and the *concours des fonctionnaires*. The first is reserved for students who have had a standard (privileged) educational background, and the second is reserved for civil servants who want to move up the bureaucratic ladder, but who lack the educational advantages of the first *concours* entrants or, as has become increasingly common, who failed to gain entry to the school through the terribly competitive *concours d'etudiants*.

The idea of creating yet a third avenue was one that Mitterrand himself held very dear, and the new "reform" is largely remembered for this ephemeral innovation. The purpose of the third avenue was to allow trade union leaders, local elected officials, and members of various associations to enter the higher civil service, and to alter the Parisian, bourgeois character of the group that administers the affairs of the country. As Mr. Le Pors put it during the parliamentary debate, there is a need "to develop a new kind of civil service."[7] The aim, or hope, of this reform was to transform the higher civil service from an elitist institution into one that reflected the diversity of French society.

This ambition was not new. It had been proclaimed repeatedly by all governments since the creation of ENA. While presenting its efforts as a major reform, the government appeared to recognize that the net effects were likely to be modest. Like previous governments, it fell back on the old argument that ENA was only a cog in a large educational machine and that the machine itself must first be overhauled. Mr. Le Pors used almost the same words that a number of previous conservative ministers had used to indicate that ENA is the prisoner of the educational system. "There can be no good reform of ENA, of a real democratization of the recruitment of higher civil servants as long as the educational system cannot guarantee a genuine equality of opportunity and assure an accurate reflection of the social realities of the nation."[8]

The government of the Left, following its predecessors of the Right, thus chose to concentrate on tinkering with access to ENA. Like previous governments, the government chose not to tamper with France's administrative structure, and it opted not to alter the structure of the *corps*. It also avoided changes to the class ranking of ENA, which determines who will enter into the *grands corps*, and it chose not to reduce the number of *corps*. The early hopes of a serious reform quickly dissipated. As André Passeron noted at the time the government was preparing the reform of ENA: "The attitude of the new rulers toward ENA has considerably evolved, not only compared to what it was prior to May 19 [1981], but even since this date. The '*énarques*' are as numerous in the ministerial cabinets of the Mauroy government as they were in the preceding governments."[9] Recruitment into ministerial cabinets did change, with certain of the *grands corps* (the *Inspection des Finances*, for example) briefly experiencing a diminished role, and at the same time other *corps* (the *administrateurs civils*) had a greater presence than in the past. This change was of brief duration, however, for by the mid-1980s, the *grands corps* had reacquired their dominant position.[10]

In the years following the Left's innovations, the *grands corps* re-established their importance in the ministerial cabinets, in the financial institutions, in industrial enterprises, and in the nationalized industries. No longer will a Socialist government be considered a threat to the *corps*. In reality, members of a *corps* have a solidarity that can even transcend political differences. Hence, the members of the *grands corps* who run the Socialist governments have come to appreciate the benefits of the elitist system as much as their colleagues who happen to belong to the Center-Right. There is almost no difference in the points of view regarding the *grands corps* between politicians on the Left or the Right.[11]

Ultimately, the Left simply concluded that there was not much advantage to be gained from a modification of the recruitment procedures into the higher civil service. Many members of the Socialist Party's leadership would lose as individuals by the abolition of the *grands corps*. They could not return to their *corps* if the need arose. They could not recruit new leaders as easily were the *corps* not in existence. They could not compensate colleagues by naming them to one *corps* or another (all *corps* allow a certain number of political appointments) for what amounts to a lifetime job.[12] All incentives pointed in the direction of the preservation of these *corps*.

As the result of the experience of the 1980s, a new consensus on elitism thus prevails today in France. The criticisms of the "system" have been stifled and the rage against "undemocratic institutions that perpetuate inequality" have been dissipated. Since the Left and Right now partake of the system, rare are its critics. No longer is there an opposition that proposes even modifications in the structures that produce the elites. Despite the evolution of the society and of the elite-forming structures, there have been no corresponding attempts to review the basis on which the elitism that characterizes French institutions rests. Whether one believes, therefore, that minor modifications are called for or whether one takes the view that serious structural reforms are in order is wholly irrelevant today.

The present consensus, however, is unhealthy. The lack of debate and the apparent agreement on the part of the major political forces is not the result of a process that involved clashes of opinion. It is a consensus reached through a negation of debate and resting entirely on the self-interest of the governing class. If nothing else, it is a reflection of the chasm that separates the world of politics from the larger society.

That the French elite disposes of considerable privileges is not a matter of conjecture. Indeed, a former director of the Ecole Nationale d'Administration, Roger Fauroux, once observed that the French higher civil service has come to resemble the aristrocracy of the ancien régime, that is, it possesses far too many privileges for the little service it renders. This severe judgment is offered by one of the quintessential products of the French elitist system: a graduate of the *Ecole Normale Superieure* and ENA, an *Inspecteur des Finances*, former president of the Saint-Gobain corporation and, lastly, minister of industry.

Many books published over the past twenty years have adequately documented the restricted social and educational base of the graduates of the major *grandes écoles*. The lack of debate on such a critical issue for the society, indeed the fear of debate itself, raises serious questions about the future of democracy in France. How does the elitist system affect the role of the elected official, of political parties, of the relationship between elite and mass levels of society? Does the elite-producing mechanisms contribute to or detract from the democratic institutions that France has fashioned so successfully over the past three decades? These questions may be more important than the capacities and the performance of the elites. No matter how efficient an elite is, there is no yardstick that will prove that a different system -- such as one based entirely on a climb through the ranks, for example -- would not have provided the same results.

The election of the Left in 1981 was expected to have dramatic consequences for the elitist structures. This critical event in the political life of France was scarcely critical in the life of the elites. The Left has merely ended up legitimizing and reinforcing a system it once criticized.

From Public Service to Self Service

The dominant elite in French society traditionally has originated from state service. It continues to do so today, though within a different kind of *Weltanschauung*. Rather than claiming a higher morality for state service, the elite now prefers to legitimize itself through the precept that it should serve society, not just the state.

The glorification of the state over two centuries created a halo over the public arena. The terms "public interest" or the "general interest," with their Rousseauian and religious overtones, had at least the function of orienting behavior in a communitarian direction. Serving the collectivity was the basis of the public ethic and it was a guidepost for public servants. Today, however, the administration has gone elsewhere for its gratifications. It has joined forces with and become indistinguishable from the political class.

Serving the public interest is today devoid of any noble connotations. The disappearance of a public-minded ethic leaves a vacuum to be filled by competing notions of morality, or allows public servants to entertain the illusion that the absence of a strongly enunciated ethic amounts to an acknowledgment that the times call for a loosening of the straitjacket of morality in which they have been confined. No longer does public virtue confront private vice. If anything, the pendulum has swung in the opposite direction and there is an inclination to equate virtue with the private sector and vice with the public.

The *grand commis* tends to view the state today as merely an antechamber leading to lucrative positions in the private sector. This inevitably places him in an inferior position vis-à-vis his interlocutor in the private sector. As Alain Minc put it: *"François Michelin et le directeur du Trésor dialoguaient de plain-pied, qu'en est-il de Bernard Tapie et d'un jeune administrateur civil?"*[13]

The image of public service has been tarnished in recent years and an important part of this is due to the cultural changes that the society has been undergoing. One of the most striking changes of all is the new respectability accorded the entrepreneur. As in the United States, "new" wealth has risen considerably in people's esteem. Wealth is no longer afraid to show its face. Power is not seen as preferable under all conditions to pecuniary gain. Wealth confers power. Hence the shift away from according public service the nobility it once enjoyed.

The private sector is considered the arena of "action," of initiative, of competition, of wizardry, and, of course, of vast wealth. In a recent survey, executives were asked what *métier* they would like to see their son go into. One can measure many of the social changes in French society through the results: the position of higher civil servant (like a university professor) was near the bottom of the list.[14]

Public service is no longer an end in itself for the *énarques*. The public servants have not remained immune to the value change that now characterizes French society. According to Minc, it takes much more of a public official today to be virtuous than it did in the past.[15]

The decline in the prestige of public service is also due, in part, to its having lost its autonomy and subordinated itself to political control. No longer is it possible for higher civil servants to be seen as independent, upright servants of the state. They very early on proclaim their loyalty to one or another political force.

The third and perhaps most important factor accounting for the decline in the prestige of public service has to do with the fact that the probity of civil servants is no longer an article of faith. Being deeply involved in politics, they inevitably find themselves assuming the methods and mores of the political arena. It may well be that the majority of civil servants remain honest, just as a large number of politicians do. But their honesty can no longer be taken for granted since they have allowed themselves to be placed in the political front line to do the bidding for their patrons. It is not simply that politics has entered public service, it is that the rules governing politics have come to seem inevitable. From this recognition it is but a short step to using the methods of those practicing in the political arena. After which come the expected and well-known rationalizations, "it's a necessary evil," "everyone does it," "you can't do good with nothing," and so on.

The changing cultural mores of the society and the evolution of political organizations and practices have loosened moral constraints on the exercise of politics. Hence, politics in France today is practiced without a stringent ethical code. The distinction between the public and private domains tends to become more and more blurred. Public service is tending to become a career for achieving self-fulfillment and self-enrichment, in more ways than one. And politics is perceived today more as a "school for scoundrels" than as an occupation involving public service, which explains why surveys reveal that two out of three French people believe that their political leaders -- across the political spectrum -- are dishonest.[16]

It was believed that the diminishing role of the state might loosen the grip of the public service elite on other sectors. In fact, Edward Balladur, as the Minister responsible for the privatization program between 1986-1988, claimed that one of the positive consequences of privatization was that it might get rid of "*cette bourgeoisie d'Etat [qui] se recrute et se reproduit dans un cercle restreint.*"[17] One might be willing to accept an undemocratic system where the chosen few "*s'entraident, se jugent, se choisissent, se cooptent, la réciprocité assurant la pérennité de l'influence,*"[18] if only there was a certainty that the best were always chosen. This not being the case, "*le vieux système devait être abandonné.*" Privatization would ensure the introduction of a more efficient and democratic system of leadership.

> En définitive, l'alternative est simple: faut-il résérver tous les postes clés à ceux qui ont reçu une certaine formation privilegiée ou faut-il faire confiance à la vie qui reclasse les talents et fait émerger les mérites? La seconde solution est bien préférable; elle est à la fois plus souple, plus juste et plus démocratique. Pour la mettre en oeuvre, il faut que l'Etat restreigne le champ de son action, se retire largement de la vie économique.[19]

If the Right believed that the "closed caste" system ought to receive a jolt from the disengagement of the state from the economy, the Left believed that this might actually take place. And yet, the self-reproducing system has survived both the fiery Leftist rhetoric of the early 1980s and the threats that privatization posed. Private shareholders have had no different impact on the choice of leaders of industry and banking from that previously exercised by the state.

Privatization appears to have had a far different impact on the elite structure than that envisaged by Balladur. The available evidence suggests that it has opened up new avenues and has encouraged civil servants to leave state service at an earlier age than in the past. A recent study of the *Inspection des Finances* shows that the rate of "*pantouflage*" increased during the 1980s. Moreover, the *Inspecteurs des Finances* make the leap into the private sector at a younger age than they did in the past. The age period that sees the greatest "*pantouflage*" is that between 38 and 40 years, that is, functionaries depart after having attained a prominent post in a ministerial cabinet and in the ministry. Simply put, "*le mouvement de moins d'Etat et de plus d'entreprise a, du point de vue de l'Inspection, commencé en 1982; depuis cette date, le nombre d'Inspecteurs au service de l'Etat diminue.*"[20]

Perhaps the most important consequence of privatization for members of the elite is that it did not lead to the emergence of a "new" elite that was unconnected to state service. The *Inspecteurs des Finances*, for example, remained in their posts after their firms became privatized. More significantly, when *Inspecteurs des Finances* did leave state service they generally found a warm welcome in private firms. *"Au total, l'Inspection constitue un vivier dans lequel les firmes privées n'hésitent pas à puiser: au cours de la période [1980s] plus de la moitié de la population des Inspecteurs pantoufleurs travaille ou a travaillé dans une firme privée."*[21] The Bauer and Danic study shows that *"vis-a-vis des 'premiers pantoufleurs' le secteur privé se montre aujourd'hui aussi accueillant (ou même nettement plus, comme en 1988) que le secteur public."*[22]

State service remains today the royal path to leadership positions in industry and finance. The political and economic changes that have transformed society have in no way lessened the attractiveness of state service. No doubt the significance of state service in and of itself has diminished. It no longer means what it once did. Yet state service remains today an instrument, and still a necessary one, for attaining objectives that are unconnected to that service. One of the most startling phenomena is that even those who attend the prestigious schools of management (HEC, ESSEC) or even graduates of the *Ecole Normale Supérieure*, are likely to seek to enter state service. In fact 30 percent of entrants into the *Inspection des Finances* between 1985-1989 came from schools of management. Rather than moving into the private sector after obtaining their management school diploma, they chose to enter ENA, work for the state and only then move into the private sector. Reaching the top of the private sector is clearly facilitated by state service. This distinctive career path is more prevalent today than in the past.

The question of why one should seek to enter state service in the first place is easily answered: to enter one of the *grands corps*. Why would one seek to enter, say, the *Inspection des Finances*? The answer, based on a study of the careers of members of this corps is:

> Hier, c'était pour servir l'Etat; et sauf exception, ce n'était qu'après avoir realisé ce rêve que l'on pantouflait pour finir sa vie professionnelle dans une grande entreprise.
>
> Aujourd'hui, c'est surtout pour devenir dirigeant d'une entreprise. Les brillants élèves qui veulent accèder rapidement au sommet d'une entreprise ont compris (ils sont brillants...) que les entreprises ne detectent pas elles-mêmes leurs dirigeants mais soustraitent ce travail aux grands corps d'Etat. Ils font donc tout pour entrer dans un grand corps et, sauf s'ils sont ingénieurs, de préférence à l'Inspection, qui assure, plus que le Conseil d'Etat ou la Cour des Comptes, des débouchés. On comprend qu'ensuite, en grand nombre, et parfois même sitôt que leurs quatre années de tournées terminées, ils pantouflent.[23]

The Appeal of Politics

Public officials in France are not held to higher moral or ethical standards than other citizens. In fact, unlike the United States, quite the contrary is the case. The laws are stretched for politicians and politicians stretch the law.

Public officials, whether elected or whether civil servants, benefit from the imposing aura of the state they represent. The elected official -- mayor, deputy, senator -- has over the years accorded himself generous material advantages. Rarely have any of these advantages been subject to public scrutiny and outrage. In part, this has to do with deference toward authority and in part, it is the consequence of a certain cynicism toward those in power. Much is expected from the state, yet, those in power are not especially expected to set an example of probity. If they manage to get things done, it will be understood if they took some unconventional means to achieve their end. Besides, the view has become widespread that those in politics are in it neither for their health nor to do good. They are there to exercise power, take care of themselves, of their friends, and of their party. If, in the process some good is done for the society, so much the better.

Politics has always been an honorable career, even if many dishonorable men have been attracted to the *métier*. Politics in France is a calling because politics itself permeates the society. Hence, exercising this profession is a way of serving the higher interests of the society. In turn, the politicians are adequately compensated by power, or the illusion of power, and the perquisites that befit this profession. Politicians receive considerable attention in the media. Often the speeches, press conferences, and movements of politicians that might not rate a mention in other societies occupy much space in the media.

There is an obsession with politicians and with politics that has only grown over the years (even as disenchantment with politicians has experienced a parallel growth). The fascination with politics and the ability of this profession to continue to attract "the best and the brightest" may be explained by three main factors: the role of the state, the relative stability of the political career, and the institution of the presidential regime.

Serving the state has been a great calling in France whether this involved serving Kings, or Emperors, or the people. Colbert, Tallyrand, and Jaurès are people who left their mark on French society through their work as politicians. In a society that accorded so much power to its state, those who controlled the state apparatus would be the beneficiaries -- or at least the representatives -- of that power. Politicians could dispense jobs, contracts, favors. The respect they have been accorded in France is the direct result of the power that the state has accumulated. Centralization has thus helped to add to the importance that politicians have traditionally been accorded in France.

Nor has this *métier* acquired a smaller role as a result of the more recent moves toward the decentralization of politics and administration. For one thing, the limelight that shines on national politicians casts a large enough glow to shine on local politicians, in part as a result of the '*cumul*' phenomenon whereby the leading national politicians were also leading local politicians. This phenomenon is uniquely French. But France has accommodated itself to this practice, whose origins lie in centralized decision making. Representing a constituency required a strong voice, and a mayor of a medium-sized town did not carry sufficient weight to be able to achieve much for his constituency. Serving as both mayor and deputy, he could represent his constituency before the central administration in one or the other capacity.

The leading politicians in France all dispose of a mayoral office, which they abandon only when they become president of the Republic. Jacques Chaban-Delmas has remained mayor of Bordeaux since 1947 and he has never felt the need to choose between being mayor of this city of over 1 million inhabitants and being a deputy, a minister, president of the National Assembly, and even prime minister. Jacques Chirac has been mayor of Paris for over a dozen years, all the while being either a deputy from another region (the Corrèze) or, on two occasions, prime minister. During all this time he has also been head of the RPR party. The only slightly anomalous aspect of Chirac's various representative roles is that he represents a constituency in the National Assembly that is located in one part of the country while being the chief elected official of a city that is both located in another part of the country and is also the largest city in the nation. Gaston Deferre ruled over the city of Marseille for over thirty years and did not abandon this political base while he was a presidential candidate or during his last years as a minister in the Socialist governments of the 1980s. Nor is the cumulation of offices a phenomenon unique to the Fifth Republic. Edouard Herriot, for example, was one of the leading politicians throughout the postwar period. He remained mayor of Lyon for forty years even as he was a minister and prime minister in the governments of the Fourth Republic. Politicians of all parties seek a local political base. And rare is the politician who is not a mayor, or a municipal councilor, or head of a regional council.

The '*cumul*' phenomenon can be explained only in part by the strength that it gives to the representative function. A more powerful reason can be found in the need to establish a political base that provides the necessary resources to maintain a political career. The greater the resources, the greater the capacity to serve one's career and one's party as well as one's ability to dispense favors.

The mayor of a small or medium-size city disposes of a staff as well as numerous other resources that go with the function. Today, as a result of decentralization, he disposes of considerable powers to construct housing and schools, to affect zoning regulations, to allocate tax revenues, and to grant building permits. Consequently, a local base for a national politician has today become important not merely for the assurance it provides when one has fallen from grace at the

national level (as when one ceases being a minister), but also, more importantly, for the power to satisfy clients who then reciprocate when the need arises.

The relationship between local authorities and clients has reached alarming
proportions in large cities. A mayor of the city of Paris is in a position to provide
many contracts -- whether for the construction of buildings, road repairs, garbage
collection, or even the furnishing of light bulbs and door handles. Such contracts
can lead to the success of an enterprise, and they generally come at a price, which
is support for the party in power. Contracts generally make allowances for the
amount to be turned back to the party that granted the contract. Obviously, the
city of Paris, which may be regarded as one of the largest enterprises in France, is
in a category of its own. But there are many other local functions that approxi-
mate the power and resources of the mayor of the city of Paris. Certain general
councils, like that of the Haute-de-Seine in the Paris region, which is one of the
richest local communities in France, accord their leaders similar powers. The
General Council of the Haute-de-Seine is headed by Charles Pasqua, a former
secretary general of the RPR and currently minister of interior. His position
within his party was considerably enhanced when he attained this post. He also
continues to serve as a senator from this department.

Politics in France continues to have an appeal as a career because of its ability to provide secure bases with considerable resources for politicians. Furthermore, because executive bodies at all levels have acquired additional powers,
mayors and the heads of the municipal, departmental, and regional councils have
become more powerful figures. The accumulation of functions has contributed to
creating secure bases for the politicians.

The second reason that makes politics an appealing career is that the development of national political parties creates a support community. One consequence of this is that it renders the political career relatively stable. All the
leading politicians in France are secure in their political base, whether this be a
mayoral office or whether it is a high-ranking position within the party. Nor are
such politicians likely to lose their seats in the National Assembly. The loss of a
place in the assembly generally only occurs when a deputy becomes a minister, at
which time he is obliged by law to relinquish his seat to his chosen stand-in.

The development of nationally organized and disciplined parties has entailed
the extinction of the atomized or independent politician. The party today provides a home, a base, a springboard for a politician. A major political career is
scarcely possible without the backing of a political party. François Mitterrand
conducted his career under the Fourth Republic outside of the major parties. The
Fifth Republic, however, consigns the political loner to the wilderness. With the
demise of the Fourth Republic Mitterrand joined and subsequently transformed
the Socialist Party into the machine that nominated him as its presidential candidate and helped him to win the presidency.

In the Fifth Republic, a national position has also regularly facilitated the development of a local power base. Many a politician who came to prominence as a member of a government was subsequently able to convert his national standing into a local position of strength. Michel Noir, a minister in the 1986-1988 Center-Right government was subsequently elected mayor of Lyon. Michel Delebarre, who acquired a remarkable reputation as minister of social affairs, subsequently became a leading politician in the Socialist Party and mayor of Dunkirk. Jack Lang and Henri Nallet both established a local power base after coming to prominence as ministers.

A centralized political system is also more apt to facilitate national prominence among aspiring politicians. This is because breaking into the national structures may pose fewer problems than making one's way up a ladder that begins at the local level and ends at the national level. The existence of highly competitive schools located in Paris creates networks that lead into a political party. When Jacques Attali and Laurent Fabius embarked on their political careers they started out as advisors to the first secretary of the Socialist Party, François Mitterrand. Like their counterparts on the Right they began opening doors for others like themselves that led to the Socialist Party. Many of those that passed through these doors today occupy leadership positions throughout French society.[24] Once inside the larger family, whether Socialist or Gaullist, there is a certain stability that the politician comes to experience. He can, at any rate, expect rewards and promotions.[25]

For all these reasons, a political career exerts a strong attraction for many an ambitious person. This includes members of France's administrative elites. Indeed, an important outlet for these officials, once they have exhausted their promotion possibilities with the state, is the political arena. In part, this is because these civil servants reach the apex of their hierarchy at an early age and so need to seek new goals. In part, it is also because these officials are in constant contact with politicians. Their functions are often not all that different from the tasks performed by their political superiors, and perhaps what the latter do appears considerably more exciting or rewarding. Thirdly, as more and more civil servants have moved into the political arena since the beginning of the Fifth Republic, a vast network has been established between the politicians and the civil servants. Many of the leading politicians in the country, on the Left and the Right, are former civil servants. Political careers can be made through the civil service elite, and since those civil servants are among the best trained in the society, the political class as a whole benefits from recruiting those considered to be among the "best and brightest."

There is a final factor that explains the pull of a political career, or at least the need to be associated with a political family: the presidentializing of the political system. This process has politicized careers that formerly might not have been deemed political. Indeed, in combination with the other changes in

French society discussed above, the impact has been to complete the eradication of boundaries between the administration and the political class.

Presidentialism and Administrative Politicization

Much has been written in recent years about the politicization of the French bureaucracy. And yet the belief remains that this is a fairly contained phenomenon, unlike the "spoils system" that is perceived to operate in the United States. Despite the important changes that have taken place in the political and administrative spheres over the past thirty years, this myth has retained much of its force. But the reality is altogether different. Today France, rather than the United States, more closely approaches, if not a spoils system, then a genuine politicization of administrative personnel. This development is the result of two simultaneous factors: on the one hand, the institutions under the state's control remained in the hands of a single political force (the Center-Right) for almost twenty-five years; on the other hand, the political system became a presidential one, a factor that assumed considerable importance in light of the fact that presidentialism was superimposed on a centralized administrative structure.

A newly elected U.S. president is far more restricted in his powers of nomination than his French counterpart. There are about 2,600,000 federal civil servants in the United States. A president names between 2,500-3,000 of these and the most important among them (cabinet secretaries, Supreme Court justices, ambassadors) must be confirmed by the Senate. Implicit in this power to effect changes at the top of the administrative hierarchy is the recognition that a president needs to have officials loyal to him and his policies even at the cost of a certain degree of instability. But, beyond the power to name a relatively small number of federal officials, a U.S. president has no say whatsoever in the placing of officials at the state and local level, nor in placing officials in other sectors of the economy and the society.

In France, what actually takes place is considerably more far reaching. First, with respect to the central administration, the highest officials are eventually replaced after the arrival of a newly appointed government. Then there are changes in other sectors where the state is present: the nationalized industries and banks, education, culture, and the audiovisual media. In short, there is practically no sector where the government does not have a say in the nominations of the directors. This is the stuff of which U.S. presidents can only dream!

This development has accelerated during the past thirty years and is the result of the bipolarization of the political (and party) system and of the presidentialization of this system. The appropriation of this power of nomination by a president may not have been inevitable. It has become so as a result of the political mores instituted by the Center-Right between 1958-1981. This political majority gradually began distributing posts to its own loyalists. It began by colonizing the upper reaches of the civil service, then extended this practice to the nationalized sector, and, finally, to sectors that had traditionally escaped the clutches of political nominations. Having been excluded from the administrative, industrial, financial, and cultural sectors for twenty-five years, the Left in 1981 proceeded to name its own loyalists to posts in all these sectors.

Much attention has been devoted to the abuse of the power of nomination by François Mitterrand. Jean-François Revel, in his castigation of the presidential system as despotic, irresponsible, monarchical, and anti-democratic, tends to place much of the blame on Mitterrand. Yet, as he himself recognizes, no president of the Fifth Republic has ever delegated (as he is legally entitled) any aspect of the power of nomination.[26] Nor does he detail the abuses of the power of nomination perpetrated by former presidents. "L'Etat-UDR" (or RPR), or "l'Etat-Giscard" were no mere fictions. Has Mitterrand stretched the power of nomination? Has he shown less concern for competence and more for loyalty? Undoubtedly. Yet, what is at issue is not who commits more faults, but rather the recognition that such abuses are endemic to the system. There is a need to consider how such abuses can be checked. Even today, however, the Right, which claims to be scandalized by the Mitterrand practice of taking care of loyalists, has not put forward any proposals that would curtail the power of nomination that all presidents of the Fifth Republic have enjoyed. Quite simply, as Jacques Chevallier observes, administrative '*alternance*' is now simply viewed as accompanying political '*alternance*.'[27]

The constitution of the Fifth Republic has encouraged the politicization of all institutions linked to the state. The result has been to give a power to successive presidents that is unlike the power possessed by any other democratically elected head of state. In Germany, the federal system limits the Chancellor's power of nominations. In Italy, the sharing of power by several political parties ensures that no one wins or loses all. In the United States, decentralization and congressional power severely limit the president's prerogatives in this domain. In France, centralization and presidentialism give the president remarkable powers to name personnel in a wide range of sectors that includes the higher civil service (which itself includes sectors as varied as transportation, justice, the police, the postal service, education, the museums, the theater, the opera, the audio-visual industry, media, banks, industries, and insurance companies). In other words, the power of nomination touches a variety of sectors that are not normally considered political.

Such a system obliges those aspiring to the top positions in all of these sectors to take sides in the political arena. Enjoying the fruits of victory requires a prior commitment, and not only from politicians. For the most part, only political loyalists will be rewarded. Providing support for a presidential candidate is the surest way to rapid promotion. Since the president and prime minister dispose of important powers of appointments to prestigious and lucrative jobs, picking the right horse assumes critical importance. Indeed, so many careers are now politically dependent that a political commitment is a sine qua non for an appointment to a multitude of posts that depend on executive prerogative. Even within a political party, aspiring politicians, or those who depend on political appointments, need to choose well among the rival political factions. As a consequence, the "independent politician" has become an oxymoron. One must choose sides and one is well rewarded for choosing correctly.

This is not strictly speaking a "spoils system," which implies a total disregard for professional competence. Nominations in France can always be justified by a minimal level of competence because France has mechanisms for producing an elite whose members may not always be qualified for specific posts but who are rarely wholly incompetent. Yet there is little doubt that political considerations are becoming more important than the possession of professional qualifications in the management of a career.

The members of France's governing elite carry out functions and occupy posts for which they were not trained. *"Les grands corps donnent en quelque sorte une habilitation à vie à l'exercise des grands décisions,"* noted François de Closets, who headed the *Commission sur l'Efficacité de l'Etat* and who concluded that it would be best if the *grands corps* were abolished.[28] The Socialist governments of the 1980s have preferred to leave the administrative structures intact and to utilize the power of nomination in much the same way that their opponents did. The lesson has not been lost on the civil servants: under the Fifth Republic, career success in the administration, in politics and in the private sector, come more easily to those who undertake political commitments. As Danièle Lockhak observes, the crisis within the public sector also encourages higher civil servants to seek gratification beyond the civil service.[29]

The presidential nature of the regime, cultural changes within the society, and the crisis within the public sector have all contributed to bringing an end to the era of a professional, "neutral" bureaucracy. It was an ideal that was not always adhered to, but it served a purpose all the same. It provided a symbol, a standard by which deviations were measured. Public service was an honored and prestigious profession. Today, that is no longer the case. The public sector is a way-station, a stepping-stone to other careers.

What was once the exception has become the norm. The criterion for a higher civil servant's climb depends today on his political choice and commitment. If political loyalty was a cause for promotion in the past, this was considered an aberration that confirmed the general principle of administrative professionalism, a principle that is no longer considered profitable. And therein lies a profound change in the manner of conducting the public's affairs.[30]

Conclusion

The immense weight of the bureaucracy in a centralized state has been a standard theme in any analysis of French society for almost two centuries. The bureaucracy filled in when politicians and political parties could not agree. In due course, the vast bureaucratic apparatus acquired a considerable degree of autonomy and many a minister complained that his choices were dictated, and often his decisions made, by the civil servants in his ministry. The power and autonomy of bureaucratic agencies led to the characterization of France as a *"République des fonctionnaires."* Civil servants seemed to be everywhere, and particularly in places where they were not expected to be: in ministerial cabinets, in ministerial posts, as presidents of the Republic, as presidents of industrial corporations and banks, and as deputies.

In abandoning even the semblance of neutrality, civil servants, in effect, have conceded their autonomy and modified their status. Hence, France today is a society in which an elitist structure furnishes civil servants with immense prestige and privileges, but where those civil servants no longer run the country behind the backs of politicians. Civil servants embrace the political wind and they submit to political choices. In one sense, politics has thus reasserted its proper role. And the major political decisions, those that move the society in one direction or another, can no longer be sabotaged by civil servants.

Politicization, then, has brought about the long-desired objective of political control of the bureaucracy. The long-term consequences of the "spoils system" are that a government will have a less efficient machine for implementing its policies, but one that is operated by ideologically or politically loyal servants. As civil servants abandon the public ethic, which appears frayed and outmoded, and embrace new practices and different ethics, they effectively come to blend much more easily with other elites in the society. Where once they distinguished themselves by rectitude and probity, they now do what "reality" imposes. Where once they took pride in serving the collectivity, today it is "individual initiative" that matters. Where once serving the public was an honor, today it is almost a source of embarrassment to be explained as "temporary." The state is there to be used as a vehicle for the promotion of a career and for eventual self-enrichment.

The stability of elite structures belies the modification that has occurred in elite practices, ethics, and mores. The process of "branching out," of becoming an "all-service" elite has inevitably brought with it a greater capacity for adaptation to changing economic, political, and cultural conditions.

The elitist structures have few detractors today, even if they have equally few who are willing to extol their virtues. These structures have achieved a degree of legitimacy that they scarcely possessed in the past. The system is no longer subject to debate and controversy. It has achieved what it has always sought -- power that can be exercised discreetly.

The system of generalized, "polyvalent" elites has always been vulnerable because of its narrow class basis. This, no longer being an issue, has effectively removed the elite as a target of attack. As the elite has blended in with the society – particularly the leadership class in finance, industry, local and national politics – it no longer provides a unique target for those seeking to account for incompetence and for fiascos. It is covered throughout by protective shields. This is one area where calls for reform and for change have been dropped from all political platforms and from public debates.

Notes

1. The works of Pierre Bourdieu, starting with *Les Héritiers* (Paris: Editions de Minuit, 1962), and culminating with *Noblesse d'Etat* (Paris: Editions de Minuit, 1989) have been the most influential in attacking the mechanisms of elite production.

2. The most comprehensive analysis of the relationship between the Left (in opposition and in power) and the administration is to be found in Jacques Chevallier, "*La Gauche et la haute administration sous la cinquième République,*" in *La Haute administration et la politique* (Paris: Presses Universitaires de France 1988), pp. 9-48.

3. *Le Monde*, 20 June 1982.

4. Yves Agnés, "L'Administration et le changement: I. Vers l'Etat-P.S.?" *Le Monde*, 29 June 1982, p. 7. See the series of articles by Agnés that includes those published 30 and 31 June 1982, in *Le Monde*.

5. See Pierre Birnbaum, eds., *Les Elites Socialistes au pouvoir 1981-1985* (Paris: Presses Universitaires de France, 1989), and A. Wickham and S. Coignard, *La Nomenklatura française: pouvoirs et privilèges des élites* (Paris: Belfond, 1986).

6. Cited in Eric Rhode, "L'ENA a-t-elle échoué?" *Le Monde de l'Education*, April 1982, p. 55.

7. *Le Monde*, 7 October 1982.

8. Ibid.

9. André Passeron, "Ni 'chasse aux sorcières' ni sabotage," *Le Monde*, 23 February 1982.

10. See Monique Dagnaud and Dominique Mehl, *L'Elite rose: sociologie du pouvoir socialiste* (Paris: Editions Ramsay, 1988).

11. See *Débat*, no. 53 (January-February 1989).

12. President Mitterrand and his governments did not hesitate to name loyalists, some of whom had neither competence nor aptitude, for jobs in the *grands corps*.

13. Alain Minc, *L'Argent fou* (Paris: Grasset, 1990), p. 59.

14. *Figaro-Magazine*, 23 June 1990, p. 74.

15. Ibid.

16. *L'Express*, 20 April 1990, p. 8.

17. Edouard Balladur, *Je Crois en l'homme plus qu'en l'Etat* (Paris: Flammarion, 1987), p. 49.

18. Ibid.

19. Ibid., p. 52.

20. Michel Bauer and Dominique Danic, *L'Inspection des Finances: 16 ans de pantouflage, 1974-1989* (Paris: ENRS-Heidrick and Struggles, N.D.), p. 13.

21. Ibid., p. 25.

22. Ibid.

23. Ibid. , p. 30.

24. See Wickham and Coignard, *La Nomenklatura française*, and Dagnaud and Miehl, *L'Elite Rose.*

25. Even a politician not known for Godfather-like qualities, Michael Rocard, has seen to it that those who have aided him in his years as prime minister have been well rewarded. See Bertrand Le Gendre, "L'Ecurie Rocard au petit trot," *Le Monde*, 30 November 1990.

26. Jean-François Revel, *L'Absolutisme inefficace ou contre le présidentialisme à la française* (Paris: Plon, 1992), p. 89.

27. Chevallier, *"La Gauche et la haute administration,"* p. 32.

28. See *Le Nouvel Observateur*, pp. 12-18, October 1989.

29. See Danièle Lockhak, "Les hauts fonctionnaires et l'alternance," *Association Française de Science Politique Colloque*, 7 and 8 February 1991, p. 17.

30. In their quest for highly remunerative posts in the private sector, higher civil servants have openly disregarded the law (article 72 of the *Code Pénal*), which forbids civil servants from occupying posts in the private sector that they previously had relations with. There have been flagrant violations of this law, and no civil servant has ever been sanctioned for a violation. The government of Michel Rocard issued a decree (January 1991) creating a *"Commission de déontologie"* that is charged with the responsibility of examining cases of civil servants who choose to go to work for an industry that they previously controlled. See *Le Monde*, 23-24 December 1990.

9

The Reconstruction
and De-Construction
of the French Party System

Yves Mény

Crudely summarized, the French party system is the manifestation of a re-sounding failure. France has never been able to transform the fundamental cleavage of political life (the Left-Right antagonism) into a system of parties capable of representing this division. While supposedly inescapable, the "modernization" of the French elite parties has never occurred, or rather has never been fully realized. And that which proved impossible to achieve while the Left-Right cleavage was at its height will be even more difficult to attain now that this cleavage has lost a great deal of its meaning and its capacity to explain political life.

If there remains anything left of French exceptionalism, it is undoubtedly located in France's difficulty in organizing and structuring intermediary organizations between society and the state and, chief among these, the political parties. The much-vaunted civil society, despite the attention it receives in political discourse or in those circles that attempt to "rethink" politics, has been but a convenient facade. It disguises the incapacity of groups throughout the society to move beyond sporadic mobilizations to a more structured and stable organization of interests; and it hides the incapacity of the political world to renew its ideas and its members. As Pierre Rosanvallon has emphasized, "To believe that the political system is viable simply because it is continually capable of devouring pieces of civil society is rather negative."[1]

The current crisis of French political parties is not new. It has become more severe, however; in addition to the historical difficulties surrounding the con-

struction of a party system, France now also faces those challenges common to
the entire Western world that flow from the economic crisis, the transformation
of values, and the collapse of communism.[2] Party systems, and the structures of
mediation more generally, have been weakened everywhere in Western Europe --
in Great Britain as well as in Italy and Germany. But the French situation is
particularly delicate even if it does not affect, at least not yet, the governability of
the country. Today it is clear that political stability, and the capacity to govern
effectively, are more a result of "the art of politics" than structure, and are the
product of institutionalized bargains rather than a solid party system in the sense
that we usually understand that term in the other European democracies.

This chapter first discusses in depth the basic weaknesses that have plagued
the French party system, including those aspects particularly pronounced during
the Fifth Republic. The second section turns to look specifically at the changes
that have in fact taken place from the late 1970s to the early 1990s. The chapter
then concludes on the pessimistic note with which it has begun -- there is little
indication amid all of the changes in France that politics has moved toward a
more structured mediation of competing interests in French society.

The Congenital Weaknesses of the
French Party System

Aside from the French Communist Party (PCF), all of the political parties
have been characterized by weakness, especially when one considers them in a
comparative perspective. Even the parties that have tried to organize themselves
more effectively have historically done so on ambiguous foundations. The Section française de l'internationale ouvrière (SFIO) was created to respond to the
challenge represented by the German Social Democratic Party within the Second
International. The Gaullist "party" in its various guises refused for a long time
even to consider itself a party and satisfied itself with being a mere tool of its
leader. The Catholics also refused the party label, claiming rather to be a "movement" (Mouvement républicain populaire: MRP) or carefully avoiding the term
"party" altogether (Progress and Modern Democracy, Centrists, etc.). It is as if
the elites, but also public opinion, have not been able to shake a basic schizophrenia: on the one hand, the conviction that profound cleavages divide the French
(at least, until recently); and on the other hand, a profound, almost visceral reluctance to translate these divisions into an organized structure. The old denigration
of divisive parties, practiced by revolutionaries and conservatives alike, remains
profoundly anchored in French culture.

Based on fragile foundations, French political parties are weakened by three
traditional traits of the political system that have been further accentuated by the
evolution of the Fifth Republic: the hold that *notables* have gained over partisan

organizations; the fragmentation and instability of parties; and the lack of personal and financial resources.

The first of these traits is the key to the others. The *notables* are a central feature of French political life, and are a kind of Republican aristocracy. Unlike the traditional aristocracy, the status of the *notable* is purely political, and can be acquired through hard work or by being annointed, or both, but not by birth. The parallel lies in the use of a local power base to achieve influence in the national political arena. Today, the most conspicuous characteristic of *notable* status comes through the cumulation of offices from the local, the regional, and the national levels. The *notables* have retained a grip on organized political life in France in a way that has profoundly retarded the growth of more "modern" political structures.

As numerous historical studies have shown, the development of large mass political organizations in France has been inhibited by a number of factors, especially the forms of French political socialization, the country's social structure (principally, the role of the peasantry), and the conditions surrounding the implementation of universal suffrage. Later attempts such as the SFIO partly failed or suffered because of the divisions among the workers. Only the Communist Party seemed to respond to the model of the modern political party, in this case in the service of a movement seeking the revolutionary conquest of power.

Until the dawn of the Fifth Republic, only the PCF could claim to escape the hold of the *notables*; their grip was firm on the Right and the Center, and deeply perverted the functioning of the SFIO. To this first exception was added another, equally deliberate: that of the Gaullist movement. The Gaullists were created -- at least so was the wish of General de Gaulle -- outside of and in opposition to the *notables*. A whole series of political, institutional, and electoral initiatives substituted a layer of new players for the elitist old guard, so as better to permit the modernization of the country. The brutal confrontation that followed ended with the apparent victory of the Gaullists in 1962.

But the worm was already in the fruit. Gaullism was actually able to install itself thanks to the support of moderate *notables*, and Pompidou himself was more in phase with the traditional structuring of the political class than with the new elites that Gaullist technocrats had tried to foster. In 1969, the defeat of the Gaullist vision was complete and the *notables* on the right regained control.

The same process of renovation would take place within the new Socialist Party (PS) under the leadership of François Mitterrand, who himself would also try with some success to substitute new elites for the old political bosses of the SFIO. But the PS ultimately experienced the same drift as the Gaullist movement, even though the reason and the processes were reversed. The Gaullists, powerful at the top, needed to sink roots, which created opportunities for the *notables* to insert themselves into the party around the country. For their part, the Socialists had roots in the form of local bastions of strength, particularly after the municipal elections of 1977, which they would use as a springboard to attain power. But the conquest from below also had the effect of turning the young Turks of the PS into *notables*. One after another would exploit to the limits the possibility of cumulating offices, which is extremely functional in the double quest for an anchorage at the base and the conquest of the summit.

One cannot emphasize enough that even if the cumulation of offices is one of the most solid and best accepted conventions of French political life, it has never been as systematic as it is today. Only a third of the deputies cumulated offices at the end of the Third Republic (35.6 percent in 1936). The figure was still only 42 percent in 1956, but the practice has increased rapidly under the Fifth Republic. The threshold of 70 percent was attained in 1973 and in 1988, 519 deputies out of 540, or 96 percent, held a local office! (See Table 9.1.) In short, the Fifth Republic, born in opposition to the *notables*, has become completely dominated by them.

Even the Communist Party, which refrained from resorting to cumulation in order to avoid what it called "municipal cretinism" (in fact, the fear that the management of local problems would affect the doctrinal "purity" of party leaders), was forced, whether it liked it or not, to submit to the political logic *of notabilization*: the alternative in reality was either to elect a red *notable* or to lose the election. In the municipal elections of 1989, there were even cases of communist mayors, who had broken with the party, defeating the official candidate of the PCF. In the city of Le Mans for example, the dissident communist mayor was triumphantly elected in the first round, despite the presence of an outsider officially backed by the party. In other words, even within the most Jacobin and most centralized party, local roots prevail over party allegiance. The PCF can console itself about this "perversion" by noting that it only really survives as an ongoing organization thanks to its local strongholds.

The second characteristic weakness of the political system has been the fragmentation and instability of parties. These two conditions are in part linked to the phenomenon of the *notables* just mentioned. In reality, quite often that which is labeled a party is really only an archipelago. At a distance, there appears to be a structural unity, but the reality is a large diversity of opinions and factions. Within such *parties*, the internal structures are "territorialized." The leaders of each "territory" are supported by a solid stronghold and a reasonably sized clientele and use the party more than they serve it. At the very least, when a local leader feels sufficiently strong without yet being capable of taking control of the party, he distances himself from it. The most extreme examples of this voluntary "marginalization" are Michel Noir in Lyon, Alain Carignon in Grenoble, Jean Monnier in Angers, Jean Royer in Tours, and Robert Vigouroux in Marseille. In other respects, party labels constitute convenient indications of orientation of the elected official on the political landscape, but tell little about real allegiances, programmatic orientations, or indeed even ideological choices.

During the Fifth Republic, it may seem that there was major progress toward institutionalizing and rationalizing the party system. The gathering of the Right under the mantel of de Gaulle and then Pompidou, the experience of a union of

TABLE 9.1 Notables in the National Assembly, 1978-1988

Offices held at election	1978*		1981		1986		1988		Total	
	no.	%	no.	%	no.	%	no.	%	no.	%
Mayor	235	48	246	50	244	42	262	45	987	46
Mayor: municipality of over 20,000 inhabitants	98	20	90	18	107	19	96	17	397	18
Adjoint	21	4	35	7	50	9	63	11	169	8
Conseiller Général**	256	52	230	47	262	45	279	48	1027	48
Mayor + cons. gén.	145	30	121	25	146	25	147	25	559	26
Regional councillor***					113	20	141	24	254	12
Mayor + regional councillor	n/a		n/a		31	5	61	11	92	4
Mayor + regional councillor + cons. gén					15	3	24	4	39	2
Any two local offices	164	33	135	27	231	40	298	52	828	39
Any one local office	363	74	364	74	450	78	490	85	1635	78
Incumbent Deputy	292	59	286	58	319	55	380	66	1277	60
Total in any of the above categories	424	86	421	86	492	86	559	97	1896	89
Total Deputies in National Assembly	491	100	491	100	577	100	577	100	2136	100

*Michel Reydellet ('Le Cumul des Mandats,' Revue de Droit Public, 1979, p. 723) gives somewhat higher figures for 1978, using Le Monde corrected by National Assembly statistics (264 mayors, 49 adjoints, 36 municipal councillors, 261 conseillers généraux, and a total of 389 local elected officials).

** Includes Paris councillors.

***From 1972 to 1986, all Deputies were ex officio regional councillors. In 1986, regional councillors were elected on the day of the parliamentary elections.

Sources: Le Monde, complemented by National Assembly figures for 1986 and 1988.

the Left, and above all the recomposition of the PS would all make one think that France would realize the benefits of bipolarization even if an English-style bipartisan system remained unrealistic. Some rejoiced in the discovery that a four-party bipolar structure would reconcile stability and pluralism. Conversely, others -- the excluded ones -- complained loudly about "the gang of four," accusing them of monopolizing the political game to the detriment of emerging forces within society.

Hardly was this summit reached when centrifugal forces regained the upper hand. Not only, as we will see below, were new forces attempting to emerge, but the traditional parties were racked by profound internal tensions. In its party congress in Rennes in 1990, the Socialist Party, which had always accepted internal factions, provided the sad spectacle of a deeply divided party, without an accepted leader and without a credible program. More seriously, the Rassemblement pour la République (RPR) and the PCF, which had in their different ways tried to maintain the unity of their party, themselves experienced the pangs of fractionalization. By the late eighties, neither of them was in a position to engage any longer in the *exclusions* or purges that would have permitted it to maintain the supremacy of the leadership or the purity of the party line. The Maastricht referendum fully revealed this implosion of the parties and the party system. For all practical purposes, only the National Front, and to a lesser extent the PCF, were able to maintain a more or less unified party line on Maastricht.

The third weakness of the French parties flows from their meager resources, in human terms as well as in organizational and financial terms. There is no need to dwell upon this well-known aspect of the French party system. Let us, however, emphasize certain elements. Traditionally, the French party has had few (or no!) militants. The case of Olivier Stirn, minister of overseas development in the Rocard government, paying unemployed workers to fill a room is certainly a caricature. But it serves as the extreme example of a tragic situation, namely the inability or the limited ability of the parties to achieve significant mobilization of a militant base. Under the Fifth Republic, only two parties (the PCF and the RPR) have been capable of attracting and seducing a respectable number of actual members. But in both cases, the image of the metro -- which fills up and empties out at each station -- has considerable validity, so significant is the turnover among militants. To a lesser extent and especially at the end of the 1970s, the Socialist Party was also capable of constructing a militant base. However, this heterogenous conglomerate constructed from diverse socialist strata -- ranging from those nostalgic for 1968 to representatives of the middle class hoping for a change, to some real opportunists -- was destined to fray with the application (or non-application) of the Socialist program. Today, the French parties are anemic, as are the unions. Both have become "professionals of representation" (politically and socially) but are no longer movements of collective mobilization.

Organizational and financial resources are equally limited. With the exception, once again, of the PCF and in certain respects the Gaullist movement,[3] the political parties are incapable of providing themselves with an effective organization. The two major factors discussed above have probably contributed to this shortcoming. On the one hand, the dominance of *notables* constitutes at once a substitute for and a barrier against a strong organization; on the other hand, the absence of militants removes a major justification that might have permitted such organization. It is significant that until 1988 -- the time, incidentally, of the law instituting the financing of electoral campaigns -- the French political parties had neither an official status nor an applicable *ad hoc* legal framework. Some were informal groupings, others resorted to using the law of 1901 regulating the right of association.

Relying neither upon the unions as typical social democratic parties tend to do, nor upon strong militantism, and not benefitting from official public financing, the parties lived -- and still live -- "from week to week" or on the basis of informal arrangements. Quite often, at the local level, the parties possess neither an office, nor any infrastructure, nor even a telephone: to look up a party in a phone book is for all intents and purposes futile, except in the big cities. In the small towns, the parties simply do not have a formal existence; elsewhere, they find refuge either in the mayor's office or in an office of the *Departement* and they survive thanks to the logistic and material support of the local authorities. The opposition obviously has even more limited resources unless there is an exceptional (and rather recent) local consensus. In this logistical and material desert, it is not surprising that obtaining resources by any and all means -- including illegal means -- has gradually become systematic.[4]

Finally, to all of these historical and structural weaknesses of the French party system, the Fifth Republic has added another by depriving the parties of one of their essential functions: the role of mediator between the population and executive power. Up to 1958, the Parliament constituted the central arena of political life even if its symbolic role took priority over reality in many respects. The Fifth Republic, paradoxically, recognizes the parties in the constitution -- a first for France, following what had been done in Germany and Italy after World War II -- even though its founder subjected them to public censure. But in reality, this innovation serves all the better to limit their role: the parties, according to the Constitution, contribute to the expression of the right of suffrage. That is all. No other function is envisioned for them and the French system is thus the exact opposite of the *Parteienstaat* or the *Partitocrazia*.

The essence of the Fifth Republic is found in Article 4: the parties are no more than useful tools in the electoral process. The parties of preceding Republics were not especially healthy. With the Fifth Republic, they have become simple electoral machines that are necessary in certain respects for the "mother of all elections," the presidential election, or to guarantee a faithful majority in Parliament. But their mission stops there and it is a small mission at that.

The Recent Evolution of the Party System:
Phases and Causes

Over the past fifteen years, the evolution of the party system has been rather chaotic and must be understood in terms of various political, electoral, and ideological and social factors. These have combined to ensure the failure of any real reconstitution of French political parties into a system that would deserve the name.

Political Factors

The attempts to reconstruct the party system in the Fifth Republic were in large measure focused on the desirability of giving the president a stable parliamentary majority. For the Right, the period from 1962 to 1974 was the golden age of the new system. Before 1962, the majority was circumstantial and fragile. After 1974, the largest party in the government was no longer the party of the president, even if it supported him. In other words, in the *septennat* of Giscard, the presidential system and the party system were no longer synchronized.

But the illusion of a new party system in the making still remained, at least in part, both through a fear of the Left and because on the Left the presidential leader/presidential party identification mechanism that had served de Gaulle so well was being reconstructed to Mitterrand's benefit. The period 1981-1986 was again optimal from an institutional and political point of view: the classic Fifth Republic political structure, headed by an uncontested leader and supported by a dominant party flanked by a minor partner. Never again as during these five years would the Fifth Republic rediscover its Gaullist characteristics.

With the Socialist defeat in 1986, the role of the parties became more uncertain and less structured. From 1986 to 1988, the Socialist Party, in opposition, supported the head of state. The UDF and RPR governed together but were in constant struggle as to who would bear the mantle of the Right in the presidential election. In 1988, François Mitterand was again victorious but declared his wish for a majority by coalition. The voters granted his wishes by giving the Socialists only enough votes to form a minority government, forcing the prime minister to create variable-geometry-majorities depending on the issues at hand.

In 1993, the picture became further blurred: neither the head of state, nor the prime minister were official candidates for the 1995 presidential election, and none of the declared candidates was a member of the government. The two declared candidates on the Left and the Right (Rocard and Chirac) were leaders of parties that seemed increasingly divided about the prospects for their respective leaders. Enter the polls, which began to show Prime Minister Edouard Balladur and Jacques Delors, president of the European Commission, as the best-placed challengers for the presidency. Potential presidential leadership has thus become less and less associated with partisan leadership. None of this can reinforce the image of the parties in public opinion nor parties' capacity to weigh in on the selection of candidates.

The moment of truth has arrived. Scholars have long assumed that the presidential election contributed to a bipolarization of the party system by simplifying the choices. In France, the presidential election has proven to be a fantastic machine for actually destroying the political parties, especially when they are already weak. The classic political party is made for parliamentary practice. The presidential party is hardly more than an electoral machine.

Electoral Factors

Up to 1979, the French electoral system, mirroring the British system, was completely "pure": from top to bottom a two-round system of majority voting (for individuals or for a list) applied. The system was reinforced, moreover, by a certain number of restrictions (higher thresholds for access to the second round, restriction of the second-round presidential contest to only two candidates, etc.) which, taken together, seemed to force France toward bipolarization.

The worm was introduced to the fruit with the recourse to proportional representation in the European elections of 1979. The motivations justifying this shift were extremely diverse but few political actors or observers could predict the trouble that it would create. And this was only the beginning of a trend: the introduction of proportional representation in communal elections beginning in 1983, followed by recourse to proportional representation for the legislative elections of 1986, the regional elections of 1986 and 1992 and for the European elections of 1984 and 1989, all led to a certain clouding of the picture and loosened the grip of bipolarization. There were a certain number of mechanical and almost automatic effects resulting from the modification of the electoral system, to which were added the games and strategies of the voters who rapidly came to understand the advantages they could obtain from such opportunities.

Just as one could, with regard to the policy agenda, show that certain decisions were dependent upon the opening of what has been labeled a policy window, so the transformation and diversification of the electoral system constituted veritable electoral windows. The electorate has become more volatile, more fluid, adjusting its behavior as a function of the economy, of men or of strategic choices much more than through allegiance to a party. This electorate, which prefers to order à la carte rather than from a fixed menu, is highly unstable and modulates its participation and its vote as a function of the stakes of the election. Consequently, abstentions, blank votes, and protest votes only grow in number and attraction to the detriment of traditional political formations and in particular the government parties.

Indeed, the crisis of the party system has made itself apparent through a noticeable level of abstention -- without however reaching levels observed in the United States -- and through a multiplication of the number of protest or extra-system parties. Abstentions have continually increased for fifteen years and for all types of elections, whether local or national. At the same time, as certain studies made at the level of the polling stations show, abstention is much less the expression of political apathy than the manifestation of subtle strategies. Marie-France Toinet and François Subileau[5] have followed the practice of abstainers in a Parisian polling station since 1978 and have shown that only four voters out of a total of 1,200 have actually not participated in any vote. One-third of the electorate participates constantly, the other two-thirds constitute constant or intermittent abstainers. But these abstentions strike primarily at the parties of government that rallied two-thirds of the registered voters in 1978 and less than half today. The refusal to vote (blank votes, abstentions) moved from 19 percent to 35 percent between 1978 and 1993. (See Table 9.2.)

TABLE 9.2   Results of the First Round of Legislative Elections

(percentage of registered voters, excluding overseas departments)

	1978	*1986*	*1993*
Mainstream parties	74	56	45
Left	37	25	19
Right	37	31	26
Non-mainstream parties	7	19	20
FN	-	7	8
Abstentions, blank ballots, and voided ballots	19	25	35
of which blank and voided ballots	2	3	4
Refusals to vote for the mainstream parties	26	44	55

Source: F. Subileau et M.-F. Toinet, "La protestation des abstentionnistes," *Le Monde*, 18 August 1993.

The rejection of the government parties is also shown in the emergence of protest parties. Although this function was long channeled through the PCF, today the party no longer wins more than 8 percent to 10 percent according to the elections and protest has become protean and changing. The ecologists who had obtained nearly 15 percent of the vote in March 1992 hardly reached 10 percent a year later. The National Front even though stabilized below 15 percent is still the fourth major French party. It has surpassed the PCF even though it has hardly been in existence ten years. But protest takes even more corporatist or picturesque forms with the Hunters and Fishers Party, fake ecologists of all types, and the "party of laughter" in the Southwest. Despite the success of the Right in resuscitating itself to some extent, which is magnified by the collapse of the PS and the electoral system, the prospects remain mediocre for those who aspire to govern the country. This is all the more true since the disaffection just discussed is even stronger among 18-29-year-olds.[6]

Ideological and Social Factors

The destabilization of the political parties over the last decade has also resulted from ideological factors. As long as the Left was in opposition, it was rather simple to denounce policies labeled as being "Rightist" by juxtaposing them to a future "Leftist" program. This caricature of course neglected the fact that the welfare state was in essence developed by governments of the Right and that the percentage of the economy cycled through public budgets increased on average by 1 percent of GNP per year during the 1970s. Everyone remembers the disillusionment of the Socialists after several months in power and their forced "U-turn," which led to their policies becoming virtually indistinguishable from those of the Right. The famous expression of Mrs. Thatcher, "There is no alternative," ultimately showed itself even more appropriate when applied to France.

The submission of successive governments to "external constraints" and to the canons of orthodox economic management had the effect of almost completely disqualifying the ideological discourse that served to bond composite and fragile parties. In the words of Olivier Duhamel and Jerome Jaffré, "The ideological differences separating Bush and Clinton have become more perceptible than those between Bérégovoy and Balladur, which is incredible for a country like ours where we have often railed against the interchangeability of the American candidates."[7] In short, the Left-Right cleavage and the discourse that fed it and revived it on appropriate occasions (nationalizations, privatizations, education, etc.) have become progressively irrelevant.[8] More and more, the fault lines (Europe, immigration, abortion) have become lines within parties rather than inter-party divisions: the Maastricht Treaty was the most striking example but is not an isolated phenomenon.

This ideological weakening has been accentuated finally by the shady dealings of the Socialists in a number of corruption scandals. A part of the success of the Socialist Party while in opposition was due to a discourse oriented toward values and strongly critical of the "forces of money" and "savage" capitalism. By reviving and modernizing an ancient rhetoric that mixed moral, populist, and class accents, the Socialist Party could all the better distinguish itself from the wealthy, from "the chateau," and from "the money that corrupts, the money that kills" (Mitterrand). The discovery that this pious discourse disguised improper practices contributed to the further accentuation of the disenchantment with politics and the disillusionment of the party militants.

This weakening of ideology and values has accompanied the weakening of sociological indicators as variables that explain electoral behavior.[9] A confused mix -- a "splintered vote,"[10] -- has been substituted for all the beautiful certainties of the past concerning class votes and the impact of the religious variable. Neither the PS, nor even the PCF, can claim to represent a working class that is more and more seduced by the Right and even by the extreme Right. The PCF is more and more rejected by the workers, who vote more for any other party than for it! The moderate Right for its part is losing ground among farmers, among the young and among those in the liberal professions, even if its electoral fortunes are better assured than those of the PS, from whom it has won back a portion of the electorate, particularly among women. The magnitude of the changes can be no better illustrated than by the fact that the National Front and the ecologists are seducing the young, while the PS has made its best gains among those above sixty years of age!

Conclusion

Twelve years after the victory of the Left, thirty-five years after the foundation of a Republic directed against the "*régime des partis*," the spectacle offered by the French party system is a sorry one. The situation testifies to the persistent incapacity of France and the French to construct a solid and stable party system. French history and culture provide in part the key to this enigma by reminding us that this phenomenon is recurrent and that it concerns all forms of social organization (groups, unions, and so forth). In spite of the changes of the past fifty years, the French still have the fundamental symptoms of an allergy to a partisan structure.

Added to this, since 1958 and 1962, is the difficulty of reconciling traditional parties with presidential leadership. The construction of the Gaullist party from scratch for the needs of first de Gaulle, then Pompidou and Chirac was a major innovation, adapting structure to the needs of the leader. But to function well, this system required several conditions: a dominant party on the Right (with the risk of interminable quarrels over leadership), an unfailing devotion to the leader, the absence of internal divisions over presidential candidacies -- conditions that are not fulfilled today. The successful story of the reconstitution of the Socialists under the leadership of François Mitterrand was in the end no different. With the electoral defeat of 1993, the PS has returned to the starting block. Everything must be rebuilt, as in 1972, but with one key asset missing: a mobilizing spirit, which will take a long time to build up again.

The balance sheet is dramatic for the parties: protest parties proliferate with no hope other than weakening even further the government parties; the moderate Right is as splintered and diverse as thirty years ago; the PCF is moribund; the PS is beginning a convalescence that promises to be very long. The most powerful party is the RPR. It would hold all the cards if only its official leader, Jacques Chirac, appeared to the French as a natural president.

In this general meltdown of the party structure and in the climate of economic, social, and moral crisis that in the early 1990s, reigns in France, it is not surprising that the French have rediscovered old habits. In the periods of turmoil, the French have always sought a father figure. The presidential elections of 1995 will demonstrate whether they are fortunate enough to find someone who will assume this role. If they do, it will not be the parties that have produced the solution. The president will in any case face the daunting task of beginning once again to mold a party system that can provide a durable base for governing and provide clear choices for a country once again in search of itself.

Notes

1. Pierre Rosanvallon, "Le déclin des passions," *Autrement -- Série Mutations*, No. 122, May 1991.

2. Janine Mossuz-Lavau, *La politique-Janus: Mobilisation autour des problèmes, offre politique en panne*, Unpublished manuscript.

3. On the related phenomena of "presidentialization" and "localization" of the Gaullist Party, see Andrew Knapp and Patrick Le Galès, "Top-down to Bottom-up? Center-Periphery Relations and Power Structures in France's Gaullist Party," *West European Politics*, Vol. 16, No. 3, July 1993, pp. 271-294.

4. Yves Mény, *La corruption de la République* (Paris: Fayard, 1992).

5. Françoise Subileau and Marie-France Toinet, "Le Protestation des Abstentionnistes," *Le Monde*, 18 August 1993.

6. Olivier Duhamel and Jerome Jaffré, *L'Etat de l'opinion* (Paris: Le Seuil, 1993), p. 11ff.

7. Ibid., p. 12.

8 . Guy Michelat, "A la recherche de la gauche et de la droite," in CEVIPOF, *L'électorat français en questions* (Paris: Presses de la F.N.S.P., 1990).

9. François Furet, Jacques Julliard, Pierre Rosanvallon, *La République du Centre* (Paris: Calmann-Lévy, 1988).

10. Philippe Habert, Pascal Perrineau, Colette Ysmal, *Le vote éclaté* (Paris: Département des Etudes politiques du Figaro and Presses de la F.N.S.P., 1992).

10

Trade and Identity: The Coming Protectionism?

Suzanne Berger

In 1981 when the Left swept to power in France, François Mitterrand proclaimed employment as the "axis" of the Socialist program. Unemployment loomed as the voters' principal concern. This "priority of priorities" was used to legitimate much in the new government's agenda: not only the reduction of weekly working hours, but also nationalizations, industrial policies, and new fiscal policies. Today there are still some who search for remedies in new domestic reforms, demanding more education for workers, longer time horizons in managerial strategies, innovations in industrial organization inspired by Japanese and German models, and so forth.[1] Some hold out hope that an upturn in the world economy or the Bundesbank's lowering interest rates might relaunch the French on a trajectory of faster economic growth and lower unemployment. But both among political elites and within the electorate, the notion that state intervention in the domestic economy can do much to roll back unemployment is rapidly losing support.

The desire for a strong French state has, however, not faded despite a common perception of the state's current domestic impotence. Indeed, the desired location for state activism seems merely to have shifted as groups throughout society increasingly conclude that the troubles of the economy begin at the borders and that solutions lie in a new protectionism. The loss of faith in government's ability to staunch the hemorrhage of jobs through intervention in the domestic economy seems counterbalanced by the belief that the openness of the European Community market vis-à-vis the rest of the world is responsible for the rise in

French unemployment, and that limiting access to French and European markets would slow or reverse this tendency.

Unemployment and the Changing Politics of Trade

Protectionism is hardly a new phenomenon in French life. Over the course of the Third Republic protectionist forces routed free traders and established a regime of tariff protection that enjoyed considerable support across the political spectrum. In the postwar period as well, there was considerable support for protection. The business community in the fifties divided sharply over trade liberalization and the Common Market. Even after the Treaty of Rome, politicians occasionally found appeals to the protectionist reflex a reliable way of boosting popularity, particularly in response to U.S. or Japanese goods.

Yet despite several notorious protectionist outbursts -- such as when the French insisted all Japanese VCRs clear customs at Poitiers (in 1982) -- one of the more significant developments of the postwar period was the broad conversion of the French to economic openness. Surveyed in 1984 about whether French frontiers should be closed to some foreign goods or whether free trade should prevail, 61 percent pronounced for free trade and only 31 percent for restrictive measures.[2] Free trade won a wide majority of support in all social classes and political electorates, except for the Communists. Another survey the same year asked whether European Community frontiers should be closed to foreign goods, and again found only 30 percent supporting such a measure.[3]

The year of these surveys is important. By 1984, the Socialists had already carried out a "U-turn" in economic policy. Layoffs mounted as industrial restructuring accelerated; and creating new jobs loomed over all other issues as the public's main priority.[4] Thus, even in a bad year, the results of these surveys reflected the solid evolution of attitudes over the course of some thirty years of trade liberalization, both within the European Community and within the GATT framework, and showed a large consensus in favor of an open economy.

This consensus has now unraveled, both among the public and among political elites. A C.S.A. *Le Parisien* survey, dated 22 June 1993, asked about limiting the import of non-European products into the Community and about limiting the entry of foreign products into France. Sixty-seven percent of the respondents agreed with both propositions.[5] Asked whether Europe should be tougher in GATT trade negotiations, even if such a stance meant a break with the United States, 62 of the respondents replied affirmatively. Within the political class all across the spectrum, the shifts have been as dramatic (see below). A real sea change in French political attitudes appears to be in the making.

The immediate trigger for the new attraction of protectionism was a sharp rise in unemployment. Yet, however abrupt the upturn in the unemployment figures, the underlying facts about job creation in France are of much longer standing, as the Raynaud report on the state of the French economy during the twelve years of Socialist government underscored. Over this period, French economic growth equalled the European Community average (2.2 percent per year on average) and was more rapid than that of Germany (2.1 percent) or the United States (2.0 percent). But France created fewer jobs than these countries did. The number of foreigners in the workforce remained quite stable: 1.34 million in 1982, 1.29 million in 1990. But the role of industry and industrial employment fell significantly. Between 1980 and 1990 French industry's contribution to value-added in the national economy fell, and the proportion of the workforce employed by industry fell by 18 percent. Most of this loss took place in big companies, which shed 20 percent of their jobs.[6]

Why rapid increases in unemployment should be blamed on foreign trade and investment patterns is puzzling. In contrast to the United States, where protectionist demands are also rising, France has not had a trade deficit, but a trade surplus.[7] Many of the new demands for trade protection evoke images of a France submerged under a flood of labor-intensive imports from East Europe and Asia, an outpouring of jobs to low-wage countries, and an unbeatable wave of high-tech imports from Japan and the United States. But in fact only 8 percent of French imports come from Asia and East Europe.[8] European Community exports to developing countries exceed imports by 75 percent.[9] Only 4 percent of French foreign investment is directed to low-wage economies. Nor can the European Community's relations with the advanced industrial world readily be identified as responsible for rising unemployment. On the contrary: the EC accounts for one-fifth of North American manufacturing imports and only 8 percent of EC manufacturing imports come from North America.[10] Even Japan -- contrary to the impression given by the avalanche of criticisms the French make concerning that country's trading practices -- plays a rather small part in France's external economic relations, accounting in 1993 for 4 percent of French imports and 2 percent of French exports, an imbalance that has been improving over the past decade.[11]

How then could France's foreign trade play a central role in the current rise of unemployment? The Arthuis Report, a Senate Finance Commission study (dated 4 June 1993) on the economic and fiscal impact of the *délocalisation* (relocation) of industrial and service activities outside France, attempted to explain this phenomenon. The report offered an analysis that pulls together into a single coherent framework a diverse set of claims about the future of France's economic relations with the outside world.[12] On all sides it is referred to as having demonstrated that three to five million jobs in France are menaced by the prospect of transfer of productive activities to low wage countries. The report has played a critical role in setting the terms of debate over trade and the state of the French economy.

The Arthuis Report starts with a definition of *délocalisation* so broad as to cover virtually all exchange:

> *Délocalisations* amount to separating the place of production or transformation of merchandise from the place of consumption, for products which could be manufactured and consumed in the same geographic area. In other words, the manager manufactures where it's least expensive and sells wherever there is purchasing power.[13]

From this it follows, according to the report, that all sectors of the economy risk seeing jobs leave France for the low-wage economies of the developing world. The costs of production in such economies are so low that French manufacturers cannot possibly compete. "When prices defy all competition, there is no more competition! Our companies are condemned to close or to delocalize in order to try to survive."[14]

The report presents an impressive series of data on the low cost of labor in various North African, Asian, and East European countries. Matters become more complicated, however, when it attempts to explain the mechanisms through which low labor costs abroad pull employment away from France, since, as the report notes, it is extremely rare for a company to close a production site within the European Community to open one outside the European Community.[15] What the report calls the "classic" form of *délocalisation* -- investing abroad to set up new production units in low-wage settings and then shipping the goods back to Europe -- plays a minor role. Even if one looks at investment in overseas production facilities by the textile and garment industries -- a critical case because of the need for heavy labor inputs -- this investment accounts for only 2.7 percent of French foreign investment. Of that sum, only 4.1 percent is destined for textile or garment production outside OECD countries.[16] Perhaps, as the report suggests, investment overseas is not the right measure of *délocalisation*; the main channel for *délocalisation* might be subcontracting or purchase through intermediaries. But even here, the Report warns, one cannot expect to find statistical confirmation. Official trade statistics -- which the report denounces as misleading -- show that imports from non-OECD countries as a share of total imports rose only 4.5 percent over the period 1984-1992.[17]

None of these shifts is very large; so why the alarm? In part, the argument against *délocalization* rests on extrapolation from a few celebrated cases where French firms have lost out to low-cost competitors or have begun to resort to foreign, low-cost subcontractors. In a section on information technology, for example, the Arthuis Report contrasts the monthly salaries of program analysts in the Philippines, India, and Barbados with those in France, and endorses the somber conclusion of witnesses who appeared before the commission that "the generalization of subcontracting appears inevitable."[18] "Out of a total of 300,000 information technologists (in France), 50,000 to 80,000 jobs could be delocalized in the next few years."[19] Perhaps. But as of 1993, the same witnesses reported only 500-800 jobs in information technologies had been subcontracted offshore. From the fact that it is possible to transfer any such jobs outside of France, the report concludes for this sector as well as others, that virtually all such jobs are menaced. By such reasoning, 84 percent of all industrial jobs are declared "*délocalisables.*"[20]

The report reaches its conclusions, not only by extrapolation from current examples, but by identifying other mechanisms that link low-wage economies to France's dilemmas. Two processes stand out. The first process is symbolized by "the parable of the wine in the water." It is a parable told by Francis Mer, president of Usinor-Sacilor, the large nationalized steel company, who uses it to explain how importing even small quantities of low-cost East European steel is enough to wreck European steel markets:

> Importing a single drop of [wine] is sometimes enough to disturb troubled French and European markets. The statements of certain politicians and economists show that they do not understand how prices are formed on our markets. I have tried to explain it to them with the following image. In their view, the European market is like a glass of oil into which one adds a drop of vinegar: steel from the East at dumping prices. The oil remains pure; the vinegar simply sticks to an edge, not mixing with the oil. One might even pick up the drop of vinegar with a spoon. Nothing changes: no diffusion effect; no marginal adjunction effect. *But our market resembles more a glass of water into which a bit of wine is allowed to fall. It will suddenly and definitively color all the water. A few percentages of steel sold at low prices disturbs the whole market.*[21]

In sum, the amount of merchandise imported (or the number of jobs exported) is not in and of itself decisive. Through demonstration effects, or through a special pricing mechanism, even a little "wine" is enough to devastate the French economy. "Once the process begins, it appears irreversible."[22]

A second factor promoting *délocalisation* relates to the role of large-scale retail stores in France, according to the report. True, the report indicates, there is no "direct causality" between big stores and *délocalisation*. These stores import little from low-cost producer countries. But they are still responsible for giving a powerful boost to this process, since by emphasizing low prices and the interest of consumers in low prices, they encourage, even force, manufacturers into *délocalisation*. Because these big stores "dominate" manufacturers, particularly in traditional sectors, they are at a minimum, "transmission belts" for the transfer of production out of France. Given the important share (about two-fifths) of the retail market controlled by the large retailers, they exert "such a financial power, dispose of unbeatable means of pressure, and are the natural and privileged intermediary of networks of importers. Massive advertising and sales in big stores assure the success of *délocalisations* and of imports of all products."[23]

The actual imports of the largest retailers today (Centres Leclerc, Carrefour, Intermarché) are less than 3 percent of their volume of trade -- so proclaiming their responsibility for the transfer of production abroad rests on no simple extrapolation of their current practices. Rather the idea derives from the destructive nature of their appeal to consumers to focus on price.[24] The bitterness of the attack on the supermarkets, assigning them blame for the troubles of manufacturers, and deducing from their very *raison d'être* the ruin of the French economy are all very familiar themes in contemporary French history, here woven into a new story about France's relations with the outside world. Indeed the report, describing a future in which 300 million (European consumers) confront 3 billion (low-wage producers), can summon up no worse image than that of "the logic of *délocalisation* transforming Europe into a vast supermarket selling goods produced elsewhere."[25]

Given the jerry-rigged scaffolding on which these arguments are supported and the shakiness of the evidence, economic analysis can hardly explain the influence of the Arthuis Report. One must shift focus altogether to discover why increasing numbers of French find convincing an interpretation that blames unprecedented levels of unemployment on savage competition and the uncontrolled entry of goods and services from the rest of the world.

A New Cleavage in French Politics?

The Arthuis Report falls into a political environment that has been transformed and polarized over the past decade by issues that have focused the attention of the public and elites upon France's borders with the rest of the world. However different the substance and context of the issues at stake, the protagonists in each of the debates evoke the same images of a France whose unprotected frontiers leave it open and vulnerable to the invasion of external, dangerous forces. Whether the intrusion feared is a flood of immigrants from North Africa or the goods of East Europe and the developing world or Japanese cars or the wheat of North America, the terms used to castigate the state's irresponsibility in lowering the guard against the dangers of the outside world are strikingly similar.

The first appearance of this cluster of images involved immigration. Beginning with the 1983 election of a *Front National* candidate in Dreux and rising rapidly with Jean-Marie Le Pen's surge to 11.1 percent in the 1984 European elections, an anti-immigrant politics came to dominate the domestic agenda.[26] Public dissatisfaction over the presence of large immigrant populations in France fused a cluster of distinct concerns into a single political issue.[27] One dimension links the immigrants to unemployment levels. Another blames the immigrants for increases in crime and the disintegration of safety in urban settings. Perhaps most significant for the role it plays in Le Pen's program and appeal is the claim that immigration threatens national integrity and national identity. Le Pen vividly described the presence of the immigrants as an "invasion" threatening to obliterate the French, as for example, in a 17 December 1980 interview in *Le Monde*:

> There is no xenophobia in my views. There are races, different peoples, and they have different territories. The invasion of the territory of one people by another people has until now been defined as a constitutive element of war. When the Huns, the Visigoths, and the Ostrogoths, chased from their lands by poverty, advance and invade the lands of their neighbors, there is no war if one opens the doors to them, if one hands over the women. They are satisfied, and if you agree to take care of their horses, they'll even treat you like a collaborator.[28]

Support for Le Pen's views on immigration and for his overall perspective has risen over time, most dramatically from 1990 to 1991, when the proportion of those surveyed describing themselves as "completely" or "rather" in agreement with his positions climbed from 18 percent to 32 percent. These levels of support proved remarkably resilient, both to Le Pen's personal reverses (as when he attacked French participation in the Gulf War as an "ill-advised adventure" and tried himself to negotiate with Saddam Hussein) and in general to the public's continuing leeriness about his ability to run the country and about the *Front National* as a danger to democracy.[29]

But even if Le Pen is unlikely to gain enough public confidence to come to power, his successes are influencing a growing number of Center Right politicians to use language and suggest reforms that can appeal to the Le Pen electorate. Alain Juppé, the *Rassemblement pour la République* (RPR) politician, now foreign minister, challenged the policy of allowing the immigrants' families to join them in France:

> Each person is free of course to remain faithful to his religion, tradition, specific culture, which may enrich the common stock. This is the pluralism inherent in democracy. But from that to allowing public agencies to distribute subsidies to polygamous family heads ... is a step too far. This is not integration. This risks dissolving the social contract that binds us.[30]

Jacques Chirac, the RPR leader, talked of the discomforts of living in public housing permeated with the smells of foreign foods. Valéry Giscard d'Estaing, the UDF leader, moved even closer to Le Pen's positions. Across the board, with rare exceptions, politicians from the Center Right began shifting toward the anti-immigrant language and program of Le Pen.

Despite the fact that the official discourse and policies on immigration of Left and Right governments were essentially the same, differences over immigration came to be the only issue on which the public saw any real distinction between parties of the Left and the Right.[31] A 1989 survey found 48 percent of the French -- and a majority of the Left electorate (Socialists, Communists, ecologists) -- favoring policies that would promote the integration of the immigrants into French society and 46 percent of the French -- and a majority of the Right electorate (RPR, UDF, National Front) -- supporting the alternative: the departure of most immigrants.[32] Analyzing these results, Olivier Duhamel and Jérome Jaffré, the editors of the 1990 SOFRES annual report, concluded: "Islam has replaced Communism as the threat to Western Europe."

Equally important for the future of French politics was the growing division over these issues among elites of both the Left and the Right. These internal divisions were already apparent in the 1989 controversy over whether Muslim girls should be allowed to wear headscarves in public schools. The Socialist education minister's decision to permit this practice provoked major splits within the Socialist and opposition parties, thus anticipating the ways in which the Maastricht referendum and the GATT issues would later divide the parties of the Left and the Right.

The political battle over ratification of the Maastricht Treaty was the second major catalyst for polarizing the political terrain on the issue of France's relations with the outside. Although 89 percent of the deputies and senators had approved the Maastricht treaty, the "yes" vote in the 22 September 1992 referendum barely passed, with 51 percent of the votes.[33] Undoubtedly, there was a variety of reasons for the magnitude of the "no" vote. At the time some commentators interpreted it as an anti-Mitterrand vote. But the continuing erosion of pro-Maastricht sentiment, even after the victory of the Right in the 1993 legislative elections, lends more credibility to an interpretation of the 1992 vote as a reflection of anxiety about national identity and fear of the loss of national control.

Although many analysts describe the voters who rejected the treaty as having shifted from support for Europe to opposition, a more careful reading of public opinion surveys that had shown large pro-Europe majorities offers a different interpretation. Annick Percheron's prescient analysis of these surveys suggested that those polled in the past had never really focused on the consequences of European integration for their personal welfare.[34] High levels of ignorance and indifference, combined with generally positive orientations toward the idea of Europe to produce a superficial, hence fragile, consensus on Europe. During the campaign before the referendum, the RPR split, and two prominent Gaullist politicians, Charles Pasqua and Philippe Séguin, mounted a brilliant attack on the treaty. For the first time in France, there was a full-blown public debate over the implications of deepening commitment to the European Community. In the course of the debate, as the voters came to appreciate the stakes in the harmonization of European practices and in the renunciation of added degrees of national sovereignty, negative reactions soared.

Thus over the course of a decade, battles over immigrants and over Europe have been opening a new cleavage in French politics. This divide cuts across the old Left and Right camps, as the Maastricht referendum results showed: the treaty was rejected by voters in the heartland of French Socialism -- Pas de Calais

-- and overwhelmingly approved in the old strongholds of Social Catholicism. The new cleavage identifies France's borders as the central point of national political debate. Thus decisions concerning trade and protection are made in a political environment that has been increasingly polarized over the issue of France's relations with the outside world.

Toward a New Protectionism

After the Marxist, or class-based, interpretations of the workings of the economy faded with the Socialist Party's acceptance of the market and the government's "U-turn" in economic policy, many heralded a long-awaited and frequently announced "normalization" of French exceptionalism. But this phase seems to have been an ideological hiatus, rather than the end of ideology. The new interpretations of economic stagnation and the impotence of policy to halt rising unemployment coincide with the categories evoked in the immigration controversy and the European question, and build an explanation of French troubles in which the core fact is the state's loss of control at the borders over forces vital to French welfare. As the Arthuis Report illustrated, the plausibility of these accounts requires a special vision of France in the world. It is this vision that unites segments of the elites from both the Left and the Right and threatens to transform the landscape of partisan politics.

The new religion of a protected France is winning converts across the political spectrum. On the Left, the Communists and the Socialists close to Jean-Pierre Chevènement have always been hostile both to Europe and to free trade. But what is remarkable is the shift of those Socialists who have been the staunchest advocates of European construction to more protectionist positions on trade with the rest of the world. By 1993 Mitterrand was proclaiming that "Europe must not dissolve itself in a vast free-trade zone."[35] He added that even if he was against protection, he favored sheltering the European Community against competition from low-wage economies.

Intellectuals, too, leaped on the new issue. They were most numerous and audible in opposition to proposals to include movies and media under new liberalized GATT rules. Artists, writers, actors, and movie directors urged the government to hold fast in resisting U.S. demands, lest all French culture be swamped by a flood of *Jurassic Parks*. Even for this group, old ideological barriers seemed to fall before the new enemy. The former Socialist minister of culture, Jack Lang, announced: "So, it's war and in a war, our nation must stand together."[36] Although the dangers to French culture preoccupied this group, intellectuals also tackled the issues of trade and the French public interest. Thus Alain Minc, in a comment that appeared in *Le Monde* under the evocative title of *"La nouvelle trahison des Clercs"* attacked the business community for promoting a free-trade GATT regime that the end of the Cold War rendered obsolete:

With the free circulation of capital and technologies, competition will be un-
bearable with the Chinese, fortified by their capitalist chromosome, their productivity, their capital, and who work as efficiently as we, for thirty times less.
The Chinese explosion is the end of the 1945 GATT model: we are moving
towards an economy where capital and technology will continue to circulate as
today, but dams will reappear between zones. The elites must reach unanimity
on this subject in order to convince the Germans, whose own difficulties will
make them receptive. To become the intelligent advocates of a Community
preferential trade system extended to industry and to services: this is the task
for intellectuals today, instead of hiding behind the mirages of economic fictions.[37]

On the Right, the government parties are split by conflicts between advocates
of more or less protectionist trade policies, more or less tolerant or repressive
policies on immigration, and more or less enthusiasm for European construction,
with a growing likelihood that the attackers and defenders in one debate will
discover themselves with the same allies and enemies the next time around. Even
among those committed to Europe, a new language appears. An interview in *Le
Monde* with Alain Juppé, the RPR foreign minister, vividly illustrated this new
amalgam of a sober, even resigned, acceptance of Europe as the necessary frame
for French action in the world, with a new activism on trade with the rest of the
world.[38] On Europe, says Juppé, what are the alternatives? Germany with 80
million inhabitants and an economy that will rapidly absorb reunification may
think it needs Europe less than before, but we French must hang on to what we
have built over the past three or four decades. The only real questions are what
kind of a Europe and what kind of GATT regime? For "is [Europe] a free-trade
zone or a territory of solidarity?" If Europe is to be more than a free-trade zone,
exchange with the rest of the world should be regulated by a preferential trade
system.

This notion of a preferential European trading system increasingly is called
upon to square the circle of how a free-trade regime might serve French interests.
It is hardly a strong solution. First of all, many of the other Community members
are hostile to the idea. And, in fact, would it really be in France's interest? Most
of France's trade surplus comes from trade outside the EC, and its intra-Commu-
nity trade is in balance or in deficit.[39]

Edouard Balladur, the RPR prime minister, perhaps recognizing the contradiction, tried to limit the damage: "Should we, as some say, close the frontiers?
The government's response is that the French economy, like the European economy
is too open to the world to sustain the closing of its markets that would result."[40]
But, prudently, he, too, began to emphasize the differences between an "artificial" and "abstract" free trade and "fair and balanced liberalism." "What is the
content of commercial and economic liberty in a world where the conditions of
competition, of life, and of production are so different." Europe, says Balladur,

depends on nurturing among its member countries a sense of common interests and solidarity: "she should not be exposed to all the winds, when others are more protected than she."[41]

Splits within the business community exacerbated dissension among political elites. In addition to the traditional hostility to market-opening measures among industrialists from such sectors as textiles, garments, and furniture, a new group of industrial protectionists had been forming around the issue of relations with Japan. The attack on Japanese entry into European car markets mounted by Jacques Calvet, head of Peugeot, widened into a general attack on free trade. By the end of 1992, Alain Gomez, president of Thomson, was calling for "abandoning the old ideology of global free-trade where everyone sells to everyone and organizing large geographic zones into trade blocs, that would be delimited and protected, though not necessarily autarkic." We need to choose between Ricardo and List, explained Gomez; and if one believes like List that nations create competitive advantage, then "a new emergent ensemble like Europe, which has not yet enjoyed such an opportunity, needs to be *fortified by a 'pedagogic' protectionism.*"[42]

As the GATT negotiations heated up in the months before the 15 December 1993, deadline for "fast-track" passage through the U.S. Congress, others leaped onto the bandwagon. An escalation of demands and of anti-Americanism that had started with farmer demonstrations against the Blair House Agreement widened to include so many and such diverse claimants that by early December 1993 it seemed France would not be able to sign on to any conceivable GATT compromise. At this point, though, the long-silent advocates of trade liberalization began to weigh in.

The first riposte to the Arthuis Report had come from an RPR deputy, Patrick Devedjian, who issued his own report on trade and the French economy.[43] Devedjian launched a full-scale attack on all the main points the new protectionists' case. He demolished the claim that *délocalisations* are responsible for rising unemployment and pointed out that France's trade surplus is largely realized with non-OECD, that is, less-developed, countries.[44] He charged that "community preference" is no more than a euphemism for protectionism. And, most important for the future lines of the free-traders' counterattack, he argued that the real offender in the arena of trade is the United States, whose self-interested and aggressive unilateralism has nothing to do with a genuinely open trade policy. "Contrary to a common idea, GATT is not the instrument of American domination, but on the contrary a tool that should be better used against the United States itself. This country, under the guise of managed trade, is implementing as much as possible a neo-protectionism."[45] Devedjian's report was denounced as doctrinaire trade liberalism by most of the members of the parliamentary commission that had supposedly produced it. The hostility within his own party to this personal initiative and to its formulation of the counterattack was so great that the report did not appear as a parliamentary document.[46]

But in fact, the regrouping of the business community and of the political class behind an acceptance of the new GATT proposals was already in the works by the late autumn. Raymond Barre publicly accused special interests of using the GATT debate to protect themselves at the expense of the public good. Gérard Longuet, minister of industry and foreign trade, testifying before a parliamentary committee reminded his colleagues that France's trade balance with low-wage countries is in surplus and pointedly argued that "if we want to sell satellites and Airbus, we have to understand that they'll be paid for in furniture, clothing, and trinkets."[47] The remarks triggered outrage and protests from traditional industries -- that is, the manufacturers of furniture, clothing, and trinkets -- but the pro-GATT forces were gaining strength. Valéry Giscard d'Estaing charged that excessive rhetoric had made France the black sheep of the trade negotiations and that France's interest lay in signing; the UDF parliamentary group leader Charles Millon declared "We have a choice between isolating ourselves, which would be regression, and a balanced opening, which would signify expansion and wealth creation."[48] Even the farmers' union, the *Fédération National des Syndicats d'Exploitants* (FNSEA), whose militance over the agricultural parts of the Uruguay Round had set off the conflagration, seemed to have decided that they had gone too far, and started backing down.[49]

In the aftermath of the GATT affair, many features of the old political landscape have reemerged. The parties of Left and Right have mostly gone back to business as usual, a return accelerated by the Balladur government's clumsy effort to slip through a radical reform of state subsidies to church schools. In 1984, when the Socialists proposed to nationalize the private schools huge numbers of protestors marched in opposition; ten years later, it was the Left that mobilized its forces on the familiar old battlegrounds of the church-state divide. But the one great fissure in the political landscape that Maastricht revealed, and that the debate over trade enlarged, remains: the Right is now deeply divided over France's relations with the outside.

The most powerful exponent of the alternative vision of France's future is Philippe Séguin, the RPR deputy and president of the Assemblée Nationale, whose dramatic speeches against the Maastricht Treaty, against free trade, and in defense of traditional conceptions of national sovereignty have been published in two recent books, *Discours pour la France* (1992) and *Ce que j'ai dit* (1993). In these works Séguin makes explicit in a way that no one else has the linkages among the set of issues that center on France's borders. In common with the others calling for new forms of protection, Séguin starts from rising unemployment. Increased joblessness risks not only the impoverishment and despair of larger and larger segments of the population, but also the unraveling of the social fabric and massive unrest. To allow the inequalities and social exclusion that unemployment produces in the name of some illusory universalism, some technocratic model of globalism, is unacceptable: "The very idea of the Republic is shattered!"[50] He endorses the Arthuis Report's conclusion that free trade is the source of rising employment and may dislocate three to five million more jobs by the end of the century.[51]

> In refusing to reconsider Europe's participation in the movement to freer trade that started during the Cold War, the European Commission is signing the death warrant not only for our industry, but for our social system and our way of life. By choosing an open Europe, or more exactly, one opened without any reciprocity, to the detriment of "Community preference," we are encouraging a diabolical cycle of social regression, which translates into a sterile multiplication of internal and external *délocalisations.*
>
> Free trade in such conditions is nothing more than the stake which ties up the European lamb, offered up to the voracity of its far more ferocious competitors.[52]

But what is really at stake, according to Séguin, goes far beyond material interests, however legitimate. Maastricht and the GATT negotiations imperil the future of France as a nation. The nation is jeopardized not only by transfers of sovereignty to other bodies, but more fundamentally, by the renunciation of the instruments through which the State's legitimacy is created. Whether the issue is trade or the European Community or the domestic market, the political choices of the State must shape a course for the country, and the prerequisite for national choices is national frontiers. "The idea of frontiers is outdated! There's a dogma to attack! For bringing back the frontiers today is the condition of any policy."[53] By giving up the means that allow it to preserve social solidarity, justice, and equality, for the sake of the illusory ideals of free markets, globalism, and Europe, the State is destroying its own foundations. "*1992 is literally the anti-1789.*"[54]

> In France, freedom and equality are stronger the more the State intervenes, whereas in other political cultures, the reverse is true [and] thus freedom is imagined to increase when public authority shrinks. In fact, this logic is foreign to our history, contrary to our idea of the Republic. ... When they say European construction is a kind of extension on a larger scale of what first the Capetian then the Republican State accomplished, I say this so-called extension is a negation: a negation of the rights of the poor, who have been the great motor of the State in France. This is the reason for the extreme fragility of the Europe of the single market: it does not protect the poor; it excludes them. It is not felt as a recourse, but as a menace. Thus its legitimacy is very weak and its survival precarious.[55]

Thus behind the debates over the state of France's economy today, there stands the still-open question of the French state. An ardent defense of the strong state, which the Socialists jettisoned along with Marxist economic doctrines, has reappeared at another point on the political spectrum. Like the Jacobins, the new protectionists' case for the state rests on its role in defending the weak against the strong, in preserving a desirable social order against the market, and in maintaining politics as the organizer of the French community. But where the Jacobins' enemies resided within, the dangers for the new protectionists lie on the borders. The possibilities of creating a wide zone of consensus across Left and Right on this vision are considerable. However improbable the resurrection of a Gaullism without de Gaulle, striking family resemblances still surface in this new body of ideas about the state. To imagine that this new demand for a strong state protecting France's frontiers will evaporate with an upturn in the economy or a presidential victory for the Right is to underestimate the strength and resilience of the nationalist vision in modern France.

Notes

1. For representative and widely discussed examples of this line of reasoning, see Michel Albert, *Capitalisme contre capitalisme* (Paris: Seuil, 1991); Dominique Taddei and Benjamin Coriat, *Made in France. L'industrie française dans la compétition mondiale.* (Paris: Livre de Poche, 1993).

2. SOFRES. *Opinion publique,* 1985 (Paris: Gallimard, 1985), p. 320.

3. SOFRES, 1985. p. 248.

4. SOFRES, 1985. p. 64. 79 percent of those polled in that year mention it among their top four priorities.

5. Jean-Michel Aphatie, "La France tentée par le protectionnisme," *Le Parisien,* 22 June 1993, pp. 2-3.

6. "Le rapport Raynaud sur la situation de la France," *Le Monde,* 20-21 June 1993, p. 15.

7. François Renard, "Commerce extérieur: une amélioration inquiétante," *Le Monde,* 3-4 October 1993. The trade surplus rose from 16.1 billion francs in the first semester of 1992 to 36.4 billion francs in the second semester of 1993. Over this period, a trade deficit with the United States has more than doubled -- despite the rising dollar. The trade deficit with Japan fell.

8. Philippe Lemaitre, "Le commerce mondial désorienté," *Le Monde,* 8 July 1993, p. 21.

9. Cited in Patrick Devedjian, *Rapport de la Mission d'information sur l'organisation du libre-échange,* Report of subcommittee of *Commission des Finances, Assemblée Nationale,* 1993, p. 12.

10. "Conjoncture: Importune Europe," *Le Monde,* 15 December 1992, p. 36.

11. Jean-Marie Bouissou, "Région: L'Asie du Nord: La France peu présente," *Le Monde,* 13 July 1993.

12. The report was produced by a parliamentary commission chaired by Senator Jean Arthuis. Arthuis is a Centrist. *Rapport d'information fait au nom de la commission des finances, du controle budgetaire et des comptes économiques de la Nation sur l'incidence économique et fiscale des délocalisations hors du territoire national des activités industrielles et de service.* France. Sénat, 1993.

13. Ibid., p. 13 (my translation in this and in the following passages of the Arthuis Report).

14. Ibid., p. 14.

15. Ibid., p. 40.

16. Ibid., pp. 114-115.

17. Ibid., p. 118.

18. Ibid., see pp. 70 ff.

19. Ibid., p. 72.

20. Ibid., p. 84.

21. Testimony of Francis Mer, in Ibid., p. 35.

22. Ibid., p. 35.

23. Ibid., p. 108.

24. Ibid., p. 109.

25. Ibid., p. 147.

26. On the electoral rise and the stability of the Le Pen vote, see Nonna Mayer, "*Le Front National*," in Dominique Chagnollaud, ed., *Bilan politique de la France*, (Paris: Hachette, 1991); Nonna Mayer, "*Explaining Electoral Right-Wing Extremism: the Case of the Le Pen Vote in the 1988 French Presidential Election*," Paper presented to the American Political Science Association Annual Meeting, Washington, 1993; Nonna Mayer and Pascal Perrineau, *Le Front National à découvert* (Paris: Presses de la Fondation Nationale des Sciences Politiques, 1989); Nonna Mayer and Pascal Perrineau, "*Pourquoi votent-ils pour le Front National?*" *Pouvoirs* 55 (1990); Martin A. Schain, "The National Front in France and the Construction of Political Legitimacy," *West European Politics*, 10 (2) April 1987; Martin A. Schain, "Immigration and Changes in the French Party System," *European Journal of Political Research*, 1988; Colette Ysmal, "The Browning of Europe: Right Wing Extremism in European Elections," Paper presented at the American Political Science Association Annual Meeting, Chicago, 1990.

27. This discussion draws on the longer treatment of these issues in Suzanne Berger, "From *Le Mouvement Poujade* to the *Front National*: Studies on the Dark Side of French Politics," in Linda B. Miller and Michael Joseph Smith, eds., *Ideas and Ideals: Essays in Honor of Stanley Hoffmann* (Boulder: Westview, 1993), pp. 313-329.

28. Interview with Jean-Marie Le Pen, *Le Monde*, 17 December 1980.

29. The French were positive about entry into the Gulf War, and no part of the electorate was more enthusiastic than the Front National's electorate.

30. Alain Juppé, in *Le Monde*, 21 March 1990.

31. SOFRES. L'Etat de l'opinion, 1990. Olivier Duhamel and Jérome Jaffré, eds., (Paris: Seuil, 1990), pp. 238-239.

32. SOFRES. 1990, p. 239.

33. Indeed one year after the referendum, polls indicated that the question would not have been approved. *Le Monde*, 21 September 1993, p. 12.

34. Annick Percheron, "Les Français et l'Europe: Acquiescement de façade ou adhésion véritable," *Revue française de science politique* Vol. 41, No. 3 (1991), pp. 382-406. See also Olivier Duhamel and Gérard Grunberg, "Référendum: Les dix Frances," *Le Monde*, 25 September 1992, pp. 1, 7; also Mayer, "Attitudes towards the Region," 1993.

35. Bruno Fanucchi, "Mitterand pour la 'préférence communautaire'," *Le Parisien*, 22 June 1993, p. 3.

36. Cited in Alan Riding, "Paris Seeks to Rally Support for Its Opposition to Trade

Talks," *New York Times*, 19 October 1993, p. A3.

37. Alain Minc, "La nouvelle trahison des clercs," *Le Monde*, 10 June 1993, p. 2.

38. Jean-Pierre Langellier and Claire Tréan, "Un entretien avec Alain Juppé," *Le Monde*, 2 September 1993, p. 1, 8.

39. Jean-Pierre Tuquoi, "Ne pas céder aux sirènes du protectionnisme," *Le Monde*, 2 October 1993, p. 27.

40. "Edouard Balladur défend sa politique économique," *Le Monde*, 20-21 June 1993.

41. Thierry Bréhier, Jean-Marie Colombani, Thomas Ferenczi, and Michel Noblecourt, *"Un entretien avec Edouard Balladur,"* *Le Monde*, 18 May 1993, pp. 9, 10.

42. Alain Gomez, "Le GATT doit mourir: Face au grand perturbateur qu'est le Japon, c'est à l'Europe d'écrire les nouvelles règles du commerce international," *Le Monde*, 28 November 1993, pp. 1, 22.

43. Patrick Devedjian, *Rapport de la Mission d'information sur l'organisation du libre-échange.* Report of subcommittee of *Commission des Finances, Assemblée Nationale*, 1993.

44. Ibid., pp. 11, 12, 22.

45. Ibid., p. 31.

46. On the controversy over the Devedjian report, see *Le Monde*, 9 October 1993, p. 16 and 15 October 1993, p. 21.

47. "M. Longuet juge impossible un développement autarcique de la France," *Le Monde*, 18 November 1993, p. 22.

48. *Le Monde*, 30 November 1993.

49. See "La FNSEA souligne que le dossier du GATT ne concerne pas seulement l'agriculture," and Jean-Pierre Tuquoi, "Commentaire: Reculade," in *Le Monde*, 19 October 1993, p. 23.

50. Phillipe Séguin, *Ce que j'ai dit* (Paris: Grasset, 1993), p. 14.

51. Ibid., pp. 80-81.

52. Ibid., p. 91.

53. Ibid., pp. 47-48.

54. Philippe Séguin. *Discours pour la France* (Paris: Grasset, 1992), p. 17.

55. Séguin, 1993, p. 40.

PART FOUR

France in the New Europe

11

France and Security in the New Europe: Between the Gaullist Legacy and the Search for a New Model

Frédéric Bozo

On peut être grand même sans beaucoup de moyens: il suffit d'être à la hauteur de l'Histoire.

—Charles de Gaulle

There have been extensive discussions about the impact of the revolutions of 1989 on French security policy in the past few years. Yet, because analysts did not immediately fully understand the magnitude of post-Cold War changes in international relations, the topic has not been exhausted. Of course, as many authors have remarked, the fading away of the Cold War logic induces the end of the specific pattern of international relations that served as the framework for France's fairly successful security policies since de Gaulle. But the end of the bipolar era does not only amount to the demise of the bloc system and, consequently, of a strong regulating structure for international relations. Indeed, ethnic conflict in the East, as well as the challenges of integration in the West suggest, albeit in two opposite ways, that the pivotal issue of the international system has again become that of the nation. This, at a time when France, too, has entered a period of introspection centered on French identity, gives a measure of the effort that is needed to embrace security issues in all their dimensions.

This conjunction of radical change outside of France and questioning within the country makes it difficult to discuss France's security policy, because the problem has to be addressed in broad, societal and historical, rather than in narrow diplomatic-strategic terms. And yet the urgency of both the international and the national agendas compels such a discussion and makes it necessary to address current issues in policy terms also. While recent events (the war in Yugoslavia, most obviously, but also the post-Maastricht crisis in European integration) have shattered most of the illusions about how easy it would be to build the "new European order," the period up to the presidential election of 1995 will indeed be crucial if any new thinking in French security policy is to emerge.

Of course, the underlying question for France is this: can the Gaullist legacy be adapted to meet the pressing challenges of the new Europe, or should France elaborate a new model in security policy? In order to answer this question, analyses (and for that matter policies) more than ever must combine historical dimensions with operational relevance. In an attempt to achieve this goal, this chapter proposes to review France's security policy after the Revolutions of 1989, then to single out the challenges France has to face in the long term, and finally, to discuss some possible options for the years to come.

The Post-Yalta Period:
Adapting the Gaullist Legacy

Since 1989, two recurrent themes have pervaded most discussions of French security policy after the collapse of the "Yalta System." First, policy has generally been assessed against the yardstick of the Gaullist experience.[1] Second, building on that assessment, it has become commonplace to argue that France has fluffed its entry into the post-Yalta period. While there is some truth in those analyses, they amount, at least in part, to foregone conclusions. Indeed, using the general's policies as an ideal type of successful approach to European security inevitably leads to belittling whatever was done after that ideal became impracticable. In fact, because the context has changed so much since the 1960s, recent French security policies must be evaluated on their own demonstrable merits.

Soon after the fall of the Berlin Wall, most analysts reached the conclusion that French diplomacy was characterized by a reluctance to acknowledge the demise of the bipolar era and by a measure of nostalgia for the order of Yalta.[2] The division of Europe, many argued, had been altogether profitable for France: the German problem was, de facto, settled; the country enjoyed an unprecedented degree of security within the Atlantic framework; yet it also managed to retain a fair degree of autonomy and influence. It was ironic, as some have noted, to see how the nation whose security concept, ever since de Gaulle, aimed at overcoming the bloc system, had become a status quo power at the time when the general's vision was fulfilled.[3] In the domestic political debate, such analyses were echoed by a French version of the "vision thing," which, very much like in the United States, developed soon after the end of the "consensual" Gulf War. Indeed, it was tempting for the opposition to denounce conservatism in foreign policy as yet another symptom of Mitterrand's inability to meet the daunting challenges that France would have to face in the years to come, whether internally or externally.

In the period immediately after the fall of the Berlin Wall, French security policy, to be sure, was essentially reactive.[4] Even though it is unlikely that Paris tried, as some have argued, to actually impede German unification, there is no denying that France was not in the front seat during the process leading up to German reunification. The Moscow treaty of September 1990 was indeed shaped by the Germans, with the agreement of the Russians and the blessing of the United States. The French, not to mention the British, played a minor role. Moreover, France was slow in acknowledging the need for an extensive transformation of the overall European architecture inherited from the Cold War era. Paris kept aloof from the reform of the Atlantic Alliance that the allies had decided to undertake in 1990-1991 at the London and Rome summits. The French at that time were also reluctant to recognize that the CSCE should play a stronger role in the pan-European dimension of security; this was remarkably clear in the context of the summit hosted in Paris in the fall of 1990. Finally, it took France a while to engage in the adaptation of its military policy to the new strategic environment. This lag was especially striking as regards the hard core of that policy, that is, the nuclear element. Paris, in effect, for quite some time, acted as if French nuclear policy would not be questioned whatever the sea change in the strategic context (e.g., France was most reluctant to acknowledge explicitly that a doctrine focusing on the early use of nuclear weapons no longer made sense).

Yet even though France's early responses to the revolutionary changes in Europe hardly escape criticism, a more nuanced appreciation of the balance sheet emerges with hindsight. Indeed, most of what has been described as conservatism may be explained by two other factors. First, future historians may well find that, Mitterrand's diplomacy in effect tried to channel the revolutionary process in European security, rather than to contain it. For instance, early French reactions to the disintegration of Yugoslavia in 1991 were, arguably, determined by the notion that (very much like in the case of German reunification) the collapse of the federation had to take place in a negotiated, orderly way rather than through unilateral, disruptive moves toward independence. In that sense, as one analyst has observed, French behavior in the security environment of the late 1980s-early 1990s was not simply nostalgic, but also anticipated the new dangers of the post-Yalta world.[5] Yet at a time of irrepressible evolution, advocates of stability often pass for defenders of the status quo. Mitterrand's concern for orderly change (whether in the case of the Germanies, Yugoslavia, or even the Soviet Union) may have been wise, yet it was inevitably taken for historical blindness -- a perception that was definitely aggravated by an unusual number of blunders in style (e.g., the Kiev trip in late 1989, or the apparent blessing of the Moscow coup in the summer of 1991).

Second, France's image as a status quo power during this period may also have been the inevitable consequence of a fundamental choice: the decision to take a quantum leap forward in European unification as the key response to the challenges of the post-Yalta era. Whether that initial choice was right or wrong, it clearly explains French *attentisme* in many instances, for example vis-à-vis NATO or the CSCE -- both institutions being, as seen from Paris in 1990-1991 as potential dissolvers of the West European integration process. At any rate, France's staunch defense of a Community that -- no less than NATO -- was historically a product of the Cold War could hardly not be seen as a way to maintain a structure that served France's interests, notably as a means to check German might. This perception, again, was fuelled by a series of political mistakes, most prominently the poor salesmanship of the European Confederation project. The idea was widely interpreted as a way to postpone EC enlargement for "decades" (as Mitterrand bluntly said in Prague) as well as to exclude the United States from pan-European arrangements. Indeed, because the strength of pro-Western and pro-United States feelings in the "other Europe" were both ignored and underestimated in Paris at that time, France's West European activism in the immediate post-Yalta period could hardly avoid the risk of antagonizing supporters of greater Europe, beginning with the East Europeans.

Of course, in the light of the recent Euro-crisis, one is forced to ask whether Maastricht has been a failure for French diplomacy, and, more specifically, for French European security policy. Indeed, the difficult -- and politically disruptive -- ratification process, the relative impotence of the EC in Yugoslavia, and the de facto breakdown of the European Monetary System as well as the divisive GATT issue (at least until the December 1993 deadline) have revealed the wide gap that remains between the ambitions of Maastricht and current realities. Although it would be outrageous to say that Maastricht is dead, as opponents of the treaty have, there is no denying that the ratification process, ironically, backfired into one of the most serious crises over European integration to date. And because of the fact that since 1989, French diplomacy has thrown all its weight into the European process and especially into its political-military dimension, which it presented as the only viable long-term response to the strategic challenges of the new Europe, the present turmoil can be seen as a major blow to France's post-Cold War security policy.

Here again, however, judgments must be made according to the correct frame of reference. To be sure, Europe's poor showing in the Yugoslav crisis has demonstrated that the common foreign and security policy (CFSP) on which France had banked so much in 1990-1991 was at best a remote objective. "Europe" has to date played a strategic role in Yugoslavia only to the extent France and Britain have. The fact that the Community hardly exists in the security dimension except through its major member states was demonstrated by Mitterrand himself, if only symbolically, when at the close of a European Council meeting in Lisbon in June 1992 he made his solitary trip to Sarajevo without warning the other heads of state. Conversely, the Yugoslav crisis has also shown the pitfalls of searching for a common European position at any cost, notably when, for the sake of the cohesion of the twelve, France and others followed Germany in hastily recognizing Slovenia and Croatia, thus putting all of Europe's weight behind a policy of which they clearly disapproved. The lessons of Yugoslavia are thus twofold: on the one hand, individual member states must retain their autonomy of decision in order to avoid collective European paralysis as a result of the reluctance of others to intervene; on the other hand, they must keep an effective veto power so as to prevent ill-advised policies from being collectively adopted by the Community against their own individual will. Clearly, the CFSP -- if or when it actually takes shape -- will have to be more of an instrument for common action whenever this proves possible on an ad hoc basis, than the single political-military arm of a much fantasized European strategic "actor." To put it in historical terms, the Maastricht process, in the security realm at least, has much more to do with the Fouchet plan than with the European Defense Community.

This, however, is no news. It merely confirms what should have been clear in reading the Maastricht Treaty, chapter V, which is but a legal and institutional framework within which common policies can be evolved. To be sure, other dimensions of the Maastricht design (mostly in the economic realm) could initially pass -- and rightly so -- for being fundamentally integrationist, that is, of a supranational, not intergovernmental essence. The failure of the EMS as well as the problems over the GATT, in that sense, have tended to "renationalize" the European unification process, at least as compared to a *certain* reading of Maastricht. But after all, only extremists on both sides, pro and con, had made such a reading and, as a result, either defended or denounced Maastricht as a federal construction. Recent events only demonstrate that both were equally far away from the truth, and that the treaty -- in security even more than in other aspects -- was in fact meant to formalize the actual stage of European unification rather than to make the United States of Europe irreversible.

As a result, the current Euro-crisis can also be seen -- and used -- as a way to overcome France's fundamental European dilemma. Ever since the early years of European integration, France indeed has been torn between two contradictory objectives: that of stimulating integration -- including in a supranationalist sense -- as a way to absorb Germany's might; and that of assuring that a unified Europe would allow France both to retain a fair degree of national autonomy and to be in a position to use the Community as a tool to increase the country's global influence.[6] That dilemma was very much at the core of France's handling of the Maastricht process -- hence the gap between a federalist declaratory policy and a confederalist operational approach in the negotiation that led to the treaty, particularly as regards the CFSP. But the comeback of a more pragmatic reading -- and practice -- of Maastricht is likely to blur the actual differences between those two approaches, thus making France's European dilemma more manageable.

In the domestic dimension, the post-Maastricht clarification could also ease traditional internal French divisions over the nature of the European unification process. Indeed, even though the ratification campaign, to a large extent thanks to the talents of Philippe Séguin, for a while reawakened those divisions, it is clear today that another EDC battle will not take place -- simply because another EDC is more improbable than ever, as Séguin himself recently recognized when he said that the dream of a "*Europe clés en mains*" had vanished.[7] Finally, it is now becoming increasingly clear that no credible strategic alternative to West European unification has emerged to date. While critics of the Maastricht process, including in France, have advocated other schemes as best suited to provide stability and security in Europe in the long term, neither the Euro-Atlantic nor the pan-European alternatives to a strong West European strategic community have been vindicated by recent events.

Thus, France may well be in a better position to reassert her leading role in European integration, including in its political-military dimension, when the time comes. This, in fact, could be the main assumption behind Prime Minister Balladur's European diplomacy. Since coming to power in March 1993, the new government indeed seems to have pursued two complementary, mutually reinforcing objectives in that realm: that of clarifying the nature of the European process, and that of relegitimizing it in France. Hence Balladur's eagerness, during the GATT renegotiation issue, to reassert ostentatiously the primacy of member states over the Commission as well as to demonstrate clearly to French public opinion that Europe could be used to better defend national interests, rather than the other way round.

Because, as argued above, European integration has been France's main multiplier of European and global influence and power over the past few decades, the post-Maastricht syndrome inescapably raises a third question: that of France's international status. Indeed, a dominant theme in the debate and analyses on French policy after the Cold War has been that of France's allegedly inevitable marginalization in European security. Soon after the fall of the Berlin Wall, most analysts pointed at the unavoidable downgrading of France's international ranking after the demise of the Yalta order. In the inevitable process of power redistribution among the actors of the European system after the end of the Cold War era, it was argued, France's relative position could only decline. Because France's somewhat artificial politico-military status, inherited from de Gaulle's policies, rested on the division of Europe, the demise of the Yalta order could not help but lead to a weakening of the country's international status, when that of other countries, starting of course with Germany, would rise.[8]

However "objective" (if somewhat too mechanical), this argument also has its limits. It rests on the disputable assumption that the new European system -- very much like the defunct East-West system -- is a zero-sum game. Yet the end of the Cold War also has had an impact on other powers and their respective international positions. With the dismantling of the Soviet Union and the difficult stabilization of Russia, Europe's main power in classical, political-military terms is no longer a superpower. Meanwhile, Germany is still far from filling the strategic vacuum left by the USSR in the heart of Europe. Far from increasing its assertiveness, let alone its aggressiveness, the impact of reunification on Germany's policy -- at least for the time being -- appears on the contrary to translate into a relative disappearance in security affairs, and not only from a strictly military point of view (the hasty recognition of Croatia, with hindsight, was arguably the exception that proves the rule). Finally, recent months have confirmed the difficulty of the United States remaining a superpower without a Soviet superpower adversary. Although the Bush administration acted as if the fundamentals of U.S. leadership in Europe remained unchallenged after the Cold War, the Clinton administration has adopted a far more realistic approach. As demonstrated in the Yugoslav case, U.S. willingness to intervene in Europe will unsurprisingly be more and more a function of its perceived national interest rather than one of the obligations of leadership.

In fact, up until now France's role in the former Yugoslavia contradicts the notion of French marginalization in European security. Although critics have discarded French policy as impotence dressed up as activism, France since 1991 has been far more involved in Europe's main crisis than others. Not only has the outbreak of war in the Balkans -- alas -- vindicated France's caveats about the need for negotiated and orderly change, but in fact, for all the obvious limits and the patent shortcomings of that policy (notably its failed attempt at having the EC play an active and cohesive role), Paris has had a leading role in *trying* to solve the crisis. France's determination to remain the number one supplier of troops to the UN gave the country a significant political margin of maneuver, when at the same time, the influence of the United States was limited by its unwillingness to commit ground forces.

The Yugoslav crisis may in fact have marked a turning point in the history of the Atlantic Alliance. Indeed, by thwarting a U.S. initiative aimed at lifting the arms embargo for the Muslims and at initiating air strikes against the Serbs -- a move that, as seen from Paris and London, would only have made things worse in Bosnia, notably for European soldiers on the ground -- France and Britain, in May 1993, essentially reversed the classical Euro-American relationship. Because it amounted to a Franco-British "veto" over a U.S. military initiative perceived as dangerous by the Europeans, some saw a mirror image of the 1956 Suez crisis in this episode. Although this comparison is somewhat far-fetched, events in the former Yugoslavia did illustrate the limits of U.S. influence in the most serious post-Yalta European crisis, thus likely setting a precedent in Euro-American and French-American relations. In a way, the pattern of relations that has emerged between the United States, France, and Britain in the past ten months resembles what de Gaulle had in mind in his 1958 memorandum: a three-power Western directorate on equal footing, with each nation capable of exerting a leading role. While this tripartite geometry hardly fits in France's present vision of a strong and cohesive Western Europe (one should indeed remember that de Gaulle's memorandum diplomacy was written *before* his major European initiatives of the early 1960s), it certainly cannot be described as marginalization.

The widespread perception of France's backward entry into the post-Cold War era thus needs to be reconsidered. To be sure, events in Europe in the past four years, because they have not developed in accordance with Gaullist anticipations of the exit from "Yalta," have fostered the impression of French marginalization in European security. Yet few countries, if any, can claim to have shaped events rather than to have endured them. And, more importantly, none had such a thorough and elaborated blueprint for the post-Cold War period as France has had since de Gaulle.

Beyond Transition:
Concerns for the Long Term

Today, however, as most of the illusions about the post-Cold War period have been shattered, one needs to go beyond this balance sheet of what was arguably a transition period. Europe has indeed entered a new strategic era -- one that is characterized by uncertainty, as it is now clear that no regulating system exists to function as a substitute to the Cold War order. Moreover, institutions inherited from "Yalta" have yet to demonstrate their adaptability and utility in the new strategic context. Finally, even though the institutions seem bound to evolve, what the nature and distribution of power among the actors will be in the longer run seems most unpredictable. While France has arguably met short or middle-term challenges, it nevertheless appears to be helpless in front of future uncertainties in security, as if the country had little or no hold over long-term trends. The reason is threefold: with the demise of the Cold War era, France has arguably lost a coherent strategic concept, a clear vision of security architecture, and a measure of influence over major geopolitical trends.

France's main security problem today, it can be argued, is that there no longer is much of a French *problématique* in security. The point goes beyond the by-now classical discussion on the consequences of the loss of the enemy. That discourse, to be sure, applies to French security policy as well -- and perhaps even more so than in the case of other western nations. The United States and Britain, as insular powers, have gone through periods in history during which they were not directly threatened. In the case of France, a geographically exposed country, the absence of an enemy may well be a totally unprecedented strategic situation.

But the Cold War system offered France more than just a threat. It endowed it with a clear international mission that went beyond the sheer protection of its own vital interests. In other words, France -- at least since de Gaulle -- had a scheme for the international system.[9] In the East-West dimension, France's stated objective was, precisely, to overcome the East-West divide. On the West-West level, France's Atlantic as well as European policies were also defined as a function of that general objective, since they aimed at the loosening of the bloc system, as well as at the emergence of a *sui generis* political-strategic Western Europe (both objectives *not* being contradictory precisely because de Gaulle's Western Europe was not conceived as a bloc). Finally, France's own strategic status also fit in that global, dynamic conception of the international system, since the refusal of military integration within the Atlantic Alliance was conceived as a way to overcome the logic of blocs, and the French nuclear effort was meant to provide the basis for West European strategic autonomy in the long run.

In short, the Cold War was a remarkable period in France's international policy in that, starting in the 1960s, it allowed a strong congruence between France's objectives for the international system and its goals and means as a nation-state. This congruence, in turn, offered three main advantages. First, in the words of Stanley Hoffmann, it allowed de Gaulle and his successors to "project a vision of the future that could serve as a guide for action."[10] Indeed French diplomacy, in all its various aspects, was embedded in a global conceptual framework that generated a sense of general coherence and direction. Second, and consequently, France's international policy gained a high degree of both transparency and of visibility, which, evidently, contributed to the country's international influence and radiance. And finally, France's ability to deliver a strong international message was, in turn, throughout most of the Fifth Republic, a strong factor in the nation's strong consent to an active foreign policy.

With the Cold War security paradigm lost, France finds itself without such a conceptual framework for its international policy. Because the new international order is not an order (as it is characterized by conflict and instability), it is hard for France to define for itself a relevant mission other than the rather vague objective of contributing to peace and stability. And because the new European system is not a system (as it lacks a set of governing rules), it is even harder to offer a coherent interpretation or a global reading of the state of international relations and its evolution. Thus, French international policy after the Cold War will have to face the challenge of empiricism.

Given the highly theorized (to say Cartesian would be a cliché) nature of French policy in the past decades, the new situation confronts France with the need for something approximating a cultural revolution. Empiricism, indeed, represents a threefold challenge if France is to keep a well-focused approach to security. First, in spite of a chaotic international environment, France's policy will have to remain internally coherent. The difficulty here is to find guidelines according to which the country should decide whether and how to act in specific security situations. Without such guidelines, the risk of contradiction or, at least, of dispersion would be great, which, for instance, may already be the case as regards France's "*tous azimuts*" participation in UN military operations. Second, even though it will be difficult to continue to deliver a strong external message in the absence of a specific mission, France will have to convince the rest of the world that its international security activism fits within a specific view of Europe and the world to which France wants to contribute, and that the country does not merely aim at confirming its status as a "great power." And finally, even though this will be a more difficult task in the absence of vital stakes or of a clear vision of the world order, French security policy must continue to generate internal consensus.

The lack of a conceptual framework after the Cold War could be felt acutely in the institutional dimension of French security policy. During the bipolar era, France had, and expressed, a clear view of what European architecture should be. The nature of security called for that. Political-military organizations (and, first and foremost, alliances) indeed played a dominant role in the overall functioning of the system as a result of its very characteristics. The prevalence of the military element in international relations and the existence of a permanent and mutual threat made the peacetime organization of common defenses the cornerstone of security. Moreover, the efficiency of mutual deterrence rested on the centralization of control over nuclear weapons and strategy within each camp. Finally, because the nuclear stalemate made military confrontation unthinkable, war, in a way, had to be waged by other means -- among which security institutions played a key role (and of course, the same was true as to relations and *rapports de force* within each bloc).

As a result, France under de Gaulle and his successors, more than other nations, based its policy on its own perspective on European security architecture and its evolution, as well as on its own specific position in the edifice. In fact, the hard core of French security policy in that period, that is, relations with NATO, was primarily an exercise in security architecture. By defining its own unique status within the Atlantic construction, while at the same time offering an alternative design for transatlantic relations, France managed to maximize her political influence in the West and beyond.

Today, however, such an approach makes much less sense than in the Cold War period. For one thing, institutional problems have become somewhat secondary as compared to the burning security problems caused by ethnic conflict and the like. Even though institutions involved in European security claim to play a major role in those problems, the war in the Balkans so far has demonstrated the opposite. Although NATO, the WEU, the CSCE, and to an extent the UN have made efforts to adapt their objectives and modus operandi to the new strategic landscape, they have achieved little in concrete terms. In fact, these institutions, in competing for an active role in Yugoslavia and elsewhere, have achieved "interblocking" rather than "interlocking" -- a situation for which France, too, shares a measure of responsibility.[11] As a consequence, the current institutional debate, in the new context, is becoming increasingly irrelevant -- not unlike discussing architecture in a house on fire.

In fact, France's plans for European security architecture are now in disarray. Even though, as hinted above, the post-Maastricht crisis has led to a welcome clarification of the European project by stressing what it is *not* about, the crisis has nonetheless reopened the question of what it *is* about, thus calling into question the very cornerstone of France's architectural vision. In the past few years, creating a West European politico-military identity had become the main ratio-nale for French NATO policies, but in the post-Maastricht context, a bipolar NATO seems quite remote. In the meantime, the transatlantic dimension of France's architectural vision has also become quite hazy. As to the once traditional pan-European dimension of security architecture as seen from Paris, it has, as argued above, been much neglected by the French since the last few years of the Cold War.

France's current weakness in the debate over security architecture in Europe represents a serious problem for the country's international policy. In the short term, this obviously weakens French diplomacy by confusing its objectives and weakening its main tool. In the long term, it could also contribute to an ominous scenario: if nothing is done, the presently poor state of security institutions might well degenerate further when in fact France, no longer a great power, has an interest in the maintenance of a strong institutional security structure. Because its own role in security can only be conceived in terms of common defense and/or of collective security, that is, in multilateral terms, when at the same time others will be able to resort to unilateral action, France needs institutional structures robust enough for it to remain an active player in the security game and, at the same time, channel potentially adverse geopolitical trends.

With neither a strong conceptual framework nor a clear architectural design for European security, France indeed finds itself confronted by a third major un-certainty: that of its leverage over the international power structure and its evolu-tion. To be sure, as hinted above, the collapse of the Soviet Union and Russia's strategic withdrawal, reunified Germany's reluctance to play an activist security role in its traditional sphere of influence, and the United States's relative disap-pearance from Europe have so far played into France's hands. Yet, here again, the longer term is more elusive. It is obvious that those key variables may change in the future: Russia could rebuild its power base and become expansionist again; Germany, after the economic and political digestion of its own reunification, could turn hegemonic in Central Europe; and the United States could do two opposite but equally dangerous things from a French point of view: it could try to restore its past leadership in Europe or, on the contrary, withdraw altogether.

The problem for France today, however, is not so much the risk that such negative trends will develop -- little can be done about that -- but rather the fact that, in the new strategic context, France is likely to have little influence over them. During the Cold War years, France, in spite of its own limited weight, had a measure of influence over those variables. In its own way, France contributed to Lord Ismay's famous triptych: by a strong yet autonomous defense posture, it played a role in containing the Soviet Union (at times, France could even have the feeling that it could contribute to contain the great Chinese geopolitical mass thanks to its nuclear deterrence -- that, at any rate, was what the famous *tous azimuts* doctrine was about); thanks to the Community and the Franco-German partnership, it helped to anchor Germany's growing might to the West; and through its *à la carte* participation in the U.S.-led Atlantic Alliance, it aimed at stabilizing U.S. involvement in European security affairs at what it considered a reasonable level.

In sum, in the Cold War system, France had a feeling that it held sway over major geopolitical trends and evolutions. But with the Cold War security framework gone and the European architecture now shaky, France is likely to lose most of that leverage, whether perceived or actual. Balancing Russia militarily no longer makes much sense in the absence of an inimical East-West relationship, and arms control and collective security do not appear to be sufficient to check Russia's potential might. Moreover, with the post-Maastricht adjustment of the European process in a confederal, intergovernmental direction and the likely widening of the Community, it will evidently become more difficult to channel German energies within a West European framework. Finally, because NATO is likely to become a much looser alliance than during the Cold War, the actual degree of U.S. involvement in European security will be less and less dependent on issues such as military integration and France's role therein.

The feeling that France is likely to have only marginal leverage over future power trends is, obviously, also fuelled by the fear that France's national power base is likely to shrink as a result of the transformation of the nature of international power -- a reflection of the by-now classical debate over the respective roles of economic and political-strategic might. In the security field, the main French anxiety (and rightly so) is indeed that of a devaluation of the nation's key political-strategic asset, that is, the *force de frappe*. The military relevance of nuclear weapons is, naturally, fading away with the end of the bipolar nuclear confrontation. In turn, the nuclear club is becoming less exclusive as a result of proliferation, and being a nuclear power provides a far less indisputable international political status than before. Meanwhile, the question of the limits of French resources arises with regard to conventional forces, at a time when such forces have regained much strategic importance due to the increasing importance of peace-making and peace-keeping. In fact, France's status today as the first military contributor to the UN may well be more a reflection of the constraints or self-restraint of other potential large contributors such as Japan or Germany than of France's actual primacy. But this status, also, could well change if either country were to become more active in peace-keeping.

De Gaulle's main achievement in foreign policy was, in many ways, to restore France as a world power while, at the same time, recognizing that it had become but a medium power. The specific Cold War international context as well as the result of the general's exceptional statesmanship made this feat possible. With both of these factors gone, this equation has to be reworked -- which, arguably, could well be the answer to the academic debate over the validity of the Gaullist legacy.

In Search of a New Model

Because the Gaullist security calculus was derived from a set of assumptions about the nature of security, the institutional framework and the underlying power structure, all of which are now being thoroughly called into question, the challenges confronting the country's security policy indeed go far beyond the need for adaptation. Yet although there is widespread agreement on the need for new thinking, new patterns of analysis or prescriptions have yet to emerge. Some analysts have stressed the necessity either to reassert French *"singularité"* or to relinquish it, as if it were an end in itself. Others have proposed a new approach to security architecture, generally focusing on the France-NATO relationship as if it were still the alpha and omega of France's security policy. In sum, few have made a serious attempt at defining what the goals of French policy should be before discussing its means.[12]

And yet France's security policy should be primarily aimed at dealing with the current focus of European insecurity. Much as the overcoming of blocs provided the rationale for the country's Cold War diplomacy, effective conflict resolution and prevention should indeed serve as its *fil rouge* for the post-Yalta era, thus restoring the sense of a French international mission. In addition, as the recent institutional debate has made clear, international organizations must be helped to contribute actively to maintaining stability if they are to survive and to serve as building blocks of a strong European architecture (which France needs). Moreover, it is only in this way that France, in spite of its limited resources, can hope to keep a measure of influence over future power shifts in European security after the Cold War. Finally, making collective security work, particularly in Central and Eastern Europe and the periphery of the former Soviet empire, would go a long way toward meeting the core French security interests in the new Europe: it would diminish the risks of the return of a hegemonic Russia, offer the most serious guarantee against the risks of German unilateralism, and help keep the United States firmly committed to the maintenance of security in Europe.

For French security policy to refocus on conflict resolution and prevention, however, is a demanding challenge, since it means, in essence, dealing with the deep-rooted problems of minorities and borders. After a long period of having been suppressed by the Yalta order, identity and territory have again become the main ingredients of conflict in Europe. In fact, as some have noted, the classical security dilemma applies to ethnic conflict with particular relevance.[13] Moreover, in Central and Eastern Europe, given the complexities of history and geography in that part of the continent, a nation-state can hardly be established but at the expense of neighboring groups or nations. And thus far, in the face of such daunting problems, collective action, as demonstrated in Yugoslavia, has only resulted in the relative paralysis of most of the security institutions involved, both on the military level (peace-keeping or peace-making), and on the political level (conflict prevention).

Of course, most of the inadequacies of collective action can be explained primarily by the fundamental internal contradictions that have marked the international community in its treatment of the crisis. (The most patent contradiction in the Yugoslav case was to acknowledge -- and even encourage through the recognition of Croatia -- the disintegration of the federation, and then to cling to the fiction of a multinational Bosnia.) Yet those contradictions are but a reflection of a fundamental problem that the international community has to face when dealing with ethnic conflict: that of the need to choose between the primacy of self-determination and the priority of stability.

There is, to be sure, a growing awareness of the need to overcome this *collective* security dilemma. Since the 1992 Helsinki conference, conflict prevention has topped the CSCE agenda. France itself has made efforts to have the international community focus on these issues. In fact, the major French diplomatic initiative in the past few months, Edouard Balladur's plan for a pact on security and stability in Europe, was meant as a major contribution to that debate. By recognizing the legitimacy of national aspirations and at the same time postulating the need to satisfy them within a negotiated framework (including the discussion of borders and minorities), the Balladur plan clearly sets out the framework within which the international community must attempt to prevent future crises.

To be sure, history suggests that a stable balance between the conflicting notions of self-determination and international order is in France's own interest. Yet defining the proper trade-off between legitimate national aspirations and international security requirements is obviously a difficult task.[14] In a way, the international community today, *mutatis mutandis*, faces a challenge similar to the one that confronted the Concert of Europe, which, until its breakdown, was essentially concerned with making national sentiment manageable for the great powers.

Yet, even though institutions such as the CSCE or initiatives such as the Balladur plan will be central to overcoming the post-Cold War *collective* security dilemma, more will be required. As the Yugoslav crisis has shown -- especially from a Franco-German perspective -- differences over ways to deal with ethnic conflict remain deep-rooted. The disagreement between Bonn and Paris over Yugoslavia was fundamentally a matter of national experience. The dispute was not, as some have argued, because of old patterns of antagonism or friendship dating back to the balance of power system, but rather because it corresponded to different traditions in nationhood: the one based on ethnicity and therefore well-inclined vis-à-vis national aspirations (particularly in the context of German unification) the other based on citizenship and thus naturally more reluctant to recognize such aspirations outright.[15]

The key lesson in Yugoslavia is that without agreement about the criteria for membership in the international community, or about which groups must be protected as minorities within existing international borders, collective security simply cannot function -- and, what is worse, security communities such as that of Western Europe can be torn apart. In short, because newly independent groups essentially fight for recognition as states or entities in their own rights, the problem of nationhood has become central from a security point of view.

The policy implications of this situation are long-term ones, and they go far beyond the traditional boundaries of strategy. To continue with the Franco-German example, the two countries' partnership will arguably need to draw renewed strength from an intense dialogue on the essentials of security and, first and foremost, on the question: what is a nation?[16] Such Franco-German dialogue is also needed in the context of European unification for reasons that go beyond traditional security concerns, for example, immigration, citizenship and so forth; this, in turn is a reflection of the fact that the security agenda after the Cold War has become fundamentally societal rather than narrowly strategic. Of course, beyond France and Germany, what is at stake, as always, is the necessity for consensus on those questions to emerge in larger circles -- in Western Europe initially, and later, beyond. Thus, in the long term, France's ability to maintain a leading role in security will rest on its ability to generate such international consensus on fundamental security issues, and to translate it into effective actions within the framework of the existing security institutions.

To be sure, the maintenance of such a framework of effective organizations is, as Mitterrand has frequently insisted since 1989, very much in the country's interest.[17] Yet it requires France's (and, for that matter, other powers') recognition that security organizations are not ends in themselves, but rather instruments at the service of collective action; as a result, they can be effective and viable in the long term only if member states are able to agree on the basics. This recognition should in fact serve as the basis of the overall French approach to European security architecture after the Cold war.

In spite of the present crisis, West European unification -- as even opponents of Maastricht recognize -- will likely remain the long-term goal of the French approach to European security.[18] In the face of turmoil in the East, the construction of a politically organized Western Europe certainly remains one of the only stable points of reference in Europe today; it may also be the only guarantee against Western European integration unraveling. And yet France's objective of promoting European security unification will be hard to pursue in the years to come. In the present context of economic stagnation and political anomie among member states and in Western Europe as a whole, the French should harbor no illusions that they can resurrect anytime soon *l'Europe stratégique* as foreshadowed in Maastricht. As a matter of fact, their capacity to give substance to the notion of a CFSP will be a function of their acknowledgment of the fact that the significance and nature of the security dimension within the West European construction is bound to evolve profoundly. In the past few years, unification in security matters was essentially presented as the natural attribute of the European

Union -- European integration, it was argued, would simply not be achieved without a strategic arm. Although this justification may still be valid in terms of historic development, it has lost much of its operational value in the post-Maastricht context of uncertainty as to the goals and nature of the European process. As a result, the security dimension of the West European construction will likely remain disconnected from the rest of the process and it will have to be defended for its own merits, that is, its actual contribution to stability in the rest of the continent.

By and large, the process of European unification in security will be of a predominantly political rather than military nature in the years to come. In the Yugoslav case, the absence of agreement among West Europeans over the nature of the crisis was indeed fraught with more consequences than their military weakness, whether individual or collective. The capacity of the European Union members to agree on fundamentals -- not their ability to manage common military operations -- will therefore be the real discriminating characteristic for a CFSP and should thus be the focus of French policies in that realm. In light of most predictable scenarios, the objective of setting up a full-blown European military apparatus in its own right does not only appear rather unrealistic, but in fact futile, given the real nature of the challenges that will have to be met. France need not abandon efforts to better structure potential West European military actions within the European Union or the WEU, as has begun to take place in recent years. But the focus of those efforts will be less sharply on a European defense identity per se than on the pursuit of pragmatic military arrangements designed to give the Europeans a measure of military autonomy, if and when it may be needed.

Finally, France now has to face the fact that not only has the widening of the European Union become inevitable, but also that the Union will be a stabilizing factor in European security all the more if it is prepared to open up. Indeed as a result of the foregoing -- in the security dimension at least -- widening Western Europe should no longer be perceived by France as a threat to deepening. After all, increasing the number of participants would neither make the possibility of dissension more probable nor that of consensus more unlikely than today. More importantly, the prospect of membership in the European Union is likely, in the years to come, to be a powerful incentive for potential applicants to settle their disputes over borders and minorities. (To be sure, the Balladur plan fits in that perspective, but to date does not seem to have fully convinced Central and Eastern Europeans who interpret it as yet another French gimmick -- much like the Confederation -- to postpone their admission to Western institutions.[19])

A revision of France's policy along the lines described could also modify the present France-NATO equation. While France's resistance to NATO reform in the past few years was essentially motivated by the fear that a rejuvenated alliance with a major role in collective security -- that is, beyond its traditional Article 5 missions -- would preempt the West European security dimension and artificially prolong U.S. hegemony, recent events are likely to assuage French misgivings on both scores. Indeed the first type of concerns made sense to the extent that the European Security and Defense Identity (ESDI) was thought of in terms of a single West European strategic actor, which could only compete with NATO. Today, however, the traditional French vision of a bipolar alliance appears more elusive, with the European pole blurred and the American one flickering. The Clinton administration recognizes the need for increased European responsibilities within the alliance, and this stance is likely to ease the traditional tension between ESDI and NATO. Indeed, the French rallied to the U.S.-sponsored concept of "separable but not separate" European forces within NATO during the January 1994 Brussels summit. Adapting the Alliance structure so that NATO assets could be used by European members even if the United States is not actively involved (e.g., in peace-keeping operations such as those now under way in Bosnia) has become crucial and could contribute to a normalization of France's NATO ties. This will, however, remain short of reintegration, which would make no sense from the point of view of France or NATO.[20]

France's concerns about U.S. hegemony in Europe continuing by virtue of a new, major NATO role in collective security writ large have also waned. Indeed the underlying French assumption since 1989 that the alliance and U.S. presence will remain overwhelming in spite of the demise of the Cold War now seems doubtful. In spite of NATO's apparently successful adaptation to the new security context, the Yugoslav crisis and NATO's marginal role therein have shown that major uncertainties remain as to its very raison d'être over the long term. As emphasized at the January 1994 summit, it is now becoming clear that, beyond institutional reform, the future of the alliance will depend on the Allies' ability to actually transform NATO into an effective instrument to enforce collective security in Europe. Conversely, the Yugoslav experience and the prospects for the implementation of a peace plan in Bosnia -- however elusive, if not theoretical -- suggests that such an instrument is indeed needed in order to implement peace-keeping on a large scale, let alone peace-making. France, once far more reluctant, has already acknowledged this evolution by taking a larger part in the preparation of such contingencies, including at the operational level. Meanwhile, the United States has come to recognize that however vital NATO is for taking on such new tasks, it is still largely maladapted to implementing collective security, as the integrated structure, a relic of the Cold War logic, lacks the flexibility necessary to deal with post-Cold War crises. Hence, it developed the idea of planning Combined Joint Task Forces (CJTF) on an ad hoc basis in an effort to introduce modularity in such operations.

To be sure, the modalities of an effective West European security and defense capacity as well as those of NATO's potential role in peace-keeping or peace-making operations remain to be settled. On both scores France is likely to continue to defend what it perceives as French and European interests, both by fostering efforts at political-military integration within the European Union/WEU (at some point, the issue of an autonomous WEU command structure will have to be raised), and by emphasizing the need to correct the "major flaw" of the alliance, that is, the weakness of political control over military authorities. Such control is indeed arguably all the more necessary in peace-making or peace-keeping because military actions on the ground are so fraught with political consequences.[21] Yet after three decades of a "troubled partnership," there is little denying that the two main factors of discord within the alliance are de facto becoming obsolete. Facts are indeed drawing the two key protagonists, France and the United States, closer to an agreement than they have been in thirty years on both the internal structure of the alliance and its function in the European system. To be sure, such a normalization of France-NATO relations should not overshadow the need for a renewed French interest and activism on the pan-European level of security, notably as regards the CSCE (which needs to be transformed into a regional collective security organization), and, for that matter, the UN (whose security council needs to be adapted with regard both to membership and functioning). Both institutions have demonstrated their limits and require serious thinking as to their roles and modi operandi, and French diplomacy should remain actively involved in that process. Moreover, as hinted above, one of the key institutional issues in the years to come will be that of defining the link between collective security organizations -- the UN and the CSCE -- and common defense organizations -- NATO and the WEU.

Finally, there is the question of leadership. The main argument of this chapter is that if France adapts its concept of security, adjusts its approach to international institutions and redefines its own position in the European system, then strategic decline is not inevitable after the Cold War. Indeed the notion that the country's influence will shrink to a degree commensurate with its actual power base is most disputable. In the Cold War system, France was a medium power with a more than medium influence because it found an appropriate international role. The same could be true after the Cold War, provided it is realized that such a role must be thoroughly redefined -- a task that, by definition, requires a sense of direction.

Yet the present phase of *cohabitation*, although far more successful in terms of the functioning of French diplomacy than the previous experience, is not favorable to this adjustment. Relations between the government and the president are good on the substance of French foreign policy; even though the international context is far more fluid than in 1986-1988, there seems to be no major dissension of the magnitude experienced then. But neither the government nor the president has the legitimacy nor indeed the margin of maneuver necessary for proposing far-reaching concepts of what the country's international security policy should be in the long term. Moreover -- not unlike the U.S. situation -- the order of national priorities is clearly not favorable to the redefinition of foreign and security policy, and not only in terms of allocation of resources. Indeed, the magnitude of economic, social, and cultural problems to be tackled domestically makes it difficult to address international issues in a constructive way. Finally, the crisis in constructing Europe, because it blurs the main traditional references of France's international policy, also makes it more difficult for the French. The current debate over French defense policy provides a case in point. While key variables of the Gaullist legacy in defense policy are evidently being called into question (the strategic significance of the nuclear element, the relevance of a mainly conscription army and, maybe -- in the absence of a vital threat -- the very notion of strategic autonomy), the drafting of a new defense White Paper, the first in over twenty years, was essentially done without any serious thinking on the nature of security problems upstream.

In fact, the fundamental reappraisal that is so badly needed may still be distant. The new start in France's security role in Europe will occur at best after the next presidential election of 1995, and then only if the candidates realize the vast challenges confronting the French nation in its international role. While leadership is essential, even more will arguably depend on the long-term evolution of the society, and, in fact, on the evolution of French identity. At a time when the focus of international relations and security in the East and the West has again become the nation, France is unlikely to remain unaffected by this general phenomenon. In the French case, ever since the advent of modern times, the state of international relations and the spirit of the nation have been indissolubly intertwined. Thus what is fundamentally at stake with regard to foreign policy in the present phase of national introspection is, to use Michel Winock's words, the distinction between an "open" conception of the nation and a "closed" one. The battle between the two conceptions is most clear in the debate over immigration, assimilation and the like. But it is also relevant from a foreign policy point of view. Indeed it will require the French to develop a generous conception of their own national identity in order for them to feel concerned and do something about the unrest caused by the identity problems of others and thus keep a leading role in security policy.

Notes

1. For an extensive discussion of the Gaullist experience and its legacy in security policy, see Philip H. Gordon, *A Certain Idea of France: French Security Policy and the Gaullist Legacy* (Princeton: Princeton University Press, 1993).

2. See this author's discussion in "Paradigm Lost: The French Experience with Détente" in Richard Davy, ed., *European Detente: A Reappraisal* (London: Sage/RIIA, 1992).

3. See, for example, Michael Stürmer, "As 'Escape from Yalta' came to pass, a strategy for Germany crumbled," *International Herald Tribune*, 7 March 1990; and Henry Kissinger, "De Gaulle: what he would do now," ibid.

4. For a critical description of French security policy in the first year after the fall of the Berlin Wall, see Claire Tréan, "La France et le nouvel ordre européen," *Politique*

étrangère, 1/91, pp. 81-90; see also Hubert Védrine and Jean Musitelli's semi-official point of view: "Les changements des années 1989-1990 et l'Europe de la prochaine décennie," ibid., pp. 165-177; and Frédéric Bozo, "French security policy and the new European order" in Colin McInnes, ed., *Security and Strategy in the New Europe* (London: Routledge, 1992).

5. Ronald Tiersky, "France in the New Europe," *Foreign Affairs*, Spring 1992, pp. 131-146.

6. See Stanley Hoffmann, "Dilemmes et stratégies de la France dans la nouvelle Europe (1989-1991)," *Politique étrangère*, 4/92, pp. 879-892.

7. "Où va la construction européenne?", Speech by Philippe Séguin given at the University of Paris-Dauphine, 1 December 1993.

8. See the discussion in Gordon, 186ff.

9. See Stanley Hoffmann "Charles de Gaulle's Foreign Policy," to be published in a book edited by Gordon Craig.

10. Ibid.

11. See Jérôme Paolini and Alexis Seydoux, "From Western Security Interblocking to Institutional Evolutionism," in *Challenges and Responses for Future European Security: British, French and German Perspectives*, European Strategy Group, 1993; and Frédéric Bozo "Organisations de sécurité et insécurité en Europe," *Politique étrangère* 2/93, pp. 447-458.

12. See for example, Didier Grange, "Pour une nouvelle politique étrangère," *Esprit*, November 1992, pp. 13-43; François Bujon de l'Estang, "France: pour une nouvelle politique étrangère," *Politique internationale*, Winter 1992/1993, pp. 177-192; and Marisol Touraine, "France-Etats-Unis: une histoire au passé?" *Politique étrangère*, 3/93, pp. 725-732.

13. Barry Posen, "The Security Dilemma and Ethnic Conflict," *Survival*, Spring 1993, pp. 27-47.

14. See Georges-Henri Soutou, "La question des nationalités à l'Est," *Politique étrangère*, 3/93, pp. 697-711.

15. On ethnicity and international relations after the Cold War, see Pierre Hassner, "Beyond Nationalism and Internationalism: Ethnicity and World Order," *Survival*, Summer 1993, pp. 49-65.

16. The Balladur plan for security and stability in Europe would, by the way, have better contributed to that had it been a Franco-German initiative from the outset.

17. See his interview with *L'Expansion*, 17 October 1991.

18. See for example Philippe Séguin, speech at University of Paris-Dauphine.

19. However the US proposed "Partnership for Peace" (a half formula with no guarantee of future membership) is likely to have a positive effect on the perception of French diplomacy in Central and Eastern Europe by shifting the *"mauvais rôle"* over to US diplomacy.

20. See Pascal Boniface, "Inutile de réintégrer l'OTAN," *Libération*, 10 January 1994.

21. See G. Trangis, "Ni splendide isolement, ni réintégration," *Le Monde*, 14 July 1993. Of course, this also means that there should be a measure of politico-military control on the part of the Security Council over NATO operations, for the alliance does not have the legitimacy to decide by itself on such interventions.

12

French Identity and
Post-Cold War Europe

Gregory Flynn

There can be little doubt that the French today are grappling with their identity. As Pierre Nora has argued, "one model of the nation is giving away to another, which is still being painfully sought."[1]   While this process has been under way for some time, it has acquired a new sense of urgency over the past few years.

One of the main reasons for this new urgency has been the revolutionary change in Europe since 1989. Uncertainties about the future shape of the continent have reinforced the already substantial political, social, and economic dilemmas brought on by the modernization and transformation of France during the postwar period. The collapse of bipolarity has also challenged basic notions of how France has defined itself.

During the postwar period, especially since the advent of the Fifth Republic, France has both perceived and described itself as occupying an exceptional position within the European system. The nation resided within the bipolar structure as a key member of the Western Alliance but it also stood above the structure as an actor less bound by its constraints. France further saw itself as a key shaper of European unity, a nation with a special role in Europe's future, and at the same time as a nation with a mission larger than Europe.

The end of a divided Europe has brought the end of the conditions that facilitated this assertion of French exceptionalism. It has brought to a head the dilemmas inherent in the decline from great power status, which France was unable to resolve in the 1950s and was thereafter able to hide under the mantle of Gaullism.

Specifically, France must now confront the consequences of being dependent for crucial dimensions of its security and economic well-being both on the behavior of its neighbors, and on their security and economic well-being. This situation is forcing France to reconsider precisely how its national interests are defined. France has long had two souls[2] -- one national and one European -- but has heretofore been capable of successfully ignoring, or at least circumventing, their incompatibilities.

None of this is to suggest that France did not depend heavily on the United States and on its European partners for both security and economic welfare during the Cold War. But the context was fundamentally different. The Cold War *system* was so rigid that France actually gained the flexibility to pursue a national vision of its role because both the Atlantic Alliance and the European integration process, although affected by France's policies, were condemned to survive. They were constituent parts of the larger system. Such systemic stalemate ensured French security: It was impossible to secure Europe without protecting France. Moreover, it was possible to have European integration on the cheap: The "negative integration" of tariff barrier reduction brought immediate gains to all and thus guaranteed the European Community's endurance without forcing the issue of national sovereignty that more adventurous moves toward "positive integration" or institution building always raised.[3]

France was thus able to "reconcile" its commitment to collective interests with its desire to defend its national prerogatives without having to make hard choices. That juggling act is going to be infinitely more difficult, if not impossible, in post-bipolar Europe. The system is once again fluid, there are real choices to be made, and it will matter more which policies France chooses to pursue. For the first time since the early 1950s, there is once again a real debate, provoked in large part by the Maastricht Referendum, about how France's national interest relates to choices at the European level. France's two souls must, at a minimum, find a new means of coexisting, with each facing new challenges from the other.

The situation today unquestionably adds a critical dimension to the debate over French identity. And yet, precisely how it relates to what we normally understand as identity is not so clear. No one would argue that recent changes in Europe have made the French feel less French. Indeed, evidence shows that even the most pro-European French men and women are French first (save, perhaps, a number of good Bretons who may well identify with both Europe and their region more than with France).[4] At the same time, the challenges of the new Europe, bringing with them a new pattern of external constraints, obviously affect how France views itself.

What the French have lost with the collapse of postwar Europe is not their identity of being French, but an integral piece of what it has meant to be French. French foreign policy in the Fifth Republic, with its symbols of *Independence* and *Grandeur*, gave form to France's sense of being a country with a unique mission. As William Wallace has argued, "Foreign policy is about national identity itself: about the sources of national pride, the characteristics which distinguish a country from its neighbors, the core elements of sovereignty it seeks to defend, the values it stands for and seeks to promote abroad."[5] The new Europe will force the French to rethink all of these dimensions. They will have to do so under conditions where it will no longer be as easy to maintain the same ambiguity about the relationship between France's sovereignty and its national interests. Moreover, there may well be no symbols as powerful as *Independence* and *Grandeur* to help control the tension between France's desire for national autonomy and the requirements of building a collective Europe. The disappearance of a permissive context confronts France with the need not only for new policies, but for something much deeper: a new expression of what it means to be French in today's Europe.

The Essence and Content of Identity

The basic case being made here is that an intimate link exists between French identity and the European order. Scholars have until now largely ignored the relationship between international context and national identity.[6] To explore this relationship, one must make some conceptual distinctions that are not normally made in the literature on identity or nationalism. Doing so, however, offers insight into the problems and prospects for French policy makers successfully dealing with the dilemmas they currently confront.

Traditionally, national identity has been analyzed primarily as a quality developed during the emergence of the nation-state. Scholars have been concerned with how populations developed an identity with the national state, rather than simply a local or regional sense of self. While there has been some debate about whether national identities are primarily based on something inherent about a collectivity or are mainly constructed, the focus remains heavily on the nation-building phase. This is certainly true for the literature on French identity.

While there are exceptions, most of this basic literature does not really consider the notion that the identity of a nation can change over time. It concentrates on what makes the citizen identify with the nation initially and has not been interested in what happens to a nation's identity as the country moves through different phases of its existence. Some would presumably consider the question irrelevant as long as the underlying sources of national cohesion had been identified. It is clear, however, that there is more to a nation's identity than the initial glue that bonded its people together. Indeed, it is clear that a nation's identity, at least in some of its dimensions, can be quite different from one historical period to another.

To capture this, it is helpful for our purposes to examine French identity not just as comprising many different dimensions, but as having two distinct components: an *essence* and a *content*. Inevitably, one must approach this analysis from the level of a citizen who gives loyalty to the nation. On one hand the *essence* of French identity can be considered to embody those qualities that make an individual identify with France instead of other potential objects of loyalty -- what it takes for someone to feel French (as opposed to German). The most obvious examples concern language and other elements of culture that separate the French from their neighbors, as well as basic expectations of what the state is to provide the individual in terms of security, welfare, and preservation of basic values; in other words, the basic social compact between the citizen and the state. The *content* of French identity, on the other hand, embodies those qualities that help define what it means to be French at a given moment. Here, the obvious examples are specific political institutions or economic approaches, and certain social and cultural patterns.[7]

Both essence and content are integral to the identity of a nation at all times. Although both can change over time, the distinction between the two lies in the time frame over which each can change and in the fact that content can change without affecting the basic identification of the individual with the nation. Using these distinctions does not really take a position on whether identity at the origin of the nation emerged from inherent characteristics or was constructed over time. It clearly does mean, however, that identity is a dynamic and not a static concept.

The essence of a nation's identity is stable (as stable, at least, as the nation itself) and change will occur rarely and only over a long period of time. But if one accepts that the identification of the individual with the nation is not only emotional but also functional, anything that were to call fundamentally into question the social compact between a state and its citizens could also affect the essence of a nation's identity. Such a circumstance could result, for example, from factors that affect the basic organization of national and international life, such as the evolution of technological and economic conditions. If the state cannot adjust to meet its population's demands under the new conditions, either the population must drop certain of its demands, or alternatively, begin to make these demands on some other institution or authority that can meet them. Elements of loyalty can thereby be transferred to a lower, regional or local level, or to a higher, European or international level, and in the process, a piece of identity will be transferred from the nation-state to the other authority. This need not result in a French citizen ceasing to feel French, but it will mean that an important part of the bonding agent has been altered, and along with it, the essence of France's collective identity.

All of this assumes, as is widely accepted today, that identity, even in its essence, is not an exclusive concept. Thus it is possible for an individual to have multiple identities -- multiple objects of loyalty -- each of which can claim priority depending on the circumstances or the issue in question. It is useful to conceive of multiple identities in terms of concentric circles.[8] For our purpose, these circles will center on the individual and move outward through various local or regional layers to the nation, and then on to the European level and beyond.

It is clear in a country like France, for example, that many individuals do have strong regional identities that dominate on many issues. At the same time, it is equally clear that these same individuals will feel French rather than German. Some may also have a well-developed sense of a European identity, holding Brussels responsible for important dimensions of the social compact. Nonetheless, most authors have concluded, as Anthony Smith has written, that national identification remains "the cultural and political norm, transcending other loyalties in scope and power."[9]

Unlike the essence, the content of national identity will change much more frequently because it is heavily determined by the context in which the nation exists at any point in time. Thus, in one period, society may be structured in a way that symbolizes an important dimension of what it means, for example, to be French. If that social structure is made obsolete by significant changes in economic conditions, however, new expression of what it means to be French under the new conditions must be found. In the process, new content will be given to identity. Indeed, until this happens, the country will experience a crisis of identity because of the change in context.

There is an intimate, indeed dialectic, relationship between the essence and content of national identity. The essence of French identity determines those inviolable basic values that must be preserved by the state and, in an important way, therefore, thus sets limits on what content can be given to French identity in shaping responses to context. In theory, at least, it is also possible for the content of French identity that has been developed in a specific historical context to become so much a part of what it means to be French that it becomes part of the essence. When this happens, adjustments to changes in context will not be able to violate certain specific values even if these values had not existed in previous times. When a nation is comfortable with its identity, both the essence and content will be in harmony with one another. In periods of change, however, the dialectic relationship between the two is brought to the fore.

Thinking about national identity in terms of these two basic components makes it much easier to understand the link between French identity, the international context, and recent changes in Europe. The essence of French identity determines a set of basic norms that France's international profile must incorporate in order for French foreign policy to find support at home. The constraints and opportunities offered by the international context determine the limits within which France must find an expression of itself through its foreign policy at any point in time. Over the years, the international context has been one of the most important in helping define the content of French identity. When there are changes to context, particularly when there are dramatic changes -- such as the collapse of the traditional European state system, France's decline from great power status, and the emergence of bipolarity; or, more recently, the disintegration of the Soviet bloc and the end of the European stalemate -- the adjustment of France's foreign policy and international profile must be substantial, all the while keeping

them compatible with basic norms that can be supported by the French population.   An important dimension of the content of French identity must be left
behind and a new one formed in the process.

The language of governing is the mechanism through which French foreign
policy actually becomes part of the content of French identity. The contribution
of foreign policy to the content of identity comes from the symbols leaders use to
justify and mobilize support for policies. We need to understand, however, when
the language of governing, of legitimizing policy, becomes so deeply ingrained
within a society that it in fact becomes a part of that society's identity. How do we
know, for example, that the symbols of Gaullism were really a part of France's
identity and not just an effective tool for managing policy?

Politicians attempt to create overarching symbols powerful enough to mobilize regularly the support necessary for what they want to do, both in domestic
policy and in foreign policy. Sometimes the same symbols even work for both.
But clearly not all such symbols become elements of the content of national identity. Successive governments, at least in democracies, may evoke quite different
symbols equally effectively. A symbol arguably becomes an element of identity
when it becomes so powerful that either it may not be changed by successive
governments, or it can prevent a party that rejects the symbol from being elected
or taken into a coalition. *Independence* and *Grandeur* clearly meet this particular test, as will be discussed below.

If national identity, both in its essence and content, provides a certain discipline to both the conduct of and domestic debate over foreign policy, periods in
which the content of national identity is called into question by a changing international context become particularly difficult in domestic politics. On the one
hand, the validity of symbols and policy is being challenged not simply by domestic dissent but by the changing context itself. The search for symbols to express a
new content of identity legitimizes dissent and debate beyond the bounds of previously acceptable frameworks; those who violate older norms are not automatically sanctioned, which opens considerably the range of positions that can be put
forward in policy debate. On the other hand, the stakes in the definition of a new
foreign policy approach are greater than the policy itself; debate is actually over
the nation's identity, which engenders even deeper passions.

This combination of conditions is responsible for the intensity of the emotions that has dominated the debate over France's adjustment to post-Cold War
Europe, most particularly played out in the verbal battles leading to the Maastricht
Referendum. François Mitterrand, in particular, has attempted to reach beyond
the symbols of Gaullism and to use Europe as a means of giving French identity
new content for the end of the century and beyond. He has done so on the premise
that only by working together will European states be capable of confronting
successfully the new range of challenges they face, including delivering on substantial elements of their respective social compacts. He has encountered,
however, the strong opposition of those who remain attached to the legacy and

symbols of Gaullism, as well as something deeper -- a special meaning that sovereignty and the state have had in the development of the essence of French identity. The result, as yet, has been inconclusive, and is likely to remain so for some time, leaving the French with a major problem as they struggle with what it means to be French in today's Europe.

The Gaullist Legacy and the
Content of French Identity

Part of the problem facing France today derives from the almost perfect fit between the content of French identity created by Gaullism and traditional French conceptions of France's uniqueness that form a critical part of the essence of French identity. The claim of France to an exceptional position in international affairs was considered an entitlement by de Gaulle, given the historic role of French power in Europe. More important, *Independence* and *Grandeur* both had roots in French history. As Philip Gordon has argued, "De Gaulle played on rather than created French ... myth."[10] The content he gave French identity during the postwar period built on critical elements deeply embedded in the essence of French identity. That content sustained a certain illusion of French autonomy by allowing France to enjoy the benefits of collectivity from both the Atlantic Alliance and the European Community, while not having to submit itself to the same strictures as its partners.[11] It permitted France to create the image of an international role for itself that was honorable for a former great European power.

Interestingly, not all French initially accepted the direction of Gaullist policy or believed in Gaullist rhetoric; de Gaulle's vision for France was in fact controversial. Indeed, one of the great ironies of de Gaulle's tenure as president is that he never enjoyed the benefits of the identity he fostered. As Anton DePorte has pointed out, the debate over France's *force de frappe*, a key to, and primary symbol of, the policy of *Independence*,

> showed that a considerable number of French people did not want to have their consciousness raised or their country's status enhanced in this way. They feared that the nuclear force, and the more assertive aspects of the General's policies in general, would isolate France from its allies and weaken rather than increase its security and influence in an alliance that was still perceived by them, and many others in Western Europe, as necessary to confront a threatening Soviet enemy. De Gaulle's policies eventually *did* change French public thinking in the ways he desired. But the 'Gaullist consensus' on defense, and on the appropriateness and feasibility of asserting French national independence (while remaining in the Alliance), was a phenomenon that he created but did not himself enjoy in his time.[12]

There can be little doubt that the international dimensions of Gaullism came to form a critical element of the content of French identity. Its basic tenets represented something that those in or contending for power could not violate without fear of political sanction. The parties of the Left, for example, would almost certainly have been condemned to the political wilderness for even longer had they not finally reconciled themselves with France's nuclear vocation in the 1970s.[13] The reforms in French defense policy initiated by Valéry Giscard d'Estaing and Général Guy Méry in the late 1970s would surely have been carried further had Giscard not been a prisoner of his Gaullist partners. This was, of course, a reflection of the political landscape of the moment, but it is also clear that no president could withstand the charges of moving France toward reintegration with NATO.

Any policy that could be attacked as sacrificing France's *Independence* was incapable of garnering or sustaining a political consensus, and no political leader since 1969 has wanted to tackle the issue head on. It was easier to live the fiction than to debate the reality. As Philip Gordon argues,

> The force and influence of the Gaullist national security legacy can be measured first by how much it appears against all odds to have guided and constrained de Gaulle's successors, particularly the latest two. Neither Valéry Giscard d'Estaing nor François Mitterrand came to office with any particular affinity for what was know as 'Gaullism'; both were sharp critics of it. Moreover, neither Giscard nor Mitterrand was ever known for his admiration of Gaullist defense thinking. ... In spite of this, neither man, despite the enormous power of the French presidency in the *domaine reservé* of foreign and security policy, altered the basic orientation of de Gaulle's defense doctrine, which had been elaborated under very different circumstances with some very different requirements.[14]

Those who followed de Gaulle as president of France, although less strident in their rhetoric and more nuanced in their policies, thus continued to sustain the myth; all have affirmed France's special status and portrayed this as normal. This was the case despite the fact that the realities of French power were implicitly acknowledged at least since the late 1970s. But the persistent belief in French distinctiveness made the continued usage of Gaullist symbols easy; they corresponded to the deeper French sense of self even if they no longer really fit the European or international context in which France found itself. Thus, as bipolarity collapsed, the central tenets of Gaullism still stood, as Stanley Hoffmann has written,

> both because they seemed apt to the situation of France in the Cold War and because they were supported by the public. Now their adequacy to the new world was questionable, but the consensus was still there -- and no president could, by breaking it, undermine his own position or effectiveness, unless he was able to build a new one around a new set of tenets and 'sell' it to the public, if not to parliament.[15]

In the debate over French policy and the future of European order, it is clear that no political leader has yet found a viable formula to foster a new consensus. This debate is not only over new policy and where France fits into the new landscape. It is a search for an entirely new structure of political communication, of symbols and political legitimation to replace that of Gaullism. Although France actually seems to have come to terms with its status as a medium power -- as a more normal European state -- it does not yet have a satisfactory way of expressing what that means.

François Mitterrand has been criticized by many observers for his indecisiveness and lack of vision in the face of the momentous changes that have occurred in Europe since 1989. Yet for all his vacillation on German unity and the collapse of the Soviet Union, he has been remarkably consistent for over a decade in his policy toward the European Community. He discovered early in his first term that *Independence* was an illusion in economic policy, and he committed France to revitalizing Europe as a means of making both more competitive in the world of the twenty-first century. Europe was to be the central, if not the only, means through which France pursued its national interest because it would give France more control over shaping its own destiny than France could possibly have alone. In the name of collective progress, he even went so far as to accept an extension of majority voting within the European Community on most of the harmonization provisions contained in the Single European Act. There was little political dissent at home, but then, these were times of heady Euro-optimism across the continent.

As the Soviet empire collapsed and Germany was reunified, Mitterrand's answer was more European integration of the traditional kind. Further integration would inextricably bind the new Germany to France and the West and would provide a stabilizing core in the face of the emerging disorder to the East. Ways had to be found for dealing with the East that did not jeopardize the process of deepening among existing Community members. Mitterrand played an instrumental role in launching the two intergovernmental conferences that led to the Maastricht Treaty, and French vision largely prevailed in shaping this blueprint for Europe's future. Moreover, for all of the fanfare about Europe taking a giant step toward Union, that Union according to Maastricht would be very much one in which the member states remained the key actors.

Mitterrand's justification for Maastricht mirrored his claims for the Single European Act: More of the right kind of integration was essential and would give France a greater voice over its own destiny than it would otherwise have. In this case, he also feared that without further steps forward, the Community could begin moving, along with the rest of the continent, toward a renationalization of perspectives and policies. *Europe*, he once again told the French, was the best means of pursuing France's national interests and enhancing France's autonomy. He clearly did not expect to unleash the depths of passion about French sovereignty that were subsequently revealed in the debate over ratification of the Maastricht Treaty.

Objectively, Mitterrand's confidence may have been justified. He was not particularly vulnerable on the other dimensions of policy. His foreign policy had violated no basic tenets of Gaullism. His rhetoric about France's role in the world struck all the right chords. He was appropriately assertive on behalf of Europe's need to develop a defense identity distinct from its partnership with the United States. Where he failed, however, was in giving the French a sense of where the nation was headed, and that it had some control over the process. This ultimately had more to do with internal politics than with foreign policy, but the new external uncertainties clearly heightened France's sense of navigating without a rudder.

Some of the dispute over the Maastricht Treaty may well have to do with the conditions under which it was presented. Mitterrand had become a weak president, and almost anything he defended was likely to provoke opposition (some of the treaty's defenders reportedly even tried to convince him to maintain a low profile so as not to accentuate a protest vote). However, as has been pointed out many times, the public in France had never before been consulted on European integration; there was a real democratic deficit stemming from the fact that integration had always been pursued from the top down. There was thus no real public experience in debating the tricky issues surrounding the concept of sovereignty. Perhaps this is why the debate actually reveals so much about the crisis of French identity.

Mitterrand clearly attempted to pursue Europe as a policy and simultaneously to use *Europe* as a symbol to legitimate policy, believing it powerful enough to help control dissent. He had never formally renounced the basic Gaullist symbols, and certainly continued to speak of France's historic role and distinctiveness. In his mind, *Europe* was clearly destined not to replace, but to take a more prominent place alongside *Grandeur* and *Independence*, even if the latter would have to undergo some reinterpretation. As strong as support for European integration is in France, however, *Europe* is not powerful enough as a symbol to dominate the fears and political cross pressures set loose over the past few years and that were brought into focus by France's European policy. Indeed, while it reassures some French, it heightens the uncertainty of a substantial number of others.

If it were just a matter of content, building Europe as a policy for pursuing French interests would fit well with the French desire for shaping grand designs. Moreover, the French are deeply committed to preserving the progress made over the past several decades in creating a new basis for relations among the Community's members. But *Europe* as a symbol also threatens the essence of French identity by endangering the traditional vision of French sovereignty.

The reality of the Maastricht Treaty is that it moves Europe a major step toward Union. Clearly, between the two grand contending visions of European unity -- the federal and the confederal -- the latter prevailed; under Maastricht, the member states remain the driving force of the unification process. But Maastricht also involves the transfer of further powers to the new Union. In its review of the treaty, the French Constitutional Court ruled that two elements of the treaty conflicted with the Constitution: first, the proposed participation of foreigners in municipal elections; and second, the provisions and protocols defining the Economic and Monetary Union. The court also ruled "that the extension of qualified majority in the Council of Ministers restricts French sovereignty (because French Ministers can be overruled by their European counterparts)."[16]

Yet, on this key issue, the court took pains to elaborate its understanding of the nature of sovereignty. It determined that France could "transfer competences" in order "to participate in the creation or in the development of an international organization."..."This pronouncement constitutes a rejection of dogmatic notions of the indivisible nature of sovereignty: sovereignty is not a hermetically sealed whole or totality, but rather a bundle of discrete state functions, or 'competences.' "[17]

This ruling might have laid the issue quietly to rest, but Mitterrand's decision to pursue ratification of the treaty through public referendum rather than by submitting it to parliament provided an opportunity for contending visions of sovereignty to be given a passionate public airing. "What emerged from the sound and the fury," as Stanley Hoffmann has aptly summarized it,

> was the need to choose between two radically different conceptions of sovereignty ... an 'absolutist' one, which happened to be deeply engraved in French culture, ... and a pragmatic and relative notion of sovereignty looked at ... not as an indivisible substance but as a bundle of competences that could be gradually pooled or transferred to common bodies, so as to substitute the efficiency of the whole for the relative inefficiency of the members.[18]

But the debate went well beyond legal arguments to the evocation of symbols that represented contending views on both the essence and content of French identity. Philippe Séguin, perhaps the key opponent of ratification, attacked the treaty as nothing less than an attempt "to transfer the 'social contract' from the national to the European level."[19] He raised "the specter of a 'normalization' and 'banalisation' of French exceptionalism, an exceptionalism declared to be the root strength of the nation."[20] Those supporting the treaty in turn raised the specter of Europe collapsing if the treaty were not ratified, and argued that France needed to strengthen rather than forsake perhaps the key tool in protecting French national interest.

In the end, the debate centered not on alternative visions of Europe but on alternative visions of France. On the one hand were those for whom the essence of French identity remains a very traditional vision of the nation-state and sovereignty. On the other hand were those for whom the essence of France's identity was more functional in nature and had evolved over time; this permitted a new content to emerge as France learned to pursue its interests through vehicles beyond the nation-state. Cross-cutting this cleavage was also a real uncertainty about where the entire European project was headed, which produced

> a gnawing fear of being caught in an enterprise that will either lead to a Federation in which the nation will lose its identity as a political unit, with its political powers going both upward, to the new central institutions of the Union, and downward, to the regions, or else result in a Baroque or Gaudiesque construction, multileveled and multispeed, manipulated above all by Germany. There is a fear that the Community begins to resemble much more the German model of Federalism and 'social market economy' than the French model of the unitary and regulatory state.[21]

The Maastricht Referendum was approved by the slimmest of margins. It was hardly a resounding endorsement of the vision of "pooled sovereignties" as a new ingredient of French identity. The reality of contemporary Europe, however, is precisely one of pooled sovereignties, nations concluding that they cannot accomplish alone certain basic elements of their respective social contracts. Although one can analyze the reasons why the French Referendum was as close as it was, one cannot also help but wonder how a project as modest as the Maastricht Treaty (in terms of real transfers of sovereignty) could evoke such overwrought emotions. Arguably, it shows the depth of the current identity crisis.

And yet, France has been governed since March 1993 by a coalition of the Right that has "reaffirmed Mitterrand's bid to increase French autonomy by working through international organizations rather than by asserting its independence of them, as the popular Gaullist current demands."[22] Despite the passions of Autumn 1992, the new government continues to pursue a vision of the French state as a "'negotiating' or bargaining state."[23] The basic underlying philosophy is that losses of sovereignty become acceptable if they bring increased control in other forms. And this philosophy is presently being applied not only vis-à-vis the European Community but increasingly with regard to NATO. In the debates over the adaptation of NATO and France's relationship with it, "the Right hopes that striking a bargain with the Americans will expand France's military and geopolitical power."[24] "While not ready to give up the Gaullist vision of the state's need to defend itself, the Right is willing to redefine that vision to suit the great constraints that international regimes impose in the 1990s."[25]

Despite the deep philosophical differences over the essence of French identity, therefore, the state itself continues to evolve, under the Right as well as the Left. There is clearly a broad range of France's political elite that sees the future of France as a normal, if distinctive, European power, one that has little choice but to adjust to the constraints of the context around it. For the near future, this vision is unlikely to be tested again by anything like the Maastricht Referendum. However, it is inevitable that the test will come sooner or later because the pressures for an extension of qualified majority voting to new domains within the European Union will persist. This pressure is the natural consequence of seeking to avoid debilitating deadlock within a Union of pooled sovereignties and as the Union expands to include new members, this pressure will only increase. But France is clearly not yet ready to take this step. Even hints that such an extension would be a part of the European Union created a furor in the National Assembly's debate over Maastricht, and the Constitutional Court's ruling has explicitly stated that qualified majority voting would restrict French sovereignty.

The dispute over GATT and the Blair House Accord illustrated just how sensitive this issue is in France. French farmers threatened the government with debilitating strikes if the accord were not renegotiated. To avoid confronting the issue head on, the government chose to focus attention on the way in which the accord was reached. It was the European Commission that negotiated Blair House under mandate from the European Council, but the results were never taken back to the member states for approval. The government argued that there can be no acceptance of an accord that has not been approved by France, and it demanded a reopening of discussions. For a time, France appeared incapable of suppressing its short-term national interests in favor of collective European judgment. The entire episode has made it harder for the French to argue at home that the Union represents the best means for pursuing French national interests even if the core of the problem lies in a disproportionately powerful sector of French society. The issue pits French identity against Europe.

At least as revealing of the current French state of mind was the dispute over the cultural provisions of the proposed GATT agreement. The United States sought to have trade in the cultural area treated under the same conditions as trade in other commercial goods. France, with considerable justification, has believed that small countries must have the right to subsidize and protect this sector as a means of preserving the nation's cultural heritage. Rather than using the language of trade negotiations, however, Mitterrand and others chose to use the language of identity to mobilize French support for policy. Mitterrand argued that "no nation can impose on another nation a way of thinking."[26] Jack Lang reinvigorated his long-standing argument against the cultural imperialism from across the Atlantic. Policy was equated with defense of identity.

The underlying issue for French identity is how much the social contract can evolve before France begins to experience deeper problems of identity and thus policy legitimation. The state has always played a very special role in the conception of France as a nation -- the very process of nation-building was intimately associated with the emergence of the centralized, unitary state. Theoretically, of course, as the purpose of the state evolves, the attachment of the population to the state should evolve accordingly. But that assumes a purely functional relationship between the citizen and the state, which is clearly not always the case. The ties that bind a nation are not only utilitarian but emotional and deeply cultural. In France, cultural identity "has never been detachable from French political institutions and programs -- it has always been tied to the state. The French state's abandonment of many of its powers over the French economy, the 'Europeaniza-tion' or 'globalization' of that economy, cannot therefore fail to affect French cultural identity."[27] Because the link between the political and the cultural has been so intimate, it will be painful to absorb the changed essence of French iden-tity into the political and public consciousness. It will remain controversial for some time to come, whether or not traditional visions have any relationship to current realities.

Because the essence of French identity is undergoing mutation, adjusting the content to the new European context will remain difficult. Europe as a policy will continue to be central to France as a means of pursuing its national interest, but *Europe* as a symbol will not carry the weight of Gaullism nor bring the same discipline to French debate. As a result, France will continue in an ambivalent relationship with itself and with European integration for some time to come. *Independence* will continue in a tug of war with *Europe* as the symbols for legiti-mizing specific policies. And it is unlikely that either will conquer the political space entirely, the former because it no longer has any meaning except as a sym-bol for what must not be sacrificed, the latter because there are too many contend-ing visions of Europe. France will be able to make sacrifices in the name of its European policy, but when policy comes into conflict with the essence (for some) of French identity, national political debate will set sharp limits on what content can be given to French identity through that policy.

In the foreseeable future, it is thus unlikely that *Europe* as a symbol will become a key element in the content of French national identity, even if it may someday supplement other symbols in a less tense way than today. There is, however, no other symbol on the horizon that will do more to reconcile the ten-sions between the continuing myth of France as a largely unfettered great power and the realities of an interdependent world that continue to impose themselves.

Conclusion

Many challenges faced by contemporary France are challenges to French identity because they call into question both key dimensions of what it has meant to be French, and the specific compact that the French people have had with their state. None of the above is meant to argue that external factors are more impor-tant than the internal to the identity problems France faces today. Indeed, the most important dimensions of France's identity problems are probably internal: the profound structural changes in French society over the past several decades have not yielded a new pattern of social harmony; immigration is challenging the myth of France as an open, absorption society; the centralized French ap-proach to economic and social management is under severe challenge by the global economy; political ideologies have collapsed and political party structures have lost much of their importance in the organization of daily life -- all subjects of other chapters presented in this volume. But it is also clear from the above analysis that the international context in Europe contributes in an important way to France's identity dilemmas both by challenging its essence and by forcing a change in its content.

The problem is that the direction in which the content must naturally move provides, at least in the short run, an increased challenge to the essence. It is going to be very difficult to separate Europe as a vehicle for pursuing France's national interests from a Europe that disputes traditional views of French sovereignty and thus a core piece of the myth of the French state. Thus, in coming to grips with the future shape of European integration, which itself cannot occur in isolation from coming to grips with the relationship between the two halves of Europe, the French inevitably must confront that myth. If that myth remains strong and thus a key to how the French define their national interest, then using Europe as a policy to pursue French interests will become exceedingly difficult because in the end it becomes almost impossible to pursue the policy without using the symbol of *Europe*. Under these circumstances, it will be almost impossible to reconcile a Europe compatible with domestic political needs with a Europe that allows France to maintain a leadership role in shaping its future. The next French president faces an acute task -- one that Mitterrand attempted to address but with only partial success -- of bringing the myth of state into line with international realities. If he fails, he will fail to have the symbols at his disposal to legitimize his policies at home, and French European policy will remain a subject of substantial political controversy.

France today is very different than the country de Gaulle inherited in 1958. While it is not a country of first rank, as the general always claimed it must be, it has accomplished an incredible transformation during the postwar period, a transformation many of its European partners have failed to achieve. France is no longer fractured; it has overcome its historic divisions even as it must confront new and difficult cleavages. France no longer requires the Gaullist rhetoric, even if it once did, to help manage its domestic affairs. Indeed, the residuals of that rhetoric, although meaningful to a hard core minority, may well have become a source of division that is keeping France from dealing more effectively with the challenges of shaping the new Europe.

The reality today is that most of France has become more comfortable with its multiple identities. The challenge is to make the adjustment so that the debate over France's role in Europe is not a debate over alternative visions of France, but over what being European should mean. This will require bringing French notions of sovereignty and the state into line with contemporary European realities. France must adjust the essence of its identity in order to give new content to that identity in the new Europe. A failure of the former will make the latter a continuing problem, weakening Europe and France in the process.

Notes

1. "La Révolution des 'Lieux de mémoire'," interview in *Le Monde*, 5 February 1993, p. 28.

2. See Rainer Riemenschneider, "The Two Souls of Marianne: National Sovereignty Versus Supranationality in Europe," in Mairi Maclean and Jolyon Howorth, *Europeans on Europe: Transnational Visions of a New Continent* (New York: St. Martin's Press, 1992).

3. See John Pinder, *The Community of Europe* (New York: Oxford University Press, 1991).

4. See Nona Mayer, "Attitudes towards the Region, Europe and Politics in 1992 France," Paper delivered at the 1993 Annual Meeting of the APSA.

5. William Wallace, "Foreign Policy and National Identity in the United Kingdom," *International Affairs*, vol. 67, no. 1, January 1991, p. 65.

6. An important exception here is William Bloom, *Personal Identity, National Identity, and International Relations* (Cambridge: Cambridge University Press, 1987). His focus is on the relationship between the individual and a state's international policies, and some of his basic concepts are very relevant to the issues being discussed here.

7. The parallel to the concept of political culture here is obvious. In both cases, we are talking about dimensions of life that help define a specific society, with which the society identifies, and that can change over time as the society adapts to changing conditions.

8. See Anthony D. Smith, "National Identity and the Idea of European Unity," *International Affairs*, Vol. 68, No. 1, January 1992, p. 67. "human beings have multiple identities, that they can move between them according to context and situation, and that such identities may be concentric rather than conflictual. ... there is plenty of historical evidence for the coexistence of concentric circles of allegiance." For the latter he cites James Coleman, *Nigeria: background to nationalism* (Berkeley, CA: University of California Press, 1958).

9. Smith, "National Identity," p. 58. The classic piece on this issue remains Stanley Hoffmann, "Obstinate or Obsolete? France, European Integration, and the Fate of the Nation-State," in his *Decline or Renewal: France Since the 1930s* (New York: Viking Press, 1974), chapter 12.

10. Philip Gordon, *A Certain Idea of France* (Princeton, N.J.: Princeton University Press, 1993) p. 18. Gordon argues that there were a number of basic guidelines to which French leaders felt compelled to abide, including: retaining the ideal of total autonomy of decision; defending the theoretical independence of the *force de frappe*; avoiding any new explicit or automatic commitments to third country security; refusing to participate in any sort of integrated military command structure; continuing to claim for France an exceptional status and special global role; denying automatic use of access to French territory in time of peace or crisis; and rejecting bloc to bloc negotiations.

11. Specifically, the putative limitations on autonomy of integration within NATO and the costs of majority rule in the Community.

12. Anton DePorte, "The Foreign Policy of the Fifth Republic: Between the Nation and the World," in James F. Hollifield and George Ross, *Searching for the New France* (New York: Routledge, 1991), p. 257.

13. Indeed, for this reason, it was one of the first steps taken by François Mitterrand (along with Charles Hernu) when he reconstituted a Socialist party in 1971. The phenomenon is similar to the realignment of the West German SPD policy on membership in NATO following the Godesberg Program.

14. Gordon, *A Certain Idea of France*, p. 163.

15. Stanley Hoffmann, "French Dilemmas and Strategies in the New Europe," in Robert O. Keohane, Joseph S. Nye, and Stanley Hoffmann, *After the Cold War: International Institutions and State Strategies in Europe, 1989-1991* (Cambridge, MA: Harvard University Press, 1993), p. 134.

16. For a complete summary of the issues involved in the ratification debates, see Alec Stone, "Ratifying Maastricht: France Debates European Union," in *French Politics and Society*, Vol. 11, No. 1, Winter 1993, pp. 70-88.

17. Ibid., p. 74.

18. Stanley Hoffmann, "Thoughts on the French Nation Today," *Daedalus*, Summer 1993, p. 72.

19. Stone, "Ratifying Maastricht," p. 76.

20. Ibid., p. 77.

21. Hoffmann, "Thoughts," p. 75.

22. Patrick McCarthy, "The 1993 Elections: Politics Transformed and Policies Continued?" FPI Policy Briefs (Washington, D.C.: Paul Nitze School of Advanced International Studies, 1993), p. 20.

23. The concept is that of Pierre Rosanvallon, *L'Etat en France* (Paris: Seuil, 1990). Cited in Patrick McCarthy, "Elections," p. 5.

24. McCarthy, "Elections," p. 26.

25. Ibid., p. 25.

26. Mitterrand speaking to the Sommet de la Francophonie, October 16, 1993, as reported on Antenne 2.

27. Hoffmann, "Thoughts," p. 77.

13

Thoughts on Sovereignty and French Politics

Stanley Hoffmann

Internal and External Sovereignty

Sovereignty has been a key word in the vocabulary of French political thought for centuries -- one immediately thinks back to the writings of Jean Bodin. The recent debate on sovereignty, which dominated the campaign over the Maastricht Treaty in the spring and summer of 1992, stands in sharp contrast to past disputes in several important ways.

Traditionally, French debates about sovereignty's meaning and location have dealt with internal sovereignty: the power to issue laws for the population and over the territory of the body politic. Political thinkers took external sovereignty -- the power to act on the world scene without foreign control or interference -- for granted. They saw this attribute as both the normal and the central characteristic of statehood, regardless of whether the state was, internally, an absolute monarchy or a republic.

Of course, the debates on internal sovereignty were hardly divorced from thinking about France in the world. Indeed, in domestic constitutional and political disputes, all parties attached considerable importance to notions of absolute and indivisible sovereignty, which in turn buttressed the attachment to and passion for external sovereignty. But the focus was on domestic order.

Debates about the French nation have been dominated by the existence of two major currents of thought.[1] The first has been the revolutionary and Republican nationalism associated with the Jacobins, later with Michelet, and largely derived from Rousseau. It attributes internal sovereignty to the nation (cf. Sieyès); moreover, Rousseau's conception of indivisible and inalienable popular sovereignty also carries over into external affairs -- one need think only of his anti-federalism. Defending the sovereignty of the state on the world scene means protecting the nation from outside aggression, just as the nation must be safeguarded at home from factional interests and parties.

The second nationalist tradition dates to the end of the nineteenth century, and represents a curious blend of plebiscitarianism (Barrès) and monarchism (Maurras). Its focus has been on the need for a strong executive. At the time, it called for the restoration of an authority, who would replace a republic described as having become the prisoner of factions, and as having succumbed to political paralysis due to an excess of checks and balances. The new State would have a single will expressed either by a popular leader or by a king. This leader or king would exercise external sovereignty as well, guided only by the national interest.

Although there were obviously vast differences between these two currents, with respect both to domestic institutions and to the definition of the national interest, the similarities concerning the world scene are striking. The Republicans who took over France in the late 1870s aimed at "turning peasants into Frenchmen,"[2] and at promoting, mainly through the school system, a kind of civic consciousness for *le peuple souverain*. At the same time the Republicans also championed the notion of *le peuple armé*, capable of defending France's external sovereignty against the dominant threat -- Germany -- and of recovering, some day, the "lost provinces" torn away in 1871.

On the Right, the new nationalists found the Republic too divided and weak. They called for *la poigne* both at home and abroad, believing that the defense of France's external sovereignty required strength and resistance to nefarious ideologies (such as international Socialism) and to the spirit of compromise embodied by a Caillaux. The feared decline of France's role in the world could only be reversed by a change of regime, that is a transfer of the location of domestic sovereignty.

Although traditional debates focused primarily on internal sovereignty and its institutional expression, all parties thus saw a direct link between internal arrangements and the protection of external sovereignty. Indeed, for each of these main currents of thought, a change in the definition or location of internal sovereignty was a way to deal with threats to external sovereignty.

In contrast, the recent Maastricht debate was doubly original. On the one hand, unlike, say, the debate over the European Defense Community in the early 1950s, the Maastricht furor concentrated exclusively on external sovereignty. In the 1950s, the "defenders of French sovereignty" (in the world) were predominantly people who also argued for a change in the location of domestic sovereignty, from the National Assembly (which was supposed to speak for the nation) to either a totalitarian party, in the case of the Communists, or, again, a strong executive, in the case of the Gaullists. In 1992, by contrast, the Constitution of the Fifth Republic was not a bone of contention.

On the other hand, the frequent ferocity of the recent debate can be explained by the fact that, for many of the French, the defense of French sovereignty abroad had come to mean something more than the protection of French *interests* from foreign encroachments, more than just safeguarding the legal and political capacity to preserve French positions, more than preservation of the necessary, if not sufficient, precondition for the cherished goods of independence and free hands in world affairs. Now it meant defending France's very *identity*.

To be sure, a connection between identity and external sovereignty is not new in the early 1990s. It was evident for the Resisters -- the Free French and the Resistance at home -- who thought that Vichy's abdication of external sovereignty in essential domains was not only a disaster for French status and interests, but also created a risk of creeping Nazification, and thus the alienation of the very soul of France. Perhaps the most savage period of dispute over French identity was 1933-1945, when the threat was widely seen as coming from both abroad and within; indeed as coming, within, from evil forces associated with mortal enemies of France abroad.

Again in the 1950s the connection is potent: the men and women who fought against the European Defense Community believed that France's identity was inseparable from the national army (a belief passionately held by de Gaulle); and those who opposed giving up French Algeria saw France's identity intimately linked to a singular capacity to assimilate immigrant foreigners and overseas natives -- a capacity that would be crippled if, say, Algerians were allowed to become Algerians instead of French. (This second belief is one that de Gaulle, who deemed immigration and the integration of immigrants necessary but knew that colonial assimilation was a myth -- flattering for France's self-image but concealing precise interests -- did not fully share.)

However, the link between identity and external sovereignty has grown more intimate over time as other challenges have receded. As, gradually, the great internal ideological cleavages that had fractured the French polity, pitting rival conceptions of France's nature and specificity against one another (lay vs. Catholic, Left vs. Right), began to weaken, the threat to "Frenchness" has increasingly been seen as coming from abroad, rather than from enemies within. Thus, the frequency of "Franco-French wars" of words over external sovereignty in the past half-century reflects not only the defensiveness of France in the international system (since 1933 at least) but the increasing sense that France's distinctiveness, France's nature, France's culture, are increasingly at stake in the international arena.

The Crisis of Maastricht

Concentrating on the external sovereignty issue as it has evolved in recent years -- the 1970s, 1980s, and early 1990s -- three things explain the intensity of concern.

First, the fear of losing sovereignty is of course made more acute by the double legacy of the Old Regime and of Rousseau: the tendency to look at sovereignty not as a bundle of discrete powers and separable state functions, but rather as a talisman, indivisible and inalienable yet eminently losable.

Secondly, not just one but two factors of international politics have fueled that fear. One is the willingness of French governments to sacrifice deliberately chunks of sovereignty, that is, to use the legal power conferred upon them by French sovereignty in order to chip away at the talisman, to transfer essential powers to others (this has been the argument of the enemies of West European integration ever since the "coal and steel pool" of 1950) or in order to open French borders to unwelcome and corrosive, inassimilable foreigners (this argument had already been made by the Right, and even by many "good Republicans" à la Giraudoux, against immigration in the 1930s, and it was picked up again by Le Pen and many others, including Giscard d'Estaing, in recent years).

The other factor is more insidious, because it can't be described as just the product of governmental laxity or faulty public initiatives. It results from global trends, particularly the increasing inability of governments to exert the powers that they *theoretically* enjoy and have not juridically given away -- that is, to perform the services that the citizenry expects from a sovereign state -- because the rulers are no longer in *actual* control of the levers. This is the case in the military realm, because individual states can no longer obtain security from attack at high (i.e., nuclear) or low (i.e., terrorism) levels. In the financial and economic domain, the increasing impotence of the state owes to the "globalization" of the world economy and the disproportion between the power and mobility of private investors and operators and the resources and regulations of national authorities.

In the past few years, for many people, the European Union has come to represent both a construct to which the French government has voluntarily transferred essential areas of jurisdiction that used to protect French interests and identity, as for instance in trade and competition policy (hence the attack on Brussels's bureaucracy); and also a process of deregulation that ensures the triumph of international private interests and speculators over the enfeebled public defenders of the national interest. Similarly, the apparent continuation of illegal immigration has been seen as both the result of bad policies (not enough arrests, expulsions and obstacles) and the consequence of the inexorable pressure of persistent hungry hordes against the porous borders of the wealthy nations.

Finally, French anxiety, already kindled by the notion of sovereignty as talisman, has been reenforced by the Gaullist legacy. One of the most important messages the French received from the first president of the Fifth Republic was the idea that the defense of French sovereignty was a matter of will, and that it could be safeguarded without sacrificing those interests whose protection or promotion could no longer be ensured by France alone and now required international cooperation. France could leave the integrated commands of NATO without impairing national security, because it could continue to cooperate with the United States and with West Germany. France could insist on reducing the part of supranationality and on preserving the principle of unanimity in the Community without giving up the idea of a common agricultural or external trade policy. Will and voluntarism would even tame the damaging trends of a world economy or monetary system that seemed out of control -- or dominated by the greatest capitalist power. These expectations proved illusory, very quickly insofar as the second kind of threat was concerned, when France discovered it could do little to prevent the supremacy of the dollar, and could only harm itself by excluding foreign investments. But then the illusion persisted that the West European enterprise would be able to reestablish the control (or controls) that the nation-state was no longer capable of exerting, *and* that this enterprise could proceed without any deliberate and massive transfers of sovereignty from Paris to Brussels, or that formal transfers would be harmless because in political terms, France would continue to be the main shaper and beneficiary of the Community's policies.

The crisis over Maastricht resulted from a conjunction of factors:[3]

(a) a sudden and belated awareness of the fact -- manifest already in the Single Act, but largely unnoticed because of the absence of any broad public debate -- that the development of the European Community involved considerable transfers of essential powers (over trade, agriculture and money, over the policing of borders, over public procurement or competition policy, etc.);

(b) a realization that the Community wasn't any more capable than the nation-state of providing control over the world economy or remedies against recession, and of ensuring military security or monetary stability; and

(c) a growing doubt about the capacity of the Community to be the kind of instrument of French interests (cf. the Common Agricultural Policy) and avenue for French influence that it had been in the past. This role, in the opinion of the "pro-Europeans" in France, had justified some devolution of sovereignty, from a nation-state now often unable to reach its national goals by purely national means, to a joint enterprise in which these same national aims would be fulfilled by pooled means. After 1989, given the drastic change in the Franco-German balance, the eminently dominant role of the Bundesbank, and France's frequent isolation in EC debates on world trade and agriculture, such arguments became harder to present.[4]

French Sovereignty and the New Europe

Most people realize that in an interdependent world economy and in a turbulent geopolitical system full independence is a dream; but this realization only raises the passion for sovereignty, whose "loss" would mean giving up this dream once and for all. Defending French sovereignty is thus becoming once again an important motto of French policy. De Gaulle had fought for it on two fronts -- against U.S. hegemony, and against the supranational sirens (in whom he thought he recognized U.S. voices).

The battle against U.S. encroachments is not over, as the Franco-American contest over agriculture and "cultural products" in the Uruguay round of GATT demonstrated. Those who mobilized against U.S. pressure (and against the apparent reluctance of the European Community's Commission to support France) argued that what was at stake were not limited French interests, but essential components of France's identity: France's identification with a fading rural past, and with those few remaining domains of mass culture (TV programs and movies) not already "taken over" by the transatlantic barbarian.

It proved both necessary and difficult for the French government to deflate the issue in late 1993 in order to reach a compromise, even though the interests at stake were simply not so vast as to justify a veto that would starkly reveal France's isolation and provoke a major Franco-EC as well as Franco-American crisis. Here, France has discovered that it has, in fact, already transferred too much power to the EC for France all alone to defend successfully traditional areas of French sovereignty -- agricultural and cultural policy -- against U.S. intrusions. An attempt at recovering sovereignty could only lead to isolation, which would spell not independence, but, in fact, increased dependence on outside currents -- increased irrelevance.

More important today are two other battles. One is the fight against unwelcome immigration. Here, the French government may well find that European cooperation will serve its definition of French interests, since practically all the members of the EC want to prevent an "invasion" from the Middle East or Africa. Remarkable indeed is the way in which the government has used an agreement (Schengen) that opens borders as a lever for restricting asylum, and for amending the Constitution so as to make such a restriction constitutional. The passivity of the Left and the fervor of the Right show how successful the far Right has been, over the years, in convincing a majority of the French that closing borders to this, the third major wave of immigration in a century, was essential for the preservation of French identity.

The other battle remains the conflict over Europe. No such domestic unanimity exists on the issue of European integration, as the fight over Maastricht revealed. Behind all the sound and the fury, a few facts stand out. First, both sides in that great debate were in an embarrassing position. The supporters of

Maastricht were often on the defensive, arguing either that the future European Union would be the only way of containing Germany, or that the Union amounted to a fair exchange of devalued sovereign power(s) against valuable influence; both are highly dubious arguments. Maastricht's opponents tried to cling both to the fraying mast of *la République* and of national independence, and to the fantasy of "another Europe," which remained undefined.

Secondly, it is a fact that almost forty-five years of European integration, despite periods of stagnation and setbacks, have created an *engrenage* that it is almost impossible for France to break. In 1993 as in 1981-1982, the champions of "another policy" -- one in which the French state would take back its financial and monetary independence, regain control of its economic priorities and of its imports, re-regulate, re-subsidize, and reflate -- have found it hard to prove that the results of such a policy would be any better than those that the current policy of European monetary cooperation and economic integration allows. In a way, the French have become the captives of a policy aimed, above all, at captivating the Germans, and have little choice but using all their still considerable skills and assets to turn the common cage into a comfortable compound.

Thirdly, despite occasional musings about a domestic political realignment in which the old and largely obsolete division between Left and Right would be replaced by a clear separation between pro-EC and anti-EC forces, the chance of such a shift occurring is very low. The electorate remains dominated by domestic concerns and traditional attachments, and it is difficult to imagine conservative anti-Europeans and Left-wing ones practicing mutual *désistements* on the second ballot. Both the Left and the Right have learned to live with their inner splits over Europe, and a coalition of anti-Europeans, although it might prevail in a referendum (agglomerations of nay-sayers are easy) would find it difficult to agree on a common policy (there *are* Socialist and Gaullist statist, dirigiste anti-Europeans, but not enough to govern together). Even Rocard, the champion, not so long ago, of an opening to the center that would have had to be based on a convergence around Europe, began to talk -- before being abandoned in his role as rescuer of the Socialist Party -- of a Europe of the Left versus a Europe of the Right. The one man who might want to force a realignment is Jacques Delors, but "objectively" this may prove impossible. More than thirty years of *bipolarisation* have created vested interests and shaped electoral behavior. It would take a return to proportional representation to pave the way to a gradual realignment, but that is not in the cards just now.

Fourth and last, since the issue of sovereignty versus Europe splits both the Left and the Right, French governments are likely to continue to practice a policy of small, gradual steps toward a united Europe -- paradoxically, just enough to keep the anti-Europeans unhappy, lamenting the frittering away of French sovereignty and the discoloring of French identity, but not enough to build a European Community that would have an identity of its own, effective powers (especially in diplomacy and defense) and institutions endowed with both popular legitimacy and efficiency. As a result, the European splinter will remain lodged in the French political foot. The debate may stay focused on sovereignty, for reasons of atavism amply listed above, and because the issue of sovereignty is always raised by international agreements (through which legal sovereignty is exercised, and operational sovereignty restricted or given away) and by arguments brought before the Constitutional Council. But in reality sovereignty, which is a bundle of powers, is likely to be increasingly split between different levels of government (abroad as well as at home); it is shared between the French state (itself increasingly decentralized), the EC and the market itself. And what this complex structure guarantees is concern about and debates on French identity, on the ability of the French *nation* to define and defend its originality even when the *state* that used to be its straitjacket loses or gives up many of the powers and functions it used to have.

The *fin-de-siècle* spectacle of a French *society* that is partly "europeanized" thanks to a single European market, of a *political process* that remains entirely French, of a *state* with distinctive institutions and practices but reduced powers, and of an embryonic, sometimes catatonic European *super-state* with areas of jurisdiction over France is certainly baroque enough to baffle Cartesian minds, admirers of French gardens, and classical theorists.

Notes

1. See my 1993 Tanner lectures on "The Nation, nationalism and after: the case of France," to be published by the University of Utah Press vol. 15, 1993.

2. Eugen Weber, *Peasants into Frenchmen: The Modernization of Rural France, 1870-1914* (Stanford, CA: Stanford University Press, 1976).

3. "Thoughts on the French nation today," *Daedalus*, Summer 1993, pp. 63-80; "Goodbye to European unity?" *New York Review of Books*, May 27, 1993.

4. On the effects of 1989 on French foreign policy, see "French dilemmas and strategies in the new Europe," in Robert O. Keohane, Joseph S. Nye, and Stanley Hoffmann (eds.), *After the Cold War* (Cambridge, MA: Harvard University Press, 1993), pp. 127-147.

About the Contributors

William James Adams is the Arthur F. Thurnau Professor of Economics at the University of Michigan. He is also an affiliated staff member of the Brookings Institution and has been a visiting professor at European University Institute, the University of Paris, and Harvard University. He is the author and editor of numerous works, including *Restructuring the French Economy: Government and the Rise of Market Competition Since World War II* (1989), *French Industrial Policy* (1986), and *Singular Europe: Economy and Polity of the European Community after 1992* (1992) as well as many articles and reviews in *The Quarterly Journal of Economics*, the *American Economic Review*, the *Economic Journal*, and the *European Economic Review*.

Suzanne Berger is Ford International Professor of Political Science at the Massachusetts Institute of Technology and a senior research associate of the Center for European Studies at Harvard University. Berger was the first chair of the Social Science Research Council Committee on West Europe and has served on the SSRC Board of Directors and on its Joint Advisory Committee on International Programs as well as on the Fulbright program oversight board, the Council for International Exchange of Scholars. Her honors include election as a fellow of the American Academy of Arts and Sciences, a Guggenheim Fellowship, and election as French-American Foundation Professor of American Civilization at the Ecole des Hautes Etudes en Sciences Sociales in Paris, France (1985-1986). In 1993 the French government named her *Officier dans l'Ordre des Palmes Académiques*. She is the author and editor of many books and articles, including *Peasants against Politics* (1972), *The French Political System* (1974), *Dualism and Discontinuity in Industrial Societies* (1980), and *Organizing Interests in Western Europe* (1981).

Frédéric Bozo is associate professsor of history and international relations at *Université de Marne la Vallée* and has taught at the *Institut d'Etudes Politiques de Paris*. Since 1988, he has been a research associate with the French Institute of International Relations (IFRI), where his focus is on European and global security affairs. Bozo holds a Ph.D. in contemporary history from the *Université de*

Paris X (Nanterre) and was educated at the *Ecole Normale Supérieure* and the *Institut d'Etudes Politiques de Paris*. He also spent a year at Harvard University as a graduate student fellow. Dr. Bozo's publications include *La France et l'OTAN. De la guerre froide au nouvel ordre européen* (1991) and many articles on contemporary European security.

Jacques E. Le Cacheux is currently acting director of the *Département des études* of the *Observatoire français des conjonctures économiques* in Paris and *Maitre de Conference* at the *Institut d'Etudes Politiques de Paris*. He also teaches at the *Université de Paris X* (Nanterre) and the *Université de Paris I* (Panthéon-Sorbonne). Le Cacheux received his Ph.D. from the European University Institute and holds a Maîtrise in Economics from the *Université de Paris I* (Panthéon-Sorbonne) and a *Diplôme* from the *Institut d'Etudes Politiques de Paris*. He is the co-author of *Vers une fiscalité européene* (1991) as well as numerous articles in *Babylone*, the *Revue de l'OFCE*, *Cahiers français*, and the *Tocqueville Review*.

David Ross Cameron is professor and chair, department of political science, and chairman of the West European Studies Council at Yale University. He serves on the executive committee of the Council on European Studies, chairs a review committee for the Council for International Exchange of Scholars, and is a member of the editorial boards of *Comparative Political Studies* and *International Studies Quarterly*. He has been a fellow at the Center for Advanced Study in the Behavioral Sciences at Stanford. His publications include many book chapters and numerous articles in *French Politics and Society*, *The American Political Science Review*, *Comparative Political Studies*, and *The Canadian Journal of Political Science*. His current work focuses on the initiation, negotiation, and ratification of Maastricht and economic and monetary union, exchange rate policy in France, and transnational relations in the European Community.

Gregory Flynn is research professor of international affairs and director of programs at the Center for German and European Studies, Georgetown University. Before joining the center in 1991, he was a senior associate at the Carnegie Endowment for International Peace in Washington and deputy director of the Atlantic Institute for International Peace in Paris. Flynn has been a visiting fellow with the *Deutsche Gesellschaft für Auswärtige Politik* in Bonn and a Fulbright Scholar at the University of Munich as well as the recipient of fellowships from both the Fritz Thyssen Foundation and the Konrad Adenauer Foundation. He has served as a consultant for the Rand Corporation and the Institute for Defense Analysis. The author and editor of numerous publications on contemporary European security and international relations, as well as on France and Germany, his books include *The West and the Soviet Union: Politics and Policy* (1990), *Soviet Military Doctrine and Western Policy* (1989), *Public Images of Western Security* (1986), *NATO's Northern Allies* (1985), *The Public and Atlantic Defense* (1985), and *The Internal Fabric of Western Security* (1981).

Stanley Hoffmann is Douglas Dillon Professor of the Civilization of France at Harvard University, where he has taught since 1955. He has been the chairman of the Center for European Studies at Harvard since its creation in 1969. Born in Vienna, Professor Hoffmann lived and studied in France from 1929 to 1955; he has taught at the *Institut d'Etudes Politiques* of Paris, from which he graduated, and at the *Ecole des Hautes Etudes en Sciences Sociales*. At Harvard, he teaches French intellectual and political history, American foreign policy, the sociology of war, international politics, ethics and world affairs, modern political ideologies, the development of the modern state, and the history of Europe since 1945. His books include *Contemporary Theory in International Relations* (1960), *The State of War* (1965), *Gulliver's Troubles* (1968), *Decline or Renewal: France Since the 30s* (1974), *Primacy or World Order* (1978), *Duties Beyond Borders* (1981), *Living with Nuclear Weapons* (1983), *The Mitterrand Experiment* (1987), *The New European Community: Decisionmaking and Institutional Change* (1991), and *After the Cold War* (1993).

Jean-Noël Jeanneney is University Professor of History at the *Institut d'Etudes Politiques de Paris* and president of the *Conseil Scientifique de l'Institut d'Histoire du temps présent*. He served as secretary of state for communication from April 1992 until April 1993 and prior to that as secretary of state for external trade from May 1991 until April 1992. Since March 1992, he has been member of the Regional Council for Franche-Comté and a member of the board of directors for Seuil publishers since 1993. He has also served on the board of directors for Agence France-Presse and as president-director general of Radio France and Radio France International. He has authored numerous books, including *Le Riz et le Rouge, cinq mois en Extrême Orient* (1969), *François de Wendel en République, l'Argent et le Pouvoir* (1976), *Concordances des temps, chroniques sur l'actualité du passé* (1987), and, most recently, *Présentation de l'Armée Nouvelle de Jean Jaurès* (1992).

Richard F. Kuisel, professor of history at SUNY-Stony Brook, writes on twentieth-century France. His books include *Seducing the French: The Dilemma of Americanization* (1993) and *Capitalism and the State in Modern France: Renovation and Economic Management* (1981). He is the author of articles on various topics in French economic and political history, including postwar economic growth, economic planning, business, Vichy, de Gaulle, and Mendès-France. He has been the recipient of fellowships from the Guggenheim Foundation, the Woodrow Wilson Center for Scholars, and the American Council of Learned Societies. His current research focuses on Franco-American affairs and he is preparing a study on the political, economic, and cultural impact of the Marshall Plan on France.

Yves Mény is currently director of the Robert Schuman Centre at the European University Institute in Florence and a professor at the *Institut d'Etudes Politiques de Paris*. He has held positions at the *Université de Paris II*, the *Université de Rennes*, and he has served as visiting professor at Cornell University, the University of Rome, New York University, and the Universities of Madrid, Bologna and the *Colegio de Mexico*. Mény has published numerous articles and books, including *Centralisation et décentralisation dans le débat politique française* (1974), *Dix ans de régionalisme en Europe* (1982), *Le système politique français* (1991), and *La Corruption de la République* (1992). He serves on the editorial board of the *Revue Française de Science Politique* and has also served as consultant for the OECD and the *Commissariat général du Plan*.

Alain-Gérard Slama teaches the history of political ideas at the *Institut d'Etudes Politiques* and writes as a columnist for *Le Figaro* and *Le Point*. In addition, his articles regularly appear in journals such as *Commentaire*, *Le Débat*, the *Revue française de science politique*, and *Droits*. His books include *Les Chasseurs d'Absolu. Génèse de la gauche et de la droite* (1980) and *L'Angélisme exterminateur. Essai sur l'ordre moral contemporaine* (1993).

Ezra Suleiman is IBM Professor in International Studies at Princeton University and director of the Committee for European Studies. He has been a fellow of the French C.N.R.S. in Paris and the recipient of Guggenheim, Fulbright, and American Council on Learned Societies Fellowships. Suleiman's publications include *Politics, Power and Bureaucracy in France* (1974), *Elites in French Society: The Politics of Survival* (1978), and *Private Power and Centralization in France* (1987). His articles have appeared in *World Politics*, *Revue française de science politique*, *Comparative Politics*, the *British Journal of Political Science*, and he is the author of numerous book chapters.

About the Book

In this volume, distinguished French and U.S. historians, economists, and political scientists explore the dimensions of France's current crisis of identity. Although every European nation has been adjusting to the dramatic transformations on the continent since the end of the Cold War, France's struggle to adapt has been particularly difficult. Responding to a mix of external and internal pressures, the nation is now questioning many basic assumptions about how France should be governed, what the objectives of national policies should be, and ultimately what it means to be French.

Rather than focusing explicitly on the problem of identity, the contributors offer differing perspectives on the issues at the heart of the country's debate about its future. They begin by examining how France's historical legacy has influenced the way the nation confronts contemporary problems, giving special attention to the manner in which past traumatic experiences, socioeconomic and cultural traditions, and the belief in French exceptionalism have shaped current political thinking. They then consider how favoring a more open approach to trade and building a strong franc have changed the culture of economic policy and created dilemmas for the rule of the state as a guarantor of welfare. They go on to explore changes in elite structures, the evolution of the party system, and the spillover of new political conditions that are driving France's efforts to establish a strong national identity in the area of trade.

Finally, the contributors examine the central influence of the changing international framework on France's self-definition, on its security policies, its relationship to the European Union, and its basic perceptions of the state and sovereignty. They also consider how the answers to these questions are affecting France's relationships with the outside world and the overriding policy dilemmas faced by all the European nations.

Index